Psyche and Symbol in the Theater
of Federico García Lorca

PSYCHE AND SYMBOL IN THE THEATER OF Federico García Lorca

Perlimplín, Yerma, Blood Wedding

BY RUPERT C. ALLEN

UNIVERSITY OF TEXAS PRESS, AUSTIN AND LONDON

The publication of this book was assisted by

a grant from the Andrew W. Mellon Foundation.

Grateful acknowledgment is made for permission to quote from the following:

Dear Abby by Abigail Van Buren and reprinted by her permission.
A Death in the Family by James Agee. Copyright © 1957 by James Agee Trust. First published in Partisan Review. Reprinted by permission of the publisher, Grosset & Dunlap, Inc.
The Fall by Albert Camus. Translated by Justin O'Brien. Published by Alfred A. Knopf, Inc., and reprinted by their permission. Copyright © 1956, 1957.
Letters of James Agee to Father Flye by James Agee. Published by Houghton Mifflin Company and reprinted by their permission. Copyright © 1971.
Obras Completas by Federico García Lorca. Copyright © 1957, 1967 by Aguilar, S. A. de Ediciones. All Rights Reserved. Reprinted by permission of New Directions Publishing Corporation, U.S. publishers of the works of Federico García Lorca and agents for the Estate of the Author.
"Someone Puts a Pineapple Together" from *The Necessary Angel* by Wallace Stevens. Published by Alfred A. Knopf, Inc., and reprinted by their permission. Copyright © 1951.
Steppenwolf by Hermann Hesse. Translated by Basil Creighton. Copyright 1929, © 1957 by Holt, Rinehart and Winston, Inc. Reprinted by permission of Holt, Rinehart and Winston, Inc.

Library of Congress Cataloging in Publication Data

Allen, Rupert C
    Psyche and symbol in the theater of Federico García
Lorca: Perlimplín, Yerma, Blood wedding.

    Bibliography: p.
    1. García Lorca, Federico, 1898–1936—Knowledge—
Psychology.   2. Symbolism in literature.   3. Symbolism
(Psychology)   I. Title.
PQ6613.A763Z534   862'.6'2   74–4285
ISBN 0–292–76418–9

FOR

Eric   *Mark*
Katie   *Belita*

AND THEIR

Nina

CONTENTS

The following abbreviations have been used for works by Lorca. All references are to the thirteenth edition of his *Obras completas* (*OC*).

DT	*Diván del Tamarit*
Libro	*Libro de poemas*
NY	*Poeta en Nueva York*
PC	*Primeras canciones*
PS	*Poemas sueltos*
RG	*Romancero gitano*

PREFACE

The present studies extend in a new direction the symbological efforts of my earlier *The Symbolic World of Federico García Lorca*. In *The Symbolic World* I wished to set forth the poetic world view of Lorca the poet, whereas now I intend to examine the fictional world view of certain dramatic figures created by Lorca.

In selecting works for study in *The Symbolic World*, it was deemed necessary to include Lorca's *sui generis* play *As Soon as Five Years Pass* because it is so obviously autobiographical in the spiritual sense. The protagonist of that drama is exceptional in the theater of Lorca, if for no other reason than that he is a young man—introverted, and engrossed in the drama of his own inner life. As such, he seems to be a psychological extension of Lorca the poet, and the play deals with general psychic (rather than "dramatic") problems on the scale of those that Lorca himself must certainly have encountered in the process of evolving spiritually. Apart from *Five Years*, however, the Lorca play is not a personal statement, but rather a dramatization of *possible* psychic and symbolic processes.

Symbol and psyche are twin concepts in symbological studies, since the one is a "statement" by the other. The psyche is a manifold of conscious and unconscious contents, and the symbol is their mediator. Since Lorca's dramatic characters are psychic entities made up of both conscious and unconscious elements, they unfold, grow, and meet their fate in a dense realm of shifting symbols.

If I have limited my survey to three dramas—*Perlimplín, Yerma,* and *Blood Wedding*—it is because these are precisely the works that seem to call for an extended commentary. Lorca's other principal plays raise no real difficulties that could justify prolonged examination of the kind employed here. That there are, however, psychological and symbological problems of a certain subtlety and complexity in *Perlimplín*, *Yerma*, and *Blood Wedding* is sufficiently evident when one assesses them in terms of the published criticism. *Perlimplín* is a good deal more complex in both symbol and psyche than it has been admitted to be; *Yerma* involves psychological complications passed over by all but two critics, José Alberich and Francisco Umbral, who have dealt with them each in his own way. In *Blood Wedding* Lorca gets into complexities of intense interest to the symbologist, and to date these have remained unexplored.

Both *Yerma* and *Blood Wedding* reflect in fictional form specific problems underlying the creative act. They are "translations" into the realm of sexuality of the creative turmoil experienced by Lorca the poet. This is especially evident in *Yerma*; and while amazement has been expressed that Lorca, being a man, could deal so knowledgeably with the woman's psyche, perhaps the present study may help to reduce that amazement by suggesting wherein Lorca's knowledge lay.

It is with pleasure that I acknowledge my debt of gratitude to the Graduate College Committee for Faculty Research Support in the Humanities and Social Sciences here at the University of Arizona. It was their generosity that made it possible for me to devote a tranquil summer to preparing the final draft of the manuscript.

Psyche and Symbol in the Theater
of Federico García Lorca

PART ONE

Psyche and Symbol in *Perlimplín*

These pages are addressed to two kinds of readers: those generally interested in the psychology of symbols, and those interested in the work of Federico García Lorca. Contemporary studies in symbology ought not to be concerned solely with a specialized understanding of symbolic material; they have the power to increase our self-consciousness, which is to say our conscious understanding of the self, by trying to attend to the directive voice of the unconscious in the service of ego. The language of this voice is the silent language of its images—its symbols.

If we seek to understand the symbol in action (there is no other way, really, to understand it), what better example could be chosen than that which Lorca has given in his works? Indeed, learning about "his" symbols means nothing else than studying the dramatic meaning of human life as staged by the unconscious—the primordial impresario, and still the most convincing one of all, whose dramas seem to have leaped, fully grown, into the eyes of Lorca. To study the work of Lorca is nearly the same thing as to study myth and folklore; and to study myth and folklore is to see Lorca's significance at the proper level.

Hence this first study, devoted to the unfortunate don Perlimplín, will begin with a preparatory inquiry into the meaning of fairy-tale symbolism. The symbolism of the wicked stepmother and the malicious dwarf will be specifically elucidated, since these point to the two forces that drive don Perlimplín to his violent and ghastly end. A reasonably full understanding of this play depends upon a prior understanding of these two themes, especially because the dwarf actually appears in the play, while the "wicked stepmother" presents herself vicariously but quite clearly in the broken personality of Perlimplín.

Then a short résumé of this "farce" will be given for the benefit of those who may be unfamiliar with it. The succeeding commentary will be concerned with reviewing the sexual symbolism of Freud and showing how Lorca exploits it in *Perlimplín*, first farcically and, finally, tragically. Though Lorca himself was not a Freudian (*Perlimplín* is his only "Freudian" work), he could recognize good dramatic material when he saw it, and the psychosexual conflicts described by Freud are nothing if not dramatic; nor is it likely that he was staged to better effect and with fuller intuitive understanding of the tragically futile and empty, neurotic personalities described in his case histories.

Who Is the Wicked Stepmother?

Fairy tales are for children, but the symbolic work of the fairy tale embraces all major aspects of human life from infancy to old age, since it is a specialized, rather than limited, form of the myth-making capacity of the human mind. While fairy tales may be for children, their intuitive representation of collective human life is not at all childish.

The fairy tale consistently depicts in a highly stylized and symbolic form the growth of the child: either the manner in which his personality is integrated into the adult community, or the manner in which it *ought* to be so integrated. It shows the struggle that goes on in the soul of the child during the period of juggling for an ideal balance between conscious and unconscious tendencies, as the child is progressively separated from the family circle and confronted with the task of adapting himself harmoniously to the realities of social life at large. The little child is all too much the slave of unconscious tendencies, while the adult often enough appears to be too much the slave of consciousness, of certain conventional social values that are frequently prized far out of proportion to their capacity to confer anything other than a superficial and fleeting happiness. Hence the need for a balance of some kind, in the absence of which there arises the threat that the psyche will be tyrannized lopsidedly either by some force representing the side of consciousness, or by unconscious drives imperfectly assimilated. The balanced goal is that symbolized by the centaur, the wise creature half horse and half man.

The fairy tale is charmingly didactic in that it teaches in the most entertaining way the highest collective ideals. These are the possible goals of collective morality, which, in everyday life, are never attained and only rarely kept in focus. In fact, generally speaking the "world as it is" turns out to be represented in the fairy tale by the wicked characters, who always end by getting their comeuppance in the most frightful ways: they are dismembered, drowned, burned, crushed, boiled in oil, rolled downhill in a barrel of spikes, eaten by savage beasts—no punishment is too cruel for them; not so that the child may learn that it is good to be bloodthirsty, but so that he may learn that such evil tendencies in his own heart are not even human and do not deserve to be honored with the name of humanity or treated humanely —even when the "world as it is" tolerates them (while scorning the "childish" fairy tale).

An excellent example of such evil fairy-tale characters, and one that occurs with monotonous regularity, is that of the *wicked stepmother.* Have stepmothers ever been that common, by comparison with a virtual absence of stepfathers? And if in the olden times there were more stepmothers than at present, were they invariably wicked?

It is easy to see that a stepchild might find wickedness where there is none; that, bereft of his mother, he might project his anxieties onto the person of Daddy's new bride—she is the "usurper"—but it is not really arguable from this that the fairy tale itself is ever the product of anxiety states. Given the consistently close symbolic grasp of worldly reality evinced by these stories it is gratuitous and unconvincing to hypothesize that any fairy tale reflects the child's mistaken view of reality, if for no other reason than that fairy tales are not simply the invention of children. It would be more correct to say that the fairy tale is an invention of the conscious and the unconscious (whatever the age of the inventors) working in close collaboration, just as is the case with the myth and the poem.

With respect to the "real" identity of the wicked stepmother then: granting a fundamental soundness to the fairy tale's grasp of world reality, it will be necessary to seek some spiritual fact in real life that is symbolized by the wicked stepmother. The problem has two aspects: (*a*) why does the stepmother abound in the fairy tale, and (*b*) why is she always wicked?

The answer is obvious enough: the stepmother symbolizes a negative aspect of the mother. Mothers abound in real life, and their negative aspect is always "wicked," by definition. In reality, of course, no mother is either good or bad; but we know well that when pushed beyond the bounds of discretion mother love (essentially good) becomes "smother love" (essentially bad). Like the morality play, the fairy tale symbolizes various spiritual tendencies in the form of different characters interacting with one another, and so a particular aspect of the mother separates out to appear in the form of a new, lopsided character. It is also possible that the fairy tale reflects a repression of the negative intuition of the mother, so that she reappears in substitute form as "somebody else."

Ideally the mother loves and cherishes her offspring and works to guide them into spiritual independence; actually a good many mothers are not so fully conscious of their task that they work toward this ideal. In the beginning, when the child is but an infant, they nourish and protect him, but frequently they do not find the wisdom to let their love grow and change as the child grows and changes. They become too attached egotistically to the child, and they sometimes turn into what is called the *mater terribilis*, the "Terrible Mother." They resent (consciously or not) all those lovable extravert qualities that will enable the child to become an independent member of society, loved and valued by his contemporaries; and they become an "unnatural" mother in that jealously they consciously or unconsciously work toward their child's downfall as an adult.

The wicked stepmother invariably appears in opposition to a beautiful and lovable stepchild. The two are in dialectical opposition, for the one could not exist without the other. This is because it is the beauty and lovableness of the child that bid fair to make him a success in the world "out there," beyond the embrace of the mother. Hence it is the extraverted qualities of the child that threaten to arouse the jealousy and fear of the mother, since they seem to threaten her function. As chess players say, they "threaten to threaten." And so one reads repeatedly in fairy tales words like these: "The woman became her stepdaughter's bitterest enemy, and day by day did her best to treat her still worse. She was also envious because her step-daughter was beautiful and lovable."[1] The stories never give any kind of motivation for this hatred, for the very good reason that the hatred is the raison d'être of the characters in the first place. To give a "reason" for it would be like giving a "reason" for the love of Romeo and Juliet.

So the Terrible Mother represents an obsolete attitude. The original attitude toward the baby becomes inflexible: the child is "always her baby," and so, as the child grows, the mother's passé attitude makes her appear to be another person, a character from another, earlier drama—no longer the child's protectress and ally, but a "second" mother who in the long run acts as if she were her child's worst enemy.

Such is the wicked stepmother of the fairy tale. The frequency with which she appears does not imply that the world is full of terrible mothers, but rather teaches that the tendency is a natural threat whenever a family comes into being. It teaches that *the tendency is always there.*

In Spanish literature a notable example of the unfortunate victim of the Terrible Mother is Lorca's don Perlimplín, the old-maid bachelor, the mama's boy who remains caught in the toils of infantile sexuality. In the play an allusion is made to Perlimplín's *infortunio,* his "misfortune," and it is that which I have just been describing.

---

[1] "The Three Little Men in the Wood," *Grimm's Fairy Tales,* p. 79 (references to *Grimm's* are from the complete edition except where noted).

Lorca is, I believe, the only Spanish dramatist to deal with this kind of misfortune; and with his sure sense of symbolic relevance, he has the case diagnosed in the play by the "character" (= psychic impulse) most deeply involved with it: the so-called *phallic dwarf*.

The Meaning of the Dwarf

Perlimplín, as absurd as his fairy-tale name, is a timid, fifty-year-old virginal bachelor who marries a wildly erotic, voluptuous young woman. On their wedding night, as they get into bed, two dwarfs draw curtains over the scene, because (as one of them says) a good man's "misfortune" ought not to be publicized. While critics have consistently interpreted this as meaning that Perlimplín is impotent, such cannot possibly be the case (it contradicts the text, if nothing else) and no doubt means that the critics have tended to jump to conclusions; for, after all, the association of the ideas "bridegroom's misfortune" and "wedding night" is bound to elicit first of all the thought of impotence. This fear in the face of an important sexual occasion is a well-known companion of men, and the impotence itself may even be an indicator of the significance that the victim attaches to the occasion.

Not only has Perlimplín been repeatedly accused of impotence, but also the two dwarfs have not been treated other than literally by the critics, just as Rumpelstiltskin, for example, is understood literally by children. It goes without saying that if one inquires into the meaning of "dwarf" he will reach some definite conclusions about Perlimplín's potency; but it is not possible symbologically to treat the dwarf literally. This is because the fairy-tale dwarf (elf, gnome, brownie, goblin, etc.) is imaginary; the manikin is a symbolic entity, and so it is meaningless to take him at face value. Such practice is quite common, however: a dream is also a symbolic entity, and yet nearly everyone is content to think of his dreams literally—in terms of their "manifest content"—and in no other way.

When the dream or the fairy tale produces a fantastic character, such as the giant or the troll or the wicked stepmother, an "understanding" of such a character must mean a comprehension of the underlying need for the fantasy—what Freud called the *latent meaning* of the dream. In real life the murderous stepmother is a very rare, pathological phenomenon; in the fairy tale she turns up in every other household. Hence, in order to understand her significance, we sought out the latent content of her role, the symbolic way in which this actually corresponds to some fact in real life, and we found it in the growing process: the growing child requires a growing mother; the mother who surrenders herself to smother love turns into an "arrested," unnatural mother.

Now the fairy-tale dwarf, like the wicked stepmother, does not correspond literally to anything in real life. As part of the "manifest content" of the story he is manifestly absurd. And yet he is a common inhabitant of Fairyland, and he is certainly no stranger to the myth. So universally does he live in the minds of men, as a matter of fact, that he must be granted an archetypal significance. Lorca himself attached a good deal of significance to the dwarf, for he made this the subject of one of his classic public lectures: "The Theory and Practice of the Elf." The diminutive figure of the sprite is at the nerve center—which is to say the sexual center—of *Perlimplín*, and so an understanding of this play has to be informed by a comprehension of the symbolic significance of the "little man," who appears the world over in countless guises.

To this end a fairy tale dealing appositely with this material will be considered, the story of Rumpelstiltskin. For clear symbological vision, however, the discussion must be preluded with a brief description of the archetypal manikin, or phallic dwarf—the material protagonist of every man's sexual aspect: for every man is confronted with the problem of how he is to deal with himself as phallus bearer—else the phallus bearer within will deal with him in ways ranging from the mischievous to the massively destructive. For Perlimplín the problem is disastrous.

It has been mentioned that in *Perlimplín* two elfin figures (*duendes*) draw curtains across the bedroom scene and sit talking while Perlimplín enjoys himself with his young bride. A question that naturally occurs is why *duendes*, precisely?

The answer readily suggests itself, since the manikin, in any of his many guises, consistently appears in myth and folklore as a phallic figure. The theme of the "little man" turns up in the form of the dwarf, the elf, the goblin, the Dactyl, the doll, the gnome; as Priapus,

Pan, Rumpelstiltskin, Tom Tit Tot, Yallery Brown; as Tom Thumb, Pinkel, Tyll Ulenspiegel, or indeed as any little boy unusually precocious, cunning, diverting, and possessing a power disproportionate to his size. Here it is easy to see the symbolic connection of the dwarf with that specialized form known as the poltergeist, a malicious little prankster known also in Yorkshire as the boggart.

The manikin is, of course, frequently symbolized by his ithyphallic *magic gifts*—daggers, swords, guns, cannons, spears, and wands. This range of symbolic ideas is represented by primitive phallic vocabulary, as in the Balinese slang vocabulary of metaphors for the phallus: "child," "kris," "spear," "walking-stick," "leg," "short leg."[2] These last two items recall the fact that the phallic dwarf is well known for his tendency to hop excitedly on one leg and to dance about in moments of triumph (cf. Rumpelstiltskin). And since a notable characteristic of the phallus is the erection, the dwarf is known both as the "ugly little man" who can swell himself, and as the shape-shifter (cf. the poltergeist). In the Latin American *Tales from Silver Lands* everyone in the village was afraid of the aggressive power of *el enano* ("the dwarf"): when tranquil he would make himself very small "like a little child," and then "he was horrible to see, for his skin was wrinkled and his whiskers hung about him." But when aggressive, he would swell up to his full size and chase after people, hopping on one leg.[3]

The hostile trickery associated with the phallic dwarf stems from the behavior of the phallus itself. In the *Timaeus* Plato describes it thus: ". . . in men the organ of generation becoming rebellious and masterful, like an animal disobedient to reason, and maddened with the sting of lust, seeks to gain absolute sway."[4] Hence the dwarf has a natural talent for the practical joke (hostility to ego-consciousness), such as leading a man to expect good fortune and then suddenly withdrawing his magic power and leaving his victim in the lurch, and looking quite ridiculous. This jokester aspect of the dwarf is reflected in the body of material well known to cultural anthropologists in the form of the Trickster Cycle of stories, to be discussed presently.

[2] Gregory Bateson and Margaret Mead, *Balinese Character*, p. 135.
[3] Charles J. Finger (ed.), *Tales from Silver Lands*.
[4] Plato, *The Dialogues of Plato*, p. 67.

The symbolism of the phallic manikin is used literally in a celebrated contemporary Colombian novel, *One Hundred Years of Solitude*, by Gabriel García Márquez. Here a woman plays idle erotic games with her lover; for example, "she would play dolls with Aureliano's gigantic creature, and paint clown's eyes on it with lipstick and a handlebar mustache with eyebrow pencil."[5] Beyond the fact that the phallus is treated like a doll here, it is described as the man's *criatura*, which means literally "creature," but which is used popularly with the meaning of "little one," or "child."[6] And the ultimate futility of these erotic games no doubt enters into the negative connotations of the manikin symbol ("clown"), since the phallus bearer Aureliano is to be the last adult male of his line.

The manikin, then, is the phallus, the "little man" who consistently seems to have purposes and desires of his own, whether or not they are in the service of ego, and in spite of whatever contrary purposes and desires ego-consciousness may dream up for itself.

The dwarf is conventionally depicted as living and working underground. He is either a miner or a creator of jewels, for, like the phallus, he represents materially creative libido: "The phallus is this hero dwarf, who performs great deeds; he, this ugly god in homely form, who is the great doer of wonders, since he is the visible expression of the creative strength incarnate."[7] "The creative dwarfs toil away in secret," says Carl Jung; "the phallus, also working in darkness, begets a living being."[8]

So to confront the phallus means ultimately to confront the problem of becoming a man. It can *fascinate* with its power and so become an obstacle to conscious development, and indeed the ancient Romans placed their infant children under the prophylactic protection of Fascinus, "the spirit or daemon of the phallus, an emblem of which [*fascinus*] was hung round the necks of infants to keep away evil influences."[9]

[5] Gabriel García Márquez, *Cien años de soledad*, p. 341. My translation.

[6] Cf. Lorca's use of the word in his lecture on the Spanish lullaby: the purpose of the lullaby, he says, is to "tame the little horses that rear up excitedly in the eyes of the child [*criatura*]" (*Las nanas infantiles*, in *OC*, p. 97).

[7] C. G. Jung, *Psychology of the Unconscious*, p. 130.

[8] C. G. Jung, *Symbols of Transformation*, p. 124.

[9] See Pliny, *Natural History*, 28:39, and accompanying footnote.

One carries his phallic potential as a secret weapon. It is concealed, but it confers upon the possessor a heroic power. The boy becomes a member of the adult male group, and in primitive cultures this often means that he joins the warrior caste. This new status is commonly conferred by the ritual of circumcision whereby the men "give birth" to a new boy—which signifies the simultaneous emergence of the dwarf (= adult phallus) and of the spirit proper to the warrior caste: ". . . by the circumcision the glans penis is freed; it emerges *like an infant* from the mother's womb."[10] By means of this new birth the boys are torn from the narcissistic stage of the child and are reborn into the phallic stage of the man. The circumcised penis seen as a phallic infant corresponds precisely to the traditional image of the dwarf wearing the pileus or the Phrygian cap.

Phallicism has received much attention in myth and folklore because it is central to our natural involvement with the phases through which both the individual human being and human cultures pass in the process of spiritual differentiation, or maturing. The psyche of the infant child is largely nondifferentiated and for the most part is identical with the instinctual life of the body that it "inhabits." This is the narcissistic stage and is marked by a more-or-less spontaneous, unconscious living in the body-mind unity, such as it is. But as the child approaches the crisis of adolescence he becomes more and more inwardly aware of the growing differentiation of his own conscious life, of the spiritual differences that increasingly mark him as a self-conscious, individual human being. As Erich Neumann puts it (speaking of the boy-child), the ego "advances to the phallic stage, where consciousness of one's body and of oneself coincides with an aroused and actively desiring masculinity."[11] This is a self-conscious acting potential of the ego, qualitatively quite different from the infant's "active" desire to suckle or to fall asleep.

But the passage from the narcissistic stage to the phallic stage ("lower masculinity") means only the preliminary self-assertion of the young masculine ego, which, as is known, is a powerful instrument in the service of instinctual drives. Typically there is as yet no question of

---

[10] Bruno Bettelheim, *Symbolic Wounds*, p. 53. My italics.
[11] Erich Neumann, *The Origins and History of Consciousness*, p. 308.

spiritual self-realization in any way transcending the demands of Mother Nature. At this stage sex means erotic gratification for the most part: "Although in the phallic phase the masculine ego consciously and actively pursues its special goal, namely the satisfaction of instinct, it is still so much the organ of the unconscious that it cannot grasp that sexual satisfaction in mating has anything to do with propagation."[12]

The young male easily sees as an appropriate and desirable goal the establishment of himself as phallus bearer or copulator, rather than propagator (in both the physical and spiritual sense). He has passed through the androgynous stage of childhood and differentiates himself as a male vis-à-vis the female. So the possession of a phallus is the all-important factor, indeed so important that this stage of psychic development is thus identified: it is the phallic stage.

The psychological description of psychic development finds, naturally, a good deal of corroboration in the traditional, intuitive description furnished by mythology and folklore. For symbols are nothing if not dynamic images depicting in the most striking manner the ever-changing relationships between consciousness and the unconscious.

The phallic stage precedes man's consciousness of himself as an individual value with a unique worth.[13] Though not nearly so unconscious as the narcissistic stage, it nevertheless must still be considered so if contrasted to the spiritual stage of the so-called higher masculinity. The difference between a little boy and a don Juan Tenorio is hardly more striking than the difference between don Juan Tenorio and a Shakespeare or a Buddha. And the phallic stage of human cultures has produced a vast quantity of symbolic material descriptive of itself at that level.

Since the great concern is with the importance of the phallus, man himself at the phallic stage is depicted either as a man attached to an enormous phallus, or else as a totally phallic being: the individual turns into a walking phallus. An extremely archaic form of the phallic male in mythology occurs in the cycle of stories belonging to a number of American Indian tribes and known under the name of the Trickster.

[12] Ibid., p. 309.
[13] Ibid.

The Trickster Cycle has been studied in anthropological detail by Paul Radin, who retells the principal episodes and discusses their ethnic meaning.[14] The stories about Trickster depict him as a foolish and ignorant male living in the midst of a tribal culture already developed. Trickster initiates himself, so to speak, into the ways of the tribe by a kind of slapstick trial-and-error method. The episodes are considered to be hilarious by the audience, who follow Trickster as he muddles through one adventure after another with no clear sense of his own bodily functions, or even of the relationship between his right side and his left side (his two hands fight with each other). He breaks all the major tribal taboos.

His entry into the phallic stage of life is remarkably depicted in the episodes involving a large and burdensome penis which he carries on his back: "He did not know what it was, nor why he should be so burdened. . . . [He thought] he could put it down as soon as he wanted to; he just did not want to, for by carrying it he could show how strong he was. . . . he derided the other animals, saying that none of them was strong enough to carry so large a burden."[15] He eventually tires of the heavy load, but when he tries to unburden himself, he finds that he cannot. "This story is . . . an account of man's gradual awakening to consciousness of his own sexuality. In the beginning, its demands are considered . . . a source of pride. But as consciousness grows, the biological urge is recognized as a burden, a daemon whose service demands time and effort that might be used for more valuable tasks. Then man begins to struggle with his daemon. His conscious self and the nonpersonal daemon are no longer in harmony, and in trying to rid himself of the compulsion within him man finds that he is being torn apart."[16]

Trickster, then, is a kind of inverted unicorn figure. The phallic burden that, in the unicorn, has been raised to the head (it emanates from the brain) is still, in the phallic stage, a threatening instinctual force with which growing self-consciousness is going to have to reckon.

It is in the phallic stage that Trickster appears as symbolic of a crea-

[14] Paul Radin, *The Trickster.*
[15] M. Esther Harding, *Psychic Energy,* pp. 121–122.
[16] Ibid., p. 122.

ture who (as Karl Kerényi points out) "is the exponent and personification of the life of the body: never wholly subdued, ruled by lust and hunger, for ever running into pain and injury."[17] Or, as Jung more radically puts it, Trickster is "an archetypal psychic structure of extreme antiquity. In his clearest manifestations he is a faithful copy of an absolutely undifferentiated human consciousness, corresponding to a psyche that has hardly left the animal level."[18]

Though Trickster, as blind impulse, possesses no moral or social values, he is nevertheless necessary to their development, since the phallic stage of psychic growth is, after all, really an instrumental stage in the dynamics of spiritual growth. He is not a curse, but a challenge.

In the mythology and folklore with which most of us are generally familiar the erect phallus as man's signal burden has most often taken the form not of a heavy load to which the male is attached, but rather of a distinct individual capable of acting separately under his own impulse. The possibility is clearly suggested in one Trickster episode in which Trickster removes his phallus and sends it across a river to have intercourse with a maiden. This is the prototype of the dwarf.

The dwarf as a man's personal challenger, as an ugly little antagonist filled with malice toward one's higher ego-consciousness, is well represented by Yallery Brown, an English dwarf whom the protagonist of one story discovers under a large stone, calling to be released. "It was no bigger than a year-old baby, but it had long cotted hair and beard"; "the face of it was old," "just a heap of wrinkles." When he grows angry he stamps a foot on the earth and looks "as wicked as a raging bull." He treats the hero maliciously, reminding him, "I was nice and safe under the stone, Tom, and could do no harm; but thou let me out thyself, and thou can't put me back again!" He dances around Tom, "looking older than ever with his grinning wrinkled bit of a face," and he sings

> For harm and mischance and Yallery Brown
> Thou'st let out thyself from under the stone.[19]

[17] Karl Kerényi, "The Trickster in Relation to Greek Myth," in Radin, *The Trickster*, p. 185.
[18] Jung, "On the Psychology of the Trickster Figure," in Radin, *The Trickster*, p. 200.
[19] Joseph Jacobs (ed.), *More English Fairy Tales*, p. 35.

This dweller in the underground realm of instinct is usually identifiable in pictorial representations by the pileus or the Phrygian cap shaped like the glans penis or "acorn" (L. *glans*), and which in ancient Italy was part of the costume appropriately worn during the orgiastic Saturnalian festivities. The wearing of the pileus symbolically turns the entire body of the man into a phallus: the body is the shaft and the head is the glans penis.

An episode in Norse mythology concerns the beginning of creation, when the Frost Giants were still the only form of life. The earth was made from their dead bodies, and "dwarfs grew 'like maggots' in the carcasses, but 'at a word of the gods they became conscious with the intelligence of men and had human form.' "[20] Here the genital symbolism of the worm that attains human intelligence foreshadows the later symbolism of the phoenix: a worm born from its ashes grows into the Bird of the Sun, worshipped particularly in the great temple at Heliopolis ("Sun City").[21] The phallic meaning of the bird is well known, and when it appears as the glorious sunbird grown from a worm it represents the perfecting of those Norse dwarfs: the spiritual heights that may be attained by the mature male are chronologically rooted in the phallic stage—and, before that, in the narcissistic stage. The infantile penis is transformed into the sign of the ithyphallic adolescent who subsequently raises his masculine potential to the spiritual level of the higher masculinity. The maggot at one level becomes a dwarf; at another level he becomes a phoenix.

The fact that the phallic stage underlies further development of the male is indicated by the function of the dwarfs in the Norse myth; when (according to one version) the world was made from the carcass of Ymir, the frost ogre, his *skull* was used for the sky (i.e., the vaulted firmament is to the earth as man's head or intelligence is to his lower, earthy body); and the dwarfs were set at the corners to hold it up,[22] which is to say that the phallic stage supports the heights of the higher masculinity. The phallic dwarf must become its mainstay; the instinctual impulse or virile libido working "down there," under-

---

[20] Sheila Moon, *A Magic Dwells*, p. 60.
[21] Herodotus 2:73.
[22] "Gylfaginning," in Snorri Sturluson, *The Prose Edda*, p. 14.

ground in the unconscious, furnishes the driving force behind man's spiritual accomplishments. A celebrated example is furnished by the music of Beethoven, which is often described as a kind of natural force; the aggressive virility of his music is one of its most impressive qualities. "It has *duende* [= dwarf]," to use the phrase of the Spanish Gypsies—a phrase noted more than once by Lorca.

The dwarf, like Trickster, is himself typically indifferent to civilized goals, and symbolically "indifference" means hostility. Such indifference is typical of the young man deeply into the phallic stage (exemplified in our own time by the terrorist groups known as Hell's Angels). In myth and folklore the dwarf is generally depicted as a creature hostile to the aims of the hero, but who is nevertheless known to be in possession of something that could be of inestimable service to him. Since the "hero story" concerns the values of society, it must be understood that the gift or power of the dwarf is taken over by ego-consciousness to be used in the service of the community. In contrast is the narcissistic stage as represented in the beginning of the Aladdin story, where autoerotic gratification, indifferent to social aims, is symbolized by the boy who rubs his magic lamp: immediately the "manikin" imprisoned within the lamp swells to the size of a genie who can gratify all wishes, which means the magic of autoerotic fantasy. As Jung puts it: ". . . with onanism one has the greatest magic in one's hands; one needs only to phantasy, and with that to masturbate, then one possesses all the pleasure of the world, and is no longer compelled to conquer the world of one's desires, through hard labor and wrestling with reality. Aladdin rubs his lamp and the obedient genii stand at his bidding . . ."[23] The story relates that shortly after Aladdin's discovery of the magic lamp the boy's mother rubbed it in order to clean it, whereupon the "hideous genie appeared," and she fainted.[24] This erotic effect of maternal hygienic measures has been frequently noted.

The power of the dwarf must be wrested from him, else he will hold the man prisoner in the trap of infantile sexuality. The fact that his power lies at the basis of the higher masculinity is reflected in the Pelasgian dwarf-idea, the Cabiri, chthonic gods, or earth spirits. They

---

[23] Jung, *Psychology of the Unconscious*, p. 188.
[24] *Arabian Nights*, ed. Andrew Lang, p. 205.

were artificers and smiths[25]—culturally advanced—but were believed to be fundamentally hostile to the culture above ground. Instinctual forces do not easily give up their immense quantities of "hoarded" libido. In the Upanishads even the cosmic life force itself (purusha) is depicted as a dwarf-god and is described as the misshapen "little man" who is, however, strangely endowed: "Without feet, without hands, he moves, he grasps; eyeless, he sees, earless he hears; he knows all that is to be known, yet there is no knower of him. Men call him the Primordial Person, the Cosmic Man."[26] He is "smaller than small," "greater than great."[27] And this phallic god was known to the Greeks as Hermes, the "generative power in the world at large,"[28] the universal fertilizer, the "giver of increase, wealth."[29] "At his home, Kyllene . . . , he was in historic times worshipped in the form of an erect phallus."[30] Probably all of us are familiar with the Hermes stele, a square column bearing the head of Hermes, and in the middle of the column is an erect phallus: a clear enough representation of the relationship intuited to exist between the phallic stage and the stage of the higher masculinity.

In the Grimm story "The Spirit in the Bottle" the notion of Hermes is combined with the imp-genie of Aladdin. The boy-hero finds the bottle underground amongst the roots of an oak tree: ". . . the boy, thinking no evil, drew the cork out of the bottle. Immediately a spirit ascended from it, and began to grow, and grew so fast that in a very few moments he stood before the boy, a terrible fellow."[31] He identifies himself as Mercurius (= Hermes) and threatens to strangle the boy as his "reward" for opening the bottle—an accurate enough picture of the young male's confrontation with his phallic power; either he assimilates it, or it will "strangle" him, that is, cut off the subject's own *spiritus*, or breath.

There is an Icelandic legend according to which the hero receives from a dwarf a magic sword. The dwarf says, "It will cut, and it can

---

[25] See H. G. Baynes, *Mythology of the Soul*, pp. 548–549.
[26] Jung, *Symbols of Transformation*, p. 126.
[27] Ibid.
[28] Richard B. Onians, *The Origins of European Thought*, p. 122.
[29] Ibid.
[30] Ibid.
[31] *Grimm's Fairy Tales*, p. 460.

be made so small that you can put it in your pocket, but it will grow to its full size when you like."[32] Here again is libidinal power described in phallic terms, but with additional magic, for the dwarf here has given the hero a talisman against impotence: ". . . it will grow to its full size *when you like*"—indicating at the least a conscious power over the sometimes capricious force. This capriciousness is part of the character of the dwarf as a fickle practical joker who may willfully refuse to let the male have what the dwarf is in charge of. As François Duyckaerts observes, "The male organ sometimes takes the form of a sword, and sometimes that of . . . an amusing but fickle sprite."[33]

In "Jack and His Golden Snuff-Box" the hero takes service with a man who has a beautiful daughter. She falls in love with him. That night the hero opens his snuffbox and out hop "three little red men." They build for him a warship with magic cannon that fire in such a way that they break the leg of the girl's bed without harming her; which is to say that with tremendous phallic power he "awakens" or initiates her in the best way possible: without hurting or traumatizing her—all this by way of fulfilling the task set by the girl's father.[34]

This same story illustrates the manikin's indifference to the "sublimation" of phallic power, for when the hero and his people "try to keep the Sunday holy" in chapel, one of the dwarfs makes the women laugh by lying on the organ pipes in a ridiculous posture, wearing his "little red nightcap [= pileus] which he never forgot to wear, a sight . . . which could not help making them laugh long and loud and heartily."[35] This intrusion of the phallic dwarf into matters of high spiritual seriousness nearly causes the castle to sink into the sea: the dwarf always threatens with devouring regression. The ithyphallic organ pipes are, of course, derived from the syrinx and the flute, the instruments long associated with little priapic Pan.

Priapus himself was known as a dwarfish, primitive (and therefore untrustworthy) humanoid, and Marie Delcourt describes as follows a statue of him in the Dresden Museum: a veiled woman is seen "leaning on the shoulder of Priapus, who is shown as an aged dwarf, wear-

---

[32] W. A. Clouston, *Popular Tales and Fictions*, I, 108.

[33] François Duyckaerts, *The Sexual Bond*, p. 129.

[34] Jacobs, *More English Fairy Tales*, pp. 84–86.

[35] Ibid., p. 93.

ing a pointed cap, and wrapped in a cloak under whose great folds one can half distinguish an organ of exaggerated size. Along his left cheek he lays the long forefinger of his right hand, as if the sculptor were using this symbol to stress the meaning of the figure. Such must have been the primitive Priapus, very different from the attractive young scamp of Hellenistic art."[36]

We have seen how the most archaic form of the phallic man appears simply in the explicit form of Trickster staggering under the heavy burden of his own mysterious and unknown penis. Then we have seen how he appears in a less explicit form as the dwarf, with his various characteristics associated with phallic libido. In his most modern form he is known as the poltergeist, the familiar spirit fond of playing scary practical jokes in the house of the psyche. And in his most transcendental guise he actually presumes to oppose Shiva, the Cosmic Dancer himself, depicted as follows: "The god is dancing on the dwarfish body of the demon *Apasmara purusa*, 'forgetfulness, loss of memory' . . . who represents ignorance, the destruction of which brings enlightenment, true wisdom, and release from the bondage of existences."[37] Here the dwarf is earthly existence itself, which "tricks" man into forgetting who he is. He falls into the bondage of instinctual life, which, for the human being, ultimately means the bondage of genitality. This Eastern idea, however, emphasizes the opposition between spirit and instinct (= forgetfulness), whereas in the Occident ("forgetful" of the possibility of multiple existences) the phallic hero is generally thought of as the precursor of ourselves. Hence "release" here means release from the lower masculinity into the higher masculinity involved with the collective ideals in the single, earthly existence vouchsafed each man. Thus St. Anthony was confronted by the ugly vision of a "cringing little black boy"—the Devil—admitting finally that he had been defeated by the enlightened saint, who had wrested from the dwarf his magic strength in order to apply it to tasks transcending the capricious expenditure of libido characteristic of the manikin.[38]

[36] Marie Delcourt, *Hermaphrodite*, p. 51.
[37] Heinrich Zimmer, *The Art of Indian Asia*, I, 122.
[38] See article on St. Anthony in the *Encyclopaedia Britannica*, 1946 ed.

In a very general way it may be said that the fairy and the dwarf oppose each other as benevolent and malevolent manifestations of unconscious forces, though bad fairies are not at all lacking in the fairy tale, and sometimes storytellers find it necessary to speak of the *good* fairy. Needless to say, "conventional" fairies in the fairy tale must be distinguished from the fairy folk of Ireland, who combine in their complex personalities the bright features of the fairy godmother with all the wickedness of which the dwarf is capable. If the Irish refer to them as "the good people" it is "to avoid vexing them," as one storyteller put it.[39] The classical dwarf is known for his phallic characteristics of shape-shifting, hopping on one leg ("crippled" walking), and excited dancing, and these motifs appear in the crippling maladies visited upon human beings by the "good people," as in the case of the poor woman who was turned literally into an Oedipus: ". . . the woman had a terrible pain in her foot. It swelled to a great size, and where the swelling was the skin looked like the bark of a tree. . . . They offered one priest twenty pounds to cure her, but he said . . . he would have nothing to do with the case. He was afraid of getting a fairy stroke himself. The foot was swelling always, and it was that size that a yard of linen was needed to go once around it."[40] Like the dwarfs, the fairy folk live underground or in mounds, and thus like the dwarfs have within their power the use of dangerous unconscious and sometimes capricious forces, which makes them untrustworthy allies. The power of such creatures must be wrested away, or they must be tricked or cheated out of it. This seems to be less advisable in Ireland than on the Continent, where the dwarf regularly goes down in defeat before the human adversary, as typified in the best known of all dwarf stories, "Rumpelstiltskin."

"Rumpelstiltskin": A Case in Point

In the Grimm story "Rumpelstiltskin," it will be recalled, a miller boasts that his daughter can spin straw into gold. The king puts her to the test, shutting her all night in a room supplied with the necessaries for the job. She naturally despairs of her life, but a dwarf visits her

[39] Jeremiah Curtin, *Tales of the Fairies and of the Ghost World*, p. 42.
[40] Ibid., p. 24.

and accomplishes the task in return for her necklace. This is repeated the following night, and he accepts her ring in payment. The third night he requires her to promise him her first-born.

The delighted king marries her and a year later a son is born. The dwarf comes and demands payment, but in response to her pleading he says that he will release her from the promise if in three days' time she can guess his name. She sends forth a messenger to collect names, and on the third day the messenger happens unseen upon a little man excitedly hopping on one leg around a fire in front of a little house. He is celebrating his anticipated triumph. His victory song includes his name, Rumpelstiltskin, and so when the queen finally "guesses" correctly, Rumpelstiltskin falls into a rage and pulls at his left leg so hard that he tears himself in two.

The preceding survey of the dwarf in legend and folklore allows for the immediate statement that Rumpelstiltskin, whatever else he might mean, represents the king himself in his sexual aspect. Symbolically, the maiden is guaranteed by her father to be fertile, since traditionally this is the characteristic most highly prized in a queen consort. The guarantee is really double, for she is the daughter of a miller, and she is said to be a magic spinner. The legendary miller presides over one of the most common activities symbolic of sexuality,[41] while the creative domestic activities traditionally associated in Europe with women—cooking, sewing, weaving, spinning—easily and quite naturally come to symbolize general creativeness as wives and mothers (cf. the metaphorical use of "distaff" to signify women). From Mexico the belief is reported that elves "appear at night, especially in the kitchen, and they play tricks on women who are cooking."[42]

In "Rumpelstiltskin" the king wants to test the guarantee before taking the maiden as his queen consort, which means (since the test itself does not immediately involve becoming pregnant) that he wants to test her capacity to cope with sexuality—since it is intuited that a

---

[41] Milling is a much used symbol of sexual intercourse; cf. the folktale of why the sea has salt, where it is a mill that forever grinds salt ($=$ semen) into the ocean ($=$ archetypal womb). In Spanish literature the best-known use of the miller as an admirable phallic figure (the successful husband who habitually gratifies his strongly sexed wife) is that of Alarcón's *Three-cornered Hat*.

[42] Américo Paredes (ed.), *Folktales of Mexico*, p. 32.

woman suffering from "frigidity" (sexual anesthesia) may represent (and sometimes is) a procreative liability with which a king ought not unnecessarily burden himself.

The story relates that the king shuts the maiden in a room all night, saying that she must spin successfully, whereupon a little dwarf comes out and does the job for her. Symbolically, this means that the king himself tests her by spending the night with her. She is an initiate and so is passive, but by the end of the night the dwarf has, indeed, been able to spin. This stunning success awakens the king's greed, and he decides to continue the testing period, which culminates in a "power play": he will have ascendancy over the first-born—and it is quite taken for granted that there will indeed be a first-born. Since "first-born" and "spinning" are made to be interdependent in the story, it can be assumed that they are causally related: spinning straw into gold is different from ordinary spinning; it is "impossible" (i.e., symbolic spinning), for it produces not mere thread, but an offspring. It is eroticism with a procreative purpose, and it produces "gold," because the offspring is a prince. Straw is symbolically related to peasant life, and the maiden who can produce noble stock from her peasant womb spins straw into gold. Further, the gold symbolizes the king's sense of success, which the maiden's initiation instills.

"Rumpelstiltskin" affords the clearest possible folk example of the psychology of phallicism both as a phenomenon within any individual psyche and as descriptive of its development at a collective, or ethnic, level.

The symbolic meaning of the story in terms of the individual psyche lies in the discovery of an *individual name*. The characteristic element of "Rumpelstiltskin," the element that sets it apart from the general run of folktales, is the culmination of the story, which centers around finding out a secret name. Indeed the story seems to be merely a preparation for this. To know a person's secret name means to gain power over him. This is a belief well attested to in primitive cultures, and primitive peoples universally practice the custom of multiple names, one of which is "secret," that is, known only to oneself or special people. So it may be said that in the story the secret name of the king is the name that identifies him in his most secret aspect: his intimate

sexual aspect. To possess conscious knowledge about any person's secret sex life is truly to have a psychological power over him. Rumpelstiltskin undertakes the magic spinning for three nights (= threatened
power over the maiden's future motherhood) but in three days the
young mother finds out his name. He takes credit for the magic spinning, but she has the child. And when the final confrontation arrives,
she destroys him—or rather she depotentiates him by forcing him to
destroy himself—by telling him who he is: a grotesque spinner with a
grotesque name who cannot now disturb the serenity of the triumphant
woman-mother.

The situation in terms of the individual man's conflict with the
phallic impulse and with the anxieties that it creates on the part of the
maiden is well exemplified by the tremendous resistance encountered
initially by Freud when he insisted on knowing the intimate sexual
aspect of his patients' personalities. In fact, the success of his psychoanalytic method depended precisely upon finding out the "sexual
name" of the neurotic patient, since Freud theorized that the neurosis
was the outward manifestation of a hidden sexual dysfunction. Freud
forced the anonymous (i.e., repressed) phallic dwarf to destroy himself by leading the patient to discover his name.

The heroine of the story is led to know the name of Rumpelstiltskin
when he is observed hopping triumphantly on one leg around a fire in
front of a little house. This is a highly dramatic symbol for the man's
aggressive role in sexual intercourse; and when the queen finally di-
vulges that she does indeed know his name, Rumpelstiltskin falls into
a rage and attacks his left leg, a symbol of wrongly used ("left," or
"sinister") ithyphallic power. He, who expected that he would dominate her through sexuality, is suddenly and unexpectedly shown that
she will dominate him and retain her natural matriarchal rights over
her offspring. This important point will be returned to in a moment
apropos of the collective, or ethnic, significance of the Rumpelstiltskin
story. But here we should consider the means whereby the queen discovers the name of the dwarf.

A puzzling element of the story is the introduction of a messenger as
the instrument whereby the queen discovers the dwarf's name. It is

puzzling because of its vagueness. The use of an indistinct, anonymous character in order to fulfill an essential function does not seem typical of the fairy tale, and it is significant to find, in an English version of this story ("Tom Tit Tot"), that the king himself plays the role of the messenger in the Grimm story, suggesting that the anonymous messenger as such is inessential to the meaning, and also that he may be a later substitution for an earlier, more direct version of the story. Possibly, too, the substitution (if such it is) may represent a contamination of the idea of anonymity (i.e., what is his name?). In the Grimm story the messenger goes about publicly inquiring names, whereas in "Tom Tit Tot" the king, who was hunting in the forest, simply recalls the excited "fire dance" of the phallic dwarf. That this activity is grounded in unconscious strivings is indicated by the fact that the king tells the maiden all about it without himself suspecting the significance that can be attached to it. He shut her all night in a room for the purpose of spinning; the night episode, once begun, was taken over by his phallic aspect that has its own secret drive to which the conscious personality is oblivious. It is the kind of situation that might be described by saying that the right hand does not know what the left hand is doing (cf. Trickster's quarreling hands).

When the queen "guesses" Rumpelstiltskin's name she automatically depotentiates his phallic aggressiveness as a psychological force in the projected union, for she has raised to consciousness her own ignorant fears of it. It is no longer the anonymous, secret figure so frequently feared by the nubile virgin. His destruction is depicted as a sudden shattering; the dwarf's power is turned against himself; it is as if she had dropped a bombshell upon him. In the Grimm version he screams, "The devil has told you that!"—which, ironically, is quite true.

The dwarf is depicted in folk literature both benevolently and malevolently (since phallic power, like any other psychic drive, is ambivalent) but is customarily thought of as sinister and not to be trifled with. His sudden appearance frequently does mean a bid for power over the individual, and often enough his "benevolence" is grudgingly given, or taken in spite of him by countertrickery. This is the primary reason that "Rumpelstiltskin" must be considered to be a paradigm of the phallic dwarf motif, because the final point in the story resides in an archetypal, sexual power struggle between husband and wife.

On the collective level this power struggle is well known to cultural anthropologists who have observed the world over that in primitive cultures a sexual conflict always arises as a result of the primitive male's fear of woman's sexuality. In order to compensate for the male's apparent lack of importance in the business of procreation (all the outward drama of pregnancy and birth belongs to the woman) the men develop phallic initiation rites that are jealously—and somewhat pathetically—guarded from the women. By means of these rites they "create" and "give birth to" men: the adolescent boys are symbolically killed and reborn through the symbolic obstetric activities of the men, and often enough the men know that if the women were to discover their "secret" the self-attributed phallic importance would be destroyed in an instant. These rites, then, form part of what is called the "womb envying" pattern: the men believe "that women, by virtue of their ability to make children, hold the secrets of life."[43] In one case at least the men, "who see their whole social order threatened by the coming of the European [since the missionary may divulge the fakery of their secret rites] threaten in tearful rage to complete the ruin" by showing their ritual objects to the women.[44]

"Rumpelstiltskin," then, recapitulates the universal and age-old "womb envy" of the male who seeks to dominate the phenomenon of procreation by the assertion of his phallic importance in the making of "gold." But the story also shows the man's primitive sense of his own insignificance. It is only by inventing an importance for himself and by guarding his secret activities from the woman that he can feel secure in his dominance. His "secret" is the mysterious hocus-pocus of the phallic initiatory rites whereby the boys are "conceived" and "born" as men; the men ultimately take the credit for spinning gold. In primitive societies, all men tend to be Rumpelstiltskins. If the women ever discover the secret, the male importance is undone. The self-aggrandizement of the men rests on a falsehood, which is proved by the fact that

---

[43] Margaret Mead, *Male and Female*, p. 102.
[44] Ibid., p. 103.

the women are hysterically forbidden to observe the rites; for if they did, they would name them for what they are and all would be over with. The men would simply fall apart in a "tearful rage."

In *Perlimplín* the sexual encounter is presided over by two dwarfs, from whom it is learned that Perlimplín is having an ecstatic time of it, and that he somehow suffers from a "misfortune." Considering what we know about the symbolism of the dwarf, we will be in a position to see how the introduction of these two "extraneous" characters really sums up the whole meaning of the play. For Perlimplín's misfortune contributes to and is part of his bride's continued contempt for him as an ineffectual lover—one who, arrested at the stage of narcissistic sexuality, cannot possibly elicit from her an erotic response. And the misfortune leads also to her symbolic cuckolding of him.

For in the morning he awakens with a large pair of golden horns. That Lorca calls for *golden* horns means that the symbol is being qualified in some peculiar way. Here the use of the gold motif is not far removed from its use in "Rumpelstiltskin." Both "Rumpelstiltskin" and *Perlimplín* involve an initiation into marriage. The king says, in effect, "Since she can make gold, I will marry her," which is to say, "The queen consort must be a mate who can produce gold." In *Perlimplín* the initiation likewise takes place at night and ends by producing gold. That Perlimplín wears horns is obviously a sign of his "misfortune"; but that they are golden may be taken as symbolic of the "golden opportunity" that he enjoyed with all the greedy appetite of the naïve phallic male. The first, full-powered manifestation of his sexual instinct is like the discovery of an inner gold mine, but the fact that he misuses it—that is, in a sheerly egotistic way—compounds his misfortune. Both "Rumpelstiltskin" and *Perlimplín* involve a sexually greedy male associated with the dwarf motif. Perlimplín, like Rumpelstiltskin, will end by destroying himself through a violent attack on his phallic aspect. Rumpelstiltskin attacks his left leg and Perlimplín stabs himself in the heart with a bejeweled dagger. In the case of Rumpelstiltskin, the king is spiritually destroyed as a dominating phallus bearer, whereas in the case of Perlimplín the destruction of the phallic drive is physical and so concomitantly destroys the entire person, itself felt to be a phallus (Perlimplín dons a cape for the occasion).

A Résumé of Perlimplín

The play is set in an eighteenth-century décor. Perlimplín is an introverted fifty-year-old virginal bachelor who lives alone with his books—which is to say, his fantasy life. He is cared for by an old and loyal domestic, Marcolfa, who forces him officiously into getting married. She believes that, since she will probably die before her master, he ought to think of the future and marry a young woman who could gradually supplant Marcolfa in running the house. Perlimplín would prefer not to make a decision of this kind, but Marcolfa insists and actually arranges a match with a voluptuous young lady named Belisa. Marcolfa sees it as a marriage of convenience, but that is hardly the case with Belisa, who is depicted as a highly sexed young woman. Perlimplín finds himself committed to an unequal match then and initially feels the greatest misgivings: "Oh, Marcolfa," he complains, "what world is this that you're getting me into?"

The foregoing is given in the form of a "Prologue," and the first scene of the play takes place on the wedding night. The scene is a bedroom with five balconies. The traditional wedding-night situation is reversed, for the bride is self-confident, whereas the groom is anxious and ill at ease. She treats him with a good deal of ironic scorn that is not really apparent to him, since his level of consciousness is truly childish. Still, he is looking forward eagerly to possessing his bride and confesses to her that he was mainly indifferent toward her until he peeked at her through the keyhole while she was dressing for the wedding ceremony. This confession of childish sexual curiosity leads Belisa to ask him about his previous love life, whereupon he confesses further that he is still a virgin.

When the moment of consummation arrives two *duendes*, or sprites—they must be played by two little boys—draw a curtain across the scene, pointing out that there are certain shortcomings that it is not decent to reveal publicly. By the end of their dialogue it is morning. The *duendes* open the curtains and depart. Perlimplín is in bed with a pair of large, golden horns on his head. He gets out of bed; he is wearing his dress coat. He goes to look outside and asks, astonished, "Why are the balconies open?"

Belisa.   Because there was a gale blowing last night.

Perlimplín. Why do the balconies have five ladders reaching to the ground?

Belisa.   Because that's the custom in my mother's country.

Perlimplín. Whose five hats are those that I see beneath the balconies?

Belisa.   They belong to the little tipplers who come and go, little Perlimplín. Love!

(*Perlimplín stands gaping at her*)

Perlimplín's anxieties are allayed, and the scene ends with his expressions of contentment with his new way of life; he is completely taken by Belisa's charms.

The second scene takes place some days later, in Perlimplín's dining room, where Marcolfa is remonstrating with her master for being a cuckold. She, being a loyal old domestic, naturally identifies with her master's honor, and she is quite upset at the events of the wedding night: "On the wedding night five persons entered by the balconies. Five! Representatives of the five races of the earth. The European, with his beard; the Indian, the Negro, the Yellow [man], and the American. And you didn't even know about it."

But Perlimplín only says, "That's of no importance." In fact, he is willing to encourage Belisa's interest in young male friends. He describes to the fascinated Belisa the physical charms of one admirer of hers, and she admits that he has been writing her passionately erotic letters. The latest communication is typical: it says in effect that her "soul" is nothing by comparison with her voluptuous body. And so Perlimplín, in an apparent access of generosity, says that he will arrange a rendezvous in the garden.

The last scene dramatizes the rendezvous. Perlimplín seems deliriously happy, while Marcolfa is overcome with shame and tenders her resignation. Perlimplín asks her to wait until morning, when she will, in any case, be "free as a bird." He finds the impatient Belisa in the garden and asks "concupiscently" if she is ready to meet her lover. She assures him that she is, and he tells her with satisfaction that this will be "the triumph of my imagination." He pulls out a dagger and goes to meet the lover, saying to the astonished Belisa: "Since you love him so, I do not want him to abandon you. And so that he can be yours completely, it has occurred to me that the best thing would be to stab him in his gallant heart with this dagger. Do you like the idea?" Belisa can see, obviously, that the situation is rapidly deteriorating. By this time Perlimplín is raving: "When he is dead, you will be able to caress him always in your bed. He will be so lovely and spruced up, and you'll never have to fear that he will stop loving you. He will love you with the infinite love of the dead, and I will be free of this dark nightmare of your magnificent body . . . Your body! That I would never be able to decipher!!!" Belisa hysterically calls for a sword with which to cut her husband's throat. But he has disappeared into the bushes and now returns, muffled in his cape, and mortally wounded. He reveals himself and tells her, as if he were the young admirer invented by himself: "Your husband has just killed me with this emerald dagger." He has stabbed himself in the breast, and as he dies he says: "He killed me because he knew that I loved you more than anyone else. While he stabbed me he cried, 'Now Belisa has a soul!' " He reviles himself in the third person: "Perlimplín killed me . . . Ah, don Perlimplín! You dirty old man, you puny puppet, you could not enjoy Belisa's body . . . The body of Belisa was for young muscles and burning lips . . . I, on the other hand, loved only your body. . . . your body! But he has killed me . . . with this burning cluster of precious jewels." His last words are an "explanation" of what has happened: "Do you understand?" he says to Belisa. "I am my soul and you are your body."

Belisa.   But what about the young man? Why did you deceive me?
Perlimplín.   The young man? (*His eyes close*)

Marcolfa, shocked with grief, tells Belisa, "Now you are a new woman. You are invested by [lit. 'clothed in'] the glorious blood of my master." Belisa cannot forget the young man whom Perlimplín had promised her, and the curtain falls as Marcolfa, disgusted, says, "Don Perlimplín, rest in peace. Just listen to her, don Perlimplín, just listen to her," for Belisa is lamenting: "But where is the young man with the red cape? Oh God: where is he?"

A Time of Freud

Perlimplín is, as shall be shown in detail, a deeply Freudian play both from the point of view of the psychological perspective and in the use of "Freudian" symbolism. Such being the case, let us recall briefly the early years of the psychoanalytic phenomenon, and review in passing the principal theoretical ideas with which Freud concerned himself.

In the year 1900, as if to celebrate the birth of the new century, Sigmund Freud published his first book, *The Interpretation of Dreams*. He was at the start of a long career, stubbornly determined to pry his contemporaries loose from their psychosexual innocence. In the next few years his psychoanalytic theory took shape. He achieved a growing celebrity and, at least into the twenties, increased public resistance and hostility; for it seemed simply incredible that the facts of "civilized" psychosexual development could be as he described them. The lurking subliminal family conflict fraught with primitive sexual desires and painful repression; the desire to murder, and the fear of reprisal in the form of castration; the true meaning of phobias and compulsions—all this implied that family life (and so human life itself) was reared on an ugly foundation of obsessive genitality. Our morals were only the fruit of our anxieties, born by necessity out of the need for all of us to suppress our pervasive incestuous lust.

One may accept or reject the main tenets of psychoanalytic theory as one chooses. But if it is now seen to be something less than a series of triumphantly discovered naked facts, it is also a good deal more than idle hypothesis. To all the skeptical critics the Freudians early developed the crushing reply that hostility to psychoanalysis was itself but one more practical proof of the theory of repression. That the reply was sufficiently motivated is evidenced by the unenlightened hostility apparent in this typical and comically prejudiced attack on Freud: "The routine translation of quite normal subconscious activities into unhealthy symbols of a sexual character, which is a practice all too common among certain practitioners, both amateur and professional, today, represents in my view no more and no less than an unbridled frolic on the part of a morbid and vicious mind of the translator."[45] The above appeared in 1936. The ignorant confusion and angry determination to attack by vilification are all too obvious. By 1936 Freud had already published all his important works, and yet it was still pos-

[45] Harold Dearden, *Devilish but True*, p. 117.

sible for the educated layman to denounce Freud's "vicious" and "morbid" interpretation of "quite normal" subconscious activities!

But the Freudians were equally at guilt when they refused to distinguish between enlightened and unenlightened criticism, and in the mid-forties Ernest Jones, always one of the greatest and most productive of Freud's disciples, was able to write in retrospect of the Jungians: "The opposition took the usual form of doubt about the existence of infantile sexuality, particularly in its relation to incestuous impulses, and every endeavour was made to reinterpret the concrete data of the unconscious into Jung's cloudy generalities and thus discount their emotional significance."[46]

During the first few decades of the twentieth century—at least until the Second World War—Freudian theory found support in the European art community, particularly among the surrealists, for whom the Freudian elucidation of dream life could not fail to be of enormous interest. There was produced a good deal of "Freudian art," that is, esthetic visions based on a belief in the essential correctness of Freud's view of the psyche and its dynamics.

Among Spanish artists, Salvador Dalí offers the richest material of this kind, no doubt because his consistent lack of spiritual depth gives the impression that he is more of a follower than a leader. Certainly a Freudian interpretation of (for example) Picasso's achievements is bound to be superficial if only because don Pablo is as great in his way as Freud was in his.

And the same is true of Federico García Lorca. Lorca, as the greatest and most innovative Spanish dramatist of the first half-century (perhaps of the entire century), and as a lyric poet of such stature that comparisons are bound to be odious, cannot seriously be called a Freudian; he is a "Lorcan." And yet *Perlimplín* is a Freudian drama.

To discuss Lorca's work generally in terms of psychoanalytic theory would be to miss the point of most of it; it would be to treat his work as biographical material contributing toward a psychoanalytic understanding of Lorca the man. But Lorca was the most innovative Spanish dramatist of his time. He realized that the Freudian theory of psychosexual development contained quantities of exploitable dramatic

[46] Ernest Jones, *Free Associations*, p. 239.

material, not only because the material itself seethes with subjective, elemental conflict, but also because publicly it was explosively controversial. One of Freud's achievements was his exposition of the dynamics of repression—and to publicize the reasons for repression seems to constitute an attack on those reasons. Hence the kind of vilification that has been cited above.

Lorca, in his major dramas, showed himself influenced possibly in only one general way by the growth of depth psychology.[47] But *Perlimplín*, a minor play, is an experiment—brilliantly successful—at working entirely within the framework of Freudian theory. The human level on which Lorca considered the theory to be relevant is indicated by the fact that don Perlimplín, the embodiment of psychoanalytic theory, is a spiritual nonentity. Freudian theory dealt first of all with neurotics, that is, victims of the postulated Oedipal situation, and Perlimplín is depicted consistently as a ridiculously incomplete and timid soul—a schlemiel.

Libido, as the life force, always one of Lorca's principal thematic concerns, is here limited to its two Freudian manifestations, first (and most important, of course), as a sexual instinct and, second, as a death drive: Freud's Eros and Thanatos. Lorca traps Perlimplín in a conflict between the pleasure principle and the reality principle—a conflict that arises when he, the embodiment of infantile sexuality, is faced with the challenge of adult sexuality. The play has never been dealt with critically in this way, which may be due only to the fact that it has never received a close reading by any critic.

Perlimplín begins as a farce and ends in tragedy, reflecting the farcical aspects of neurosis, which, if untreated, are almost certain to shrivel up the life of the sufferer. But the everyday social manifestations of neurosis characteristically appear as something comic. The social attitude toward alcoholism, for example, is largely dominated by jokes and pleasantries. Phobias and compulsions are a kind of partial "insanity" whereby the individual creates for himself an incongruous adjustment to reality. Herein lies the comedy. The adjustment must be incongruous because it springs from a psychic compromise of a most peculiar kind—the compromise that Karl Menninger and his associ-

---

[47] See my discussion below of *Yerma*, apropos of unconscious goals.

ates call *dysorganization*, or *dyscontrol*. In distinguishing between this compromise and what otherwise might be called "disorganization," Menninger really sums up the seemingly comic incongruity: for dysorganization does not mean "lack of" organization, but rather "bad" organization: "There *is* organization in these ['neurotic'] conditions; it has not been lost or destroyed, but only impaired. . . . The dysorganization reflects a concomitant effort to avoid disorganization."[48] When the dyscontrol is relatively mild it appears as "a slight but definite detachment of the person from his environment, and—simultaneously— from his loyalty to reality. He becomes, as his friends would testify, a little (more) unrealistic."[49]

Hence the possibility of laughing at such behavior. It is not tragic, precisely because the neurotic individual, in reconstructing partially the world he lives in, is trying to avoid a total (and therefore tragic) withdrawal from the real world.

"Dyscontrol" and "dysorganization" are used by Menninger in order to avoid the diagnostically irrelevant problems of labeling "neuroses." For present purposes they are useful, since they avoid the very technicalities that Lorca himself avoids. Lorca was not competent to create a character strictly in terms of Freudian psychopathology, for he was not a psychoanalyst. He avoided the technical aspects of the neurotic personality and concentrated instead on the main principles of psychoanalysis. Perlimplín clearly suffers some form of dysorganization, which cannot be dramatized in detail, because to do so would be to turn the play into a patently artificial and self-conscious attempt to dramatize Freud. And Lorca was, first of all, a dramatist, not a special pleader.

Perlimplín *and Freudian Symbology*

Amor de don Perlimplín con Belisa en su jardín (The love of don Perlimplín with Belisa in his garden) is dated 1931. Freud's *The Interpretation of Dreams* appeared in 1900, his *The Psychopathology of Everyday Life* in 1901, and the Spanish translation of these works (in the *Obras completas* of Freud) came out in 1922. Thus it is more

[48] Karl Menninger, *The Vital Balance*, p. 157.
[49] Ibid., p. 174.

than likely that in the twenties Lorca became familiar, either directly or indirectly, with these first two popular books of Freud. It is *The Interpretation of Dreams* particularly that established in the public mind the notion of "Freudian symbols," which is to say, generally, a gross sexual interpretation of everyday symbols and, specifically, the interpretation of these symbols as the disguised expression of infantile-sexual desires.

In *Perlimplín* Lorca is not involved with Freudian symbolism in a naïve, uncritical way; for the most part he is playing with it. His other, "serious," works are not particularly Freudian, since the symbolism in them is never of an infantile-sexual kind. That is to say, in contrasting *Perlimplín* with other plays by Lorca, a distinction must be made between sexual symbolism per se, and Freudian symbology, which holds that the unconscious use of symbols gives disguised expression to wishes originating in infancy[50]—repressed now, of course. This origin gives the symbols their peculiarly naïve, childish quality, and it is also this whereby "adult" sexual symbolism is to be distinguished from "Freudian" symbolism. In Lorca's play *Yerma*, for example, the protagonist, a frustrated would-be mother, compares herself to a field waiting to be sown, which is a direct and undisguised allusion to fertile union. Yerma knows to what she refers, and her wish to be impregnated cannot, in itself, be called infantile. Her use of the agricultural metaphor is hardly more than a manner of speaking. The unfulfilled wish that she expresses is conscious, hence the lack of disguise. Then again, the reference is to conventional adult sexuality as the means to procreation. Yerma is not concerned with eroticism or with the immediate reduction of libidinal tension.

Readers of Lorca are familiar with his symbolism relating to life, death, and sexuality and know that nothing is to be gained by attempting to interpret it in terms of psychoanalysis, since this means removing a symbolic disguise in order to reveal repressed desires; nor is the infantile history of Yerma sufficiently implied by the data of the play to warrant and Freudian second-guessing by the critic.

Lorca's most "psychological" play, *As Soon as Five Years Pass*, is likewise not amenable to psychoanalytic interpretation, since it in-

---

[50] Sigmund Freud, *The Interpretation of Dreams*, p. 589.

volves the "holistic" problem of individuation, that is to say, the need to establish harmony among the historically current elements of the protagonist's psyche; and further, it deals with the meta-Freudian relationship between the personal psyche and the transpersonal unconscious.[51]

Perlimplín, however, is cut from a different cloth, for in it Lorca portrays not only a regressive figure but also an infantile character. His regressiveness consists in his futile attempts to come to terms with the problem of sexuality itself, and its meaning in life as apart from procreation: this is to say, Lorca is dealing with eroticism as a problem. He builds up the plot in terms of the Freudian perspective, and one senses a certain deliberateness about it. He does not convey the impression that he is a dramatist seriously "inspired" by Freud. Rather, he seems to see in psychoanalytic theory the opportunity to exploit dramatically a certain body of material. He evidently finds the Freudian material "interesting," rather than crucial for himself in a metapsychological way. It does not touch him intimately (he sets it at a distance— in the eighteenth century), but it offers a wealth of matter for theatrical exploitation.

The plot and the dialogue are both simple and unadorned. This is a characteristic that recalls *The Interpretation of Dreams*, which is full of dramatic dream episodes recounted in the form of bare résumés. As we examine *Perlimplín* for its Freudian content we will see the appearance in it not only of typically Freudian theory, but also of the mode of representation characteristic of the Freudian dream, including the use of devices described by Freud in *Dreams*: dream distortion, manifest-latent contrasts, displacement, body symbolism, condensation, censorship, wish fulfillment, absurdity, objectification; we will see the use of infantile material pondered by Freud: infantile-sexual curiosity, and the infantile drive toward ego-domination.

The basis for all this is Lorca's decision to use an infantile protagonist, which means (given Perlimplín's age) an extremely regressive male who has rarely ever "tested reality," and who still lives what is largely a fantasy life.

---

[51] The substance of this paragraph represents my conclusions reached in a lengthy seventy-six–page analysis of *Five Years* in Rupert Allen, *The Symbolic World of Federico García Lorca*.

Typical Lorcan symbolism never strikes one as arbitrary, far-fetched, gratuitous, or merely ingenious; rather, it seems to grow organically out of the material itself. His dramatic characters are typically involved with the problems that assail adults, not children—whereas *Perlimplín* is concerned with infantile sexuality. When infantile sexuality continues to be a serious problem in adult years, the result is commonly a neurosis. And this theme itself is Freudian: it simply did not exist as a possible subject of discourse before Freud, who was severely criticized and denounced for his introduction into psychology of the notion of infantile sexuality. Infantile sexuality is, indeed, necessarily associated with the name of Freud, since psychoanalysis is rooted in the study of the psychosexual dynamics of early childhood. And so Lorca's creation of a character with this kind of neurotic shortcomings might easily be expected to manifest itself in terms of the Freudian perspective and in terms of Freudian symbology.

Perlimplín is in every way but chronologically a child: his name is diminutive, he is a virgin, and he has always lived apart from world reality, under the motherly protection of an older woman, the faithful Marcolfa. Everything about him reveals that he is neurotic, above all because he labors under the child's naïveté concerning the psychosexual facts of life. His conscious behavior is determined by infantile attitudes that have remained largely intact. This psychosexual regression is, of course, the phenomenon of crucial significance in psychoanalytic theory.

Further, Lorca combines the ideas of childishness and preadult sexuality through the use of a character and subtitle taken from children's comics—the old *aleluyas*, or crude "funnies" intended for children. It is as if Lorca were to subtitle his play "comic strip." But he also adds the adjective "erotic," so that the complete title translates something like this: Love of Don Perlimplín with Belisa in his Garden: Erotic Funnies in Four Scenes.

One commentator says that Lorca calls his *aleluya* "erotic" so as to "set it apart from the childish . . . ones."[52] But this can hardly be the case, since it is evident enough that he uses the allusion to *aleluya* in the first place precisely in order to establish the play's relationship with

[52] Ernesto G. Da Cal, *Literatura del siglo XX*, p. 259.

an infantile genre. To suggest that Lorca is trying to avoid the infantile connotations of the *aleluya* is to beg the question of why he chose
that genre to begin with. No: one must recognize that the reference
to an *aleluya erótica* is another way of alluding to the Freudian topic
par excellence: infantile (= *aleluya*) sexuality (= *erótica*). The title
could be restated thusly in terms of its Freudian connection: Love of
Don Perlimplín with Belisa in his Garden: Infantile Sexuality in Four
Scenes.

It has been noted that Freud, in *Dreams*, gave particular attention
to the symbolic sexual connotation of everyday objects; he wanted to
show that psychoanalytic theory applies to everyone, not just to neurotic persons. More than once he makes this point, as in the following
instance: ". . . we must recognize that the psychical mechanism employed by neuroses is not created by the impact of a pathological disturbance upon the mind but is present already in the normal structure
of the mental apparatus."[53] This seems obvious now, after all these
years of exposure to depth psychology, but in the early years of the
century it was a controversial point. "Crazy" people were commonly
thought to be qualitatively different in the head, and even so eminent
a psychological authority as Havelock Ellis was able, in 1911, to argue
that Freudian symbology applied only to the neurotic mind,[54] as if the
dreams of "normal" people had a different latent content—an attitude
like that of the indignant American lady who informed Ernest Jones
that "while repressed ideas might have something to do with the
dreams of Europeans they certainly didn't in her country, since Amer-
icans had no repressed ideas."[55] Around the turn of the century it was
the tendency on the part of the educated public (i.e., the "Victori-
ans") to believe that their conscious life, cleansed and sterilized of all
"dirty" material, was essentially different from the sick mind of the
neurotic, or the "sex fiend," or the sexual monomaniac. Hence the
vicious criticism directed against the man who maintained that everyone's dream life was composed of a "clean" manifest content and a
"dirty" latent content; that the disguises were successful precisely be-

[53] Freud, *The Interpretation of Dreams*, p. 607.
[54] Ibid., p. 373. This note was added to *The Interpretation of Dreams* in 1914.
[55] Jones, *Free Associations*, p. 192.

cause they were not, on the whole, frighteningly bizarre, but rather because they were based on the most mundane, prosaic symbolism. After his *Dreams* Freud pursued this attempt at persuading the public at large in his second work, significantly entitled *The Psychopathology of Everyday Life*—not the "psychology" of everyday life.

The material dealt with by Freud in these works appears to be intricately interwoven into *Perlimplín*. Even the *garden* mentioned in the title gives pause. Anyone familiar with the history of Occidental literature is aware of the sexual connotation of this symbol (in Spanish literature the *locus classicus* is *La Celestina*) but such awareness had generally disappeared from the middle-class Victorian consciousness. In *Dreams* Freud approaches the subject of the garden by speaking of the house in general as eminently appropriate for the symbolization of sexual activity, and he extends this to include the biblical "vineyard, the seed, and the maiden's garden in the *Song of Solomon*": "The ugliest as well as the most intimate details of sexual life may be thought and dreamt of in seemingly innocent allusions to the kitchen; and the symptoms of hysteria could never be interpreted if we forgot that sexual symbolism can find its best hiding-place behind what is commonplace and inconspicuous."[56] Freud then goes on to give a woman's "flowery" dream set in a garden-orchard, and remarks with gentle malice (as he occasionally liked to do), "The dreamer quite lost her liking for this pretty dream after it had been interpreted."[57] The dream is one of the lengthier ones (two pages) recorded in *Dreams*, and the sexual elements are strongly emphasized by the use of capital letters. It is filled with genital and pubic symbols and references to seduction, copulation, and the like.

Now the mere fact that Lorca refers to a garden in the title of *Perlimplín* is not, of itself, sufficient to warrant a Freudian interpretation; but the play is, after all, about the erotic problems encountered by a newly married couple. It should be noted that only the last scene of the play is set in a garden, and that it is not there that Perlimplín's "love" takes place—though it *is* there that he is an "erotic success" (a point that is going to require some discussion). The "love" referred

---

[56] Freud, *The Interpretation of Dreams*, p. 346.
[57] Ibid., p. 347.

to in the title as the subject of the play could quite as justifiably be taken to be a reference to the consummation scene, which takes place not in Perlimplín's garden, but in his bedroom. In this sense there is no difficulty at all in understanding the "garden" of the title to be an allusion to the bride herself. As a matter of fact, there is an ambiguity in Spanish of the possessive adjective in the title, which cannot be rendered in English, since it could mean simultaneously "the love of don Perlimplín with Belisa in his [her] garden." The published translation by James Graham-Lujan and Richard O'Connell avoids the ambiguity by rendering the title as *The Love of Don Perlimplín and Belisa in the Garden.*[58]

As the play begins, the stage direction calls for Perlimplín to be wearing a *casaca*, the eighteenth-century gentleman's dress coat, cut full with wide sleeves and at least thigh length; as a man's large, outer garment, it is symbolically cognate to the greatcoat or overcoat (G. *Mantel*) discussed variously by Freud in *Dreams*. *Mantel* is specifically "cloak"; but all such large male outer garments (raincoat, cloak, mantle, overcoat, greatcoat) signify in Freudian symbology either condom or phallus.[59] The two garments that will be used by Perlimplín are precisely the dress coat and the cloak. As the ineffectual lover, Perlimplín is identified by his more socially formal *casaca*; the cape that he wears in the last scene successfully disguises him as an exciting seducer.

The exposition of the play makes it abundantly clear that Perlimplín has resisted all his life the challenge of living and growing. He has remained as much as possible in the narcissistic stage, and Marcolfa's attempts to push him into the phallic stage (at this late date) occasion the greatest anxieties. It is the problem of the "onward urging" life force that Perlimplín has consistently resisted, and Jung's description of it shows the general course of Perlimplín's life in résumé form: "The onward urging, living libido which rules the consciousness of the son, demands separation from the mother. The longing of the child for the mother is a hindrance on the path to this, taking the form of a

---

[58] García Lorca, *Five Plays*, trans. James Graham-Lujan and Richard O'Connell.
[59] See pp. 186, 206, 356 of Freud, *The Interpretation of Dreams*. On p. 356 Strachey specifically gives *Mantel* and "overcoat" as equivalents.

psychological resistance, which is expressed empirically in the neurosis by all manners of fears, that is to say, the fear of life . . . The fear springs from the mother, . . . from the longing to go back to the mother, which is opposed to the adaptation to reality."[60] Perlimplín, toward the end of the play, will recall fondly how contact with Belisa reactivated his early childhood memories of his mother.

The play starts with a dialogue between Perlimplín and Marcolfa, represented as a protective, hence maternal, figure. She suggests that he should think of getting married, because she could die "at any time now." Clearly the prospective wife is supposed to take over the maternal role, since Perlimplín is not accustomed to fend for himself. But when Marcolfa tells him that he must get married, he reacts by attempting to avoid the subject, pretending a lack of interest. She insists "energetically," whereupon he responds by showing great *anxiety* (he answers *angustiado*, "distressed"). Broaching the subject of adult sexuality stimulates anxiety on the part of the child. This is a widely known Freudian principle: "It is . . . a matter of daily experience that sexual intercourse between adults strikes any children who may observe it as something uncanny and that it arouses anxiety in them."[61] Here Perlimplín is not an "observer" but is rather being nagged to expose his virginal and vulnerable ego to conjugal sex. He expresses his anxiety in terms of an infantile fear, which, he says, has persisted into his adult life: "When I was a child a woman strangled her husband. He was a shoemaker. I've never forgotten it. It has always been my intention not to marry. My books are enough for me. What good will it do me?" Since Perlimplín associates matrimony with violent murder, it is necessary to take into consideration the Freudian observation that young children frequently interpret the "primal scene" as a struggle between their parents. In one instance discussed by Freud a child patient "had subsumed what happened between his parents under the concept of violence and struggling; and he had found evidence in favour of this view in the fact that he had often noticed blood in his mother's bed."[62] Now there is no internal evidence that Perlimplín

[60] Jung, *Psychology of the Unconscious*, p. 335.
[61] Freud, *The Interpretation of Dreams*, p. 585.
[62] Ibid., pp. 584–585.

actually witnessed the "primal scene," but it is clear that he makes a direct association between marriage and a violent attack. He is unique among Lorca's characters in making specific reference to a childhood memory as the basis for an anxiety, and this kind of material lies at the very heart of psychoanalytic theory. Perlimplín's recollection is obviously put forth as a childish excuse and sounds very much like what Freud called "screen memories." Memories from early childhood are highly selective and represent (in accordance with the Freudian repressive mechanism) a *displacement* of original, personal events by a substitute recollection. Here, Perlimplín gives as the reason for his personal and intimate fear of marriage his memory of an event that occurred not in his own family, but between two anonymous strangers. It goes without saying that any traumatic childhood experience shaping later attitudes toward marriage is to be sought first of all within one's own family circle. To maintain that one's fear of marriage has been crucially conditioned by the early childhood memory of a bad marriage between two strangers must be interpreted as a displacement of the original source of anxiety.

Further, it is significant that Perlimplín's recollection takes the form of the wife attacking the husband, and not the other way around, since open sexual aggression is usually attributed to the man. Perlimplín's fear of woman's "mysterious" and "dangerous" sexuality as something savage that could cause his death is both irrational and infantile: it is based on his ignorance of the topic traditionally "forbidden" to children. The classical manifestation of the adult male's fear of woman's sexuality takes the form of the neurotic belief in the *vagina dentata*, the aspect of the female that threatens to "strangle" man's phallic libido.

In the discussion of the dwarf-symbol the phallic symbolism of the foot and leg was duly noted, and the Freudian interpretation of "foot" is only too well known, since *Oedipus* means "swell-foot." The two motifs are linked in the Grimm story "The Elves," where it is told that at midnight "two pretty little naked men" came to do a shoemaker's work, thus delighting him and his wife and enriching their lives immeasurably.[63] Hence there is no need to doubt the phallic associations

[63] *Grimm's Fairy Tales*, p. 198.

of Perlimplín's poor shoemaker, whose activity was peremptorily suspended by his mate.

And so in an effort to avoid the dangerous topic of matrimony Perlimplín says that his books "are enough." He prefers the narcissistic fantasy stage (reading books) to the imagined, fearful violence of adult sexuality.

Marcolfa tries to suggest to him the erotic delights of married love. At this point Belisa is heard singing offstage. The song itself is openly erotic and characteristically Lorcan:

> Love, love.
> Between my closed thighs
> the sun swims like a fish.

To repeat, this is characteristically Lorcan, and not Freudian. Belisa is singing openly, without disguise, of her genital fire, and Lorca evidently wants to avoid associating Belisa with Freudian symbolism here since she, as Perlimplín's "antagonist," is the person capable of dealing with adult sexuality. She, unlike children, understands and uses sexual symbolism for avowedly erotic purposes. The motif of the song belongs to ancient (adult) tradition and appears in folk literature in the form of the golden fish of fertility, as in the Greek tale "The Twin Brothers," where the childless wife gives birth to twins when she eats a small portion of the golden fish caught by her husband.[64]

Marcolfa continues to nag Perlimplín about his future, and then attention is drawn to Belisa's open balcony. She is standing there "half nude" (*medio desnuda*). The association of Belisa with the balcony is a directly visual symbol, something seen rather than heard. In Freudian symbolism it means a visual representation of the maternity motif: Perlimplín's wife-to-be is imagined as a surrogate mother.

Freud gives a good deal of attention to this kind of architectural symbolism and, in interpreting one man's dream involving pears on a window sill, observes that, concerning the patient's mother, "the window-sill was the projection formed by her bosom—like balconies in dreams of houses. . . . His feeling of reality [i.e., he thought it was an unusually 'real' dream] after waking was justified, for his mother

[64] Georgios A. Megas (ed.), *Folktales of Greece*, p. 37.

had really suckled him, and had done so, in fact, for far longer than the usual time. . . . The dream must be translated: 'Give (or show) me your breast again, Mother, that I used to drink from in the past.' "[65] Elsewhere Freud points out that in dreams the façades of houses can evoke "recollections of a baby's climbing up his parents or nurse," and that the dreamer "often clutches hold of 'projections' " in these façades.[66]

Perlimplín's marriage is arranged, and he rightly anticipates it fearfully as a traumatic event: as an event that will thrust him across a new threshold into a reality with which he is not prepared to deal. What is more, it is being done to him; his is the passive submission of a child who feels constrained to make even the most important decisions in life out of obedience to adult authority, and he complains: "Ah, Marcolfa! What world are you getting me into?"

At this point Perlimplín does a childish thing, which is to ask his "mother," so to speak, to bring him a drink of water, because he is terribly thirsty—this, immediately following Marcolfa's remark that she is thrusting him into the world of matrimony. But Marcolfa, instead of bringing him the water, whispers something in his ear. He answers in disbelief, "Is it possible?" by which one is to understand no doubt that Marcolfa is interpreting for him his thirst as an erotic symbol. Since she was expected to bring him a glass of water, the Freudian interpretation lies near at hand. In *The Psychopathology of Everyday Life* Freud gives the lengthy and amusing story of one man's involvement with such a vessel—in this case a vase, which is, says Freud, "an unmistakable symbol of a woman."[67] And so Marcolfa undoubtedly tells Perlimplín that his terrible thirst will be quenched only when Belisa herself "brings him a glass of water."

This Prologue ends with the visual symbol of a flock of birds, made of black paper, flying across the balcony. In a general sense this certainly must be understood to be an ill omen, and Freud himself mentions the "ill-omened flight of birds";[68] but the bird is a familiar phallic symbol, even apart from Freud. It comes in for special discussion in

---

[65] Freud, *The Interpretation of Dreams*, pp. 372–373.
[66] Ibid., p. 355.
[67] Sigmund Freud, *The Psychopathology of Everyday Life*, p. 172.
[68] Ibid., p. 259.

Dreams apropos of the flying dream. Besides making reference to the German slang term for copulation (*vögeln*, from *Vogel*, "bird"),[69] Freud writes at greater length: "Dr. Paul Federn . . . has put forward the attractive theory that a good number of these flying dreams are dreams of erection; for the remarkable phenomenon of erection, around which the human imagination has constantly played, cannot fail to be impressive, involving as it does an apparent suspension of the laws of gravity. (Cf. in this connection the winged phalli of the ancients.)"[70] The fact that in *Perlimplín* the birds are black and of paper (= artificial) associates them simultaneously with sexuality and with death (cf. the blackbird as a harbinger of death). Perlimplín's phallic attitude is "artificial": neurotic, regressive, infantile, not "natural" to a grown man, since he seeks in the woman maternal protection rather than an erotic partner. The birds are visually associated with the balcony (= Belisa), and his need to approach his bride via her maternal aspect will ultimately bring about his death.

The first scene proper of the play takes place on the wedding night, in Perlimplín's bedroom, and Lorca calls for six doors: five of them open onto balconies, while the sixth communicates with the rest of the house. Marcolfa enters carrying a candelabrum (multiple candles corresponding to the multiple balcony doors?), which is one of Freud's famous phallic symbols. In one dream a woman "was putting a candle into a candlestick," and Freud comments: "Some transparent symbolism was being used in this dream. A candle is an object which can excite the female genitals."[71] And here he quotes a "well-known students' song" involving the autoerotic use of candles.[72] Lorca's stage direction is suggestive, since the occasion has arrived in the play when Belisa is supposed to be "excited" by her husband.

Enter Perlimplín. He looks into the next room and talks to Belisa. Visually this emphasizes his imminent relationship to her, since Lorca calls for an arrangement whereby Perlimplín is supposed to talk to her, standing in front of the entrance to the room where she is preparing herself for the consummation of the marriage. "Rooms in dreams are

---

[69] Freud, *The Interpretation of Dreams*, p. 583.
[70] Ibid., p. 394.
[71] Ibid., p. 186.
[72] Ibid., p. 187.

usually women ['Frauenzimmer'],'' says Freud; "if the various ways in and out of them are represented, this interpretation is scarcely open to doubt."[73]

The bride is wearing a lacy negligee for the occasion, and Perlimplín tells her that she looks like a frothy ocean wave and so causes him, he says, to feel the same fear that he used to feel for the ocean when he was a child—another infantile recollection put forth by him as the ostensible basis for a sexual anxiety. Of course it is latently no different from his previously expressed anxiety, since here he is using the ocean as a devouring womb symbol. He continues: ever since the wedding ceremony, he says, "my house is full of secret sounds [*rumores*], and water grows warm by itself in the glasses." Perlimplín (it shall be learned) is beginning to recover from his fright at the thought of this initiation. He is beginning to become excited (*rumores* = libido),[74] and he is aware of new libidinal sensations.

It must be noted here that the sex life of this fifty-year-old virgin has been exclusively autoerotic, a point that will be brought out later in the play. At the present moment, faced with a real erotic object (as opposed to the autoerotic fantasy), he finds his house "filled with secret sounds"—sounds of libidinal stirrings. When he says that "water grows warm by itself in the glasses," the operative word is *sola* ("by itself"), meaning here "not artificially stimulated." His thirst is actually going to be quenched (for the first time!) by the living body of a real woman in his house.

This symbolism is low keyed, in that Perlimplín compares the erotic encounter to a glass of water growing warm (literally, "tepid"). Belisa, on the other hand, is under the influence of sexual libido with an adult orientation. Her own erotic thirst is limitless, she says: "My thirst can never be quenched, like the thirst of the stone faces that pour water into the fountains." The stone face that spews forth a stream of water

---

[73] Ibid., p. 354.
[74] In his "Madrigal de verano" (*Libro*, pp. 209–211) the blood circulating within a woman's bosom produces "the *rumor* of your breasts." In "Thamar y Amnón" (*RG*, pp. 464–467) the blood becomes in a woman's finger tips "the *rumor* of a confined rose." In Act Two of *Así que pasen cinco años* the Mannequin speaks of the "warm *rumor*" of sexual union (p. 1100). In "Elegía del silencio" (*Libro*, pp. 217–219) the warmth of the sun (macrocosmic libido) is described as "the golden *rumor* that falls upon the blue mountains."

through its mouth gives the opposite impression of drinking, but the symbolism is implicit: Belisa is like a fountain; the stone face spewing forth the never-ending phallic stream symbolizes the approach of the insatiable male who never ceases to fill the fountain. The unending phallic source is ceaseless sexual appetite directed at the insatiable woman.

As Perlimplín awkwardly seeks a way to break the ice, he comes to confess to a piece of infantile sexuality of the crudest kind: for he tells Belisa that he peeked at her through the keyhole while she was dressing for the wedding ceremony. This is not voyeurism in the technical sense (repetitive neurotic behavior) but rather a spontaneous manifestation of infantile-sexual curiosity, discussed variously and at length by Freud, of course; it was a facet of the first of his famous theories that angered the public, as noted by Ernest Jones in his autobiography. Referring to the years preceding World War I, Jones speaks of how, among his educated friends and medical colleagues, he encountered "astonishment at the then novel idea" of infantile sexuality.[75] In *Dreams* a typical instance of this "novel idea" describes "a scene of early childhood in which the child, probably driven by sexual curiosity, had forced his way into his parents' bedroom."[76] In *The Psychopathology of Everyday Life* Freud speaks of a patient who "flung open the door," interrupting the analytic session immediately preceding her own, and notes that "it soon turned out that she had been demonstrating the curiosity that in the past had caused her to make her way into her parents' bedroom."[77] These "sexual researches of children" make their appearance in *Perlimplín* in the form of the confessed attempt to satisfy curiosity by spying on a woman's toilette. Why should Perlimplín have done this, when that very evening he knew he would have full access to his bride? Undoubtedly because his anxious ignorance of what to expect led him to formulate the notion of securing a preview, so as to forearm himself with some kind of certain knowledge; one aspect at least of his initiation would be familiar to him—a visual knowledge of Belisa's nudity.

---

[75] Jones, *Free Associations*, p. 150.
[76] Freud, *The Interpretation of Dreams*, p. 459; see also pp. 326, 346.
[77] Ibid., p. 214.

He says that when he saw her naked he first "felt love." This appears to be the most superficial kind of love attachment, meaning as it does the reaction to an erotic discovery. Evidently he gulped in amazement at what he saw (it was like "the deep incision of a lancet in my throat"—to note the symbolic use of the trauma, literally, "wound") and experienced a sudden erotic tension. As he admits, it was his first (visual) sexual encounter with a real, live naked woman. Belisa is rightly "amazed."

The scene of the consummation is "censored" by the device of a gray curtain drawn by two *duendes*, or sprites. In the stage direction Lorca explains that the part of the two *duendes* must be played by two little boys. The quantity of mythological and folk material concerning the manikin has shown that he plays the phallic role traditionally and universally; but he can nevertheless be considered a "Freudian" symbol in the sense that Freud first "reminded" the modern world of the sexual meaning of what appeared to be one more innocent symbol, since "Freudian interpretations" in the popular sense mean the unveiling of ideas with a sexual content long repressed by urban Occidental consciousness. And so Freudian explanations like the following (from *Dreams*) were not initially received with much credence: "Children in dreams often stand for the genitals; and, indeed, both men and women are in the habit of referring to their genitals affectionately as their 'little ones.' Stekel is right in recognizing a 'little brother' as the penis. Playing with a little child, beating it, etc., often represent masturbation in dreams."[78] As far as the general educated public was concerned these were the obscene ravings of a sexual monomaniac.

While it has been suggested that the two *duendes* exercise a censoring function, naturally this is not meant in the strictly Freudian sense, though Lorca's contrivance here bears a similarity to dream censorship. The dwarfs "veil" the erotic action of the play, partly out of a sense of "decency," but they do not hide the action in the sense that their dialogue displaces attention from what is happening behind their curtain. On the contrary, their conversation concerns nothing but that. Still, Lorca is playfully using a sexual symbol whose manifest content is not

[78] Ibid., p. 357.

immediately revealing of its latent content—or so it would seem, since no critic of this play has pointed out the sexual meaning of the *duendes*.

It has already been noted that the critics of *Perlimplín* have concluded that the consummation scene is meant to portray a failure—the groom's alleged impotence. Also noted was the probable source of such a conclusion, for one *duende* says that the public should not look upon the "misfortune" of a "good man." But the assumption of impotence is absolutely untenable and contradicts the text at several points, apart from the fact that it is unnecessary and irrelevant. The nature of Perlimplín's misfortune has been mentioned—his infantile sexuality confronted by Belisa's adult sexuality—and later it will be discussed in greater detail. For the present it should be noted that the consummation scene implies the "staging" of phallic activity, and that the *duendes* discuss it symbolically as an ongoing activity. The first remark is a greeting from one to the other: "So: how are you getting along in the pleasant little darkness?"[79]

The "dialogue" here is actually one continuous commentary representing a single point of view, with alternate lines given to each *duende*. Disregarding this stichomythic formality, one may read it as follows:

It is good [for me, a sprite] to conceal other people's shortcomings, to draw a curtain over them. Let the audience undertake to figure them out. Because [N.B.] if these things are not covered up with all kinds of precautions they will never be revealed.

And without this hiding and revealing, what would the poor people do?

Let me check the curtain to make sure that there is no open crack; for tonight's open crack is darkness tomorrow. How amusing!

When things are obvious, man thinks there is no need to uncover ["discover"] them—and so he has recourse to murky things in order to discover in them secrets he already knew.

That's why we are here! We sprites!

This is a strange bit of dialectical play with the notions of light and darkness, knowledge and ignorance, and the thread of logic is by no means obvious, which in itself is part of the mischievous play of

[79] The text reads *lo oscurillo*, from *oscuro*, "dark." Hence I have rendered the diminutive as "pleasant little [darkness]."

the sprite. The remarks disclose that disguise (or suppression) is the best stimulus to curiosity. If something is presented openly and without inhibition, it is typically accepted at face value. Of course the business of hiding and discovering here refers to sexual matters. Sexuality is never "obvious." The "obvious" exploration of sexuality is pornographic and is concerned exclusively with the physical aspects of sex. But the "murky" aspect of eroticism is psychosexual. The straightforward representation of "obscenity" (as in the permissive contemporary theater) has an impact that does not incline the spectators to consider the meaning of it all. But by the use of symbols—here the sprites —Lorca presents a certain aspect of sexuality, which, because it is "hidden" in symbols, protects "poor people" from their own discomfiture. "They" (i.e., the audience of the twenties and thirties) need the disguise of the symbol, because their conscious life is predicated on the need for the repression of their own psychosexuality. Such is the Freudian mechanism of repression. The Freudian symbol sets the audience at a comfortable distance from the sexual content and so allows them to consider it with a certain equanimity impossible in the face of raw lust. But if the innocent symbol can be made to yield its secret, this will turn out to be something that was already known unconsciously, by direct experience; for it was this knowledge that produced the symbol in the first place.

The sprites appear to make a lewd double entendre: "tonight's open crack is darkness tomorrow." They laugh at this, and so it can easily be taken as an obscene joke, but it is a frightfully relevant piece of obscenity; for if it is understood as a reference to Perlimplín's discovery of Belisa, then what appears to him "openly enjoyable" tonight is going to turn out to be a terrible enigma on the morrow. And at the end of the play, as he lies dying, he will cry out in anguish and despair that Belisa's body is a dark nightmare that he could never decipher.

The sprites, as symbolic of Perlimplín's phallic aspect, know what weaknesses inhere in his ego-consciousness. Like Rumpelstiltskin they savor thoughts of their own consequent autonomy; they make jokes about Perlimplín's erotic risk taking. One of them says that he has known Perlimplín "since his childhood," and that he also knows

Belisa well. One night, he says, he fell asleep in her boudoir and woke up "in the claws of her cats." They find this highly amusing.

Freud, in *Dreams*, elucidates the meaning of "cat" as a sexual symbol: "Many of the beasts which are used as genital symbols in mythology and folklore play the same part in dreams: e.g., fishes, snails, cats, mice (on account of the pubic hair)."[80]

In *Perlimplín* the reference to Belisa's cats is quite untypical of Lorca since to him the "mythological" use of beasts serves a more general spiritual purpose than the psychosexual one.[81] But the analogy in *Perlimplín* between this allusion and Perlimplín's recollection of the woman who strangled her husband is too close: the phallic dwarf, during the consummation scene, recalls jovially the possibility of being destroyed by the woman's sexuality (the claws are a more explicit symbolic reference to the neurotic fear of the *vagina dentata*). The fact that Belisa is said to have "cats," rather than "a cat," can easily be explained in Freudian terms. Indeed, it needs to be explained, since it is difficult to see how the *duende* could awaken in the claws of two or more cats. But the difficulty of the image is one that Freud found solvable in terms of the following rule: "The *temporal repetition* of an act is regularly shown in dreams by the *numerical multiplication* of an object."[82] Thus the sprite is saying that he was nearly destroyed by the obsessive sexuality of Belisa (= repeated demand for sex; recall her comparison of her own erotic drive to that of the incessantly receptive stone fountain).

But how is it that the *duende* who has "known" Perlimplín all his life could also be well acquainted with Belisa? The question is answerable only in terms of the logic of symbols; and it has been noted at length, in the preliminary study of the manikin, how the dwarf represents an instinctual force from the nonpersonal level of the psyche. The dwarf is not a personal aspect of the psyche, but rather an archetypal aspect of the instinct out of which one's own ego-consciousness was born, or "fragmented" (i.e., split off). One's dwarf is no different

---

[80] Freud, *The Interpretation of Dreams*, p. 357.
[81] Cf. Lorca's use of the cat symbol in *Así que pasen cinco años* and my discussion in Allen, *The Symbolic World of Federico García Lorca*, pp. 62–63.
[82] Freud, *The Interpretation of Dreams*, p. 373.

when he appears within oneself than when he appears in anyone else. If the dwarf knows one man, he knows all men, which is why Ernest Jones' indignant American lady appears absurd, believing as she did that national boundaries extend into the realm of the unconscious.

The one sprite says that he "fell asleep" in Belisa's boudoir once, and that he awakened "in the claws of her cats." Whenever we speak of the activities of unconscious figures, we must bear in mind that we have to do with a mirror world, as pointed out by Layard: ". . . it is a psychological fact of universal application that the unconscious (that is to say, the collective, not the personal unconscious . . .) is the mirror opposite of the conscious."[83] There are all kinds of reasons why such should be the case, though perhaps everyone intuits directly the meaning of mirror symbolism (as in Alice's adventures in *Through the Looking-Glass*, or in the reversed procedures of the black mass), even if he does not stop to intellectualize it. But one of the mirror aspects of the unconscious lies in the fact that, when consciousness is awake, the unconscious sleeps, and vice versa. The meaning of the terms "awake" and "asleep" really depends upon the frame of reference called consciousness. Even when a person dreams at night, he still says that he is asleep, though the dream quite obviously is a form of consciousness, often much more vivid and acute than the daily waking state.

So if both the conscious and the unconscious aspects of the psyche are taken into account, it has to be recognized that, when a person is "asleep" and dreaming, *that* is precisely the time when unconscious aspects—regularly repressed—"awaken." Thus, the *duende* once fell asleep in Belisa's boudoir—that is, he was repressed; when he "awoke" he found himself in a dangerous situation. Since the sprite is a psychic element typically repressed in the presence of ego-dominance, he can "awaken" only when conscious attention flags so as to open the floodgates of associative thought processes. Thus the fact that he "awoke" means conversely that Belisa fell asleep—or that she was in some other state not dominated by ego-consciousness. It does not have to mean that Belisa was entertaining a lover, nor does it have to have an autoerotic significance. What it does mean, regardless of the "nonconscious" state alluded to (dream state, erotic ecstasy, autoerotic fantasy), is that Be-

[83] John Layard, *The Lady of the Hare*, p. 193.

lisa's sexuality has the power to castrate, in the psychological sense. The woman who treats man not as a companion in eroticism, but merely as the phallus bearer or copulator who services, is taking possession of his manhood for her own devouring purposes. A strong and experienced erotic male partner can treat this as a challenge and force erotic equality in the sexual battle, which is finally the source of deepest joy to both partners. But the strongly sexed woman (as the "nymphomaniac") seeks in her fantasy to overpower and to appropriate for her own intrapsychic needs the sexual "vibrations" of the male. That Belisa is so has already been indicated by her speech in which she describes herself as sexually insatiable ("my thirst is never quenched"). She is, indeed, the kind of strangulating woman feared by Perlimplín, and her daemonic greed will seek out like a predator the phallic libido of any lover. Of course this does not threaten the *duende*, but only the individual lover; for the *duende* lives multiple lives (like Belisa's cats!) in the unconscious of all men. If he "awakens" to find himself in the claws of her obsessive sexuality, this is of no consequence to him—and so he laughs easily at the memory of Belisa's frantic greed.

For now, the sprites observe that "Perlimplín's soul, little and frightened like a newborn duckling, is being enriched and sublimated in these moments"—and again they laugh, because what seems so marvelous to Perlimplín right now is going to result in his own violent death.

The *duck* is a figure well known in the fairy tale and appears in a number of stories as an enchanted person. Marie-Louise von Franz, who has studied this mythic and folk symbol in some detail, concludes that "the duck symbolizes a psychic being, which on the one hand represents a principle of consciousness (sun), but on the other hand is dominated by the feminine (pond, etc.)."[84] She mentions the sun because of the motif of the "golden duck," which is said to swim in a celestial pond. The general symbolic importance of the duck is related to that of all aquatic birds and fowls, which are at home in the three realms of earth, water, and sky. But, being a "primitive" animal (by comparison with the more highly evolved brain of the mammals), the

[84] Marie-Louise von Franz, "The Problem of Evil in Fairy Tales," in *Evil*, p. 115.

duck "is the germinal principle of consciousness, wholly devoted to the service of the unconscious."[85] The well-known phallic symbolism of the bird has already been recalled, and its appearance here as an aquatic fowl recalls the *phallic swimmer* of the Trickster Cycle, where Trickster removes his phallus and sends it across a river in order to copulate with the chief's daughter. The phallic male becomes wholly absorbed in swimming like a duck. In those moments he is transformed—an "enchanted person," as in the fairy tale—and, as Kerényi says of Trickster, "his identity with this swimming part of himself— a veritable *pars pro toto*—does not cease."[86]

This material is of obvious relevance to the case of don Perlimplín. That his soul is being "enriched" by his initiation into a new world— the "pond" of Belisa's sexuality—can hardly have any reference to impotence; on the contrary, he is greedily satisfying himself in an egotistic way—given his character, how could it be otherwise? The manikin, as has been seen, represents an unconscious force, which, if not assimilated by consciousness, will overtake the ego—and that is exactly what is happening to Perlimplín. His spirit is now reduced to the status of a duckling swimming happily and unconsciously in the waters of a world new to him. But that world is equally well symbolized by the *duendes* themselves, who recognize little Perlimplín as their potential victim. And this seems funny to them.

As dawn approaches, the two dwarfs prepare to leave, and what appears to be a typical Lorcan image occurs when one of them says, "Five cold camellias of the dawn have opened in the walls of the bedroom." This is characteristic of Lorca, but the Freudian foundation of this play points to the relevant passage from *Dreams.*

Of course what is meant is that the sun is shining through the five balcony windows of the bedroom. But why does Lorca use precisely the image of the camellia? In the dialogue that follows, it will be learned that "five men" have entered the room during the night in order to have sexual relations with Belisa. These five men correspond to the five balconies, of course, which is to say that Lorca has originally imagined multiple windows to be matched by multiple sexual acts.

---

85 Ibid.
86 Kerényi, in Radin, *The Trickster*, p. 182.

The fact that now the early morning light is described as five cold camellias is related symbolically to the multiple coitions.

The camellia is the most specific of the many images shared by *Perlimplín* and *Dreams*. Freud, apropos of a dream in which camellias appear, says that this has to do with "an allusion to the *Dame aux camélias* who, as we know, usually wore a white camellia, except during her periods, when she wore a red one."[87] According to Lorca's use of the symbol, the morning light filtering through the balcony windows is like cold camellias, and so here one ought to recall the Freudian meaning of "balcony" and "window," as entrances to a bedroom. Perlimplín has satiated himself during the night (a circumstance to be discussed) and Belisa, by morning, is described genitally as a "cold flower" of the early dawn, which has "opened," that is, has been transformed by a ghastly night of sex with her unsatisfactory bedmate. It goes without saying that she is a different person now, for the night with Perlimplín has been a turning point. She, who had been waiting for one thing, has received something entirely different. Her sexual future is at stake now. Perlimplín is erotically a mere child, and he has not known how to arouse her. Thus her sexuality in marriage "blooms" only as a "cold camellia," considerably in contrast to the "hot plumage of swans" that she had lasciviously imagined previous to the consummation. She now finds herself consigned to a married life whose beginning is like a cold dawn. This is something she cannot tolerate, and her struggle to free herself of the cold prospect will soon destroy the erotic dolt to whom she is married.

The *duendes* depart, the curtain is raised, and Perlimplín and Belisa are seen in bed just as they awaken in the early morning. It is in this scene that the most farcical use of Freudian symbolism occurs, involved as it is with two of the symbols most closely associated with the sexual interpretations of Freud: the hat and the ladder. Chapter Five of *Dreams*—"Representation by Symbols"—contains a short section entitled "A Hat as a Symbol of a Man (or of Male Genitals),"[88] and elsewhere Freud goes to some lengths to explain why "steps, ladders or

---

[87] Freud, *The Interpretation of Dreams*, p. 319.
[88] Ibid., pp. 360–362.

staircases, or . . . walking up or down them, are representations of the sexual act.''[89]

In this scene Perlimplín looks out a balcony window, and the reader will recall the following dialogue:

Perlimplín.   Why are the balconies open?
Belisa.   Because there was a gale blowing last night.
Perlimplín.   Why do the balconies have five ladders reaching to the ground?
Belisa.   Because that's the custom in my mother's country.
Perlimplín.   Whose five hats are those that I see beneath the balconies?
Belisa.   They belong to the little tipplers who come and go, little Perlimplín. Love!
(*Perlimplín stands gaping at her*)

The image of five hats, or phalli, at the bottom of five ladders (multiple coitions) leaning against five entrances (female genitals) into the bedroom where Belisa lies abed on her wedding night is hardly less than a farcical exaggeration of Freudian symbolism. In fact it seems that the desire to play with such symbolism furnishes the motive for what would otherwise be a gratuitous bit of imagery.

An analytical discussion of these five hats and ladders must be deferred until the following scene, when Marcolfa makes fresh reference to them by adding data. The present discussion will skip to the end of the scene where Lorca again calls for flocks of paper birds to fly about the balconies, without stipulating, however, that they should be black in color. Morning bells are to be heard ringing at the same time. If any importance is to be attached to the fact that the birds are not black, it might very well be that this is meant to convey Perlimplín's subjective impression of the night he has just spent with Belisa. He clearly has performed his role, since he exclaims to his bride, "For the first time in my life I am happy!" The fact, too, that bells are pealing while the birds flit around the balconies can be understood easily within Freudian symbology as an expression of Perlimplín's temporary euphoric and egoistic contentment with his own performance. Anyone familiar with the Freudian point of view will have no trouble interpreting the sexuality presented by the image (acoustic here) of the ringing bells.

[89] Ibid., p. 355.

Apart from the traditional association with wedding bells, the ringing bell is a natural image of coitus (cf. the slang use in English of "dong" —the sound of a bell—as penis, the "clapper").[90] Perlimplín considers that he has performed well, though what he has done is to enjoy Belisa's body in an Oedipal fashion, which is to say that he has taken without giving, just as the little boy takes egoistically what mother has to give. The mother expects this—it is in the nature of things—but what must be Belisa's reaction? For Perlimplín Belisa's body is an extension of himself, an object of selfish gratification. Subsequently, when circumstances carry him beyond this point of view, he will then see her body as a "dark nightmare" impossible for him to "decipher." Lorca thus will confront Freud's "pleasure principle" with the "reality principle."

The play now passes to Scene Two, laid in Perlimplín's dining room. Lorca calls for a special stage effect here: "The lines of perspective are delightfully wrong" (i.e., awry, out of drawing). The table, with all the objects painted on it, looks like a "primitive Last Supper." The symbolism here is not Freudian in the visual sense, but rather in the psychological idea behind the impression that the stage set is supposed to make. By all rights, Perlimplín should have moved from the "pleasure principle" to the "reality principle," but he has not done this, nor will he be capable of doing so, since the reality principle will always remain a "dark nightmare" to him. Perlimplín does nothing more than to extend the narcissistic pleasure principle to include the body of Belisa. She is an external object that he uses in order to masturbate. As long as he can do this in a mindless and selfish way without taking into consideration his bride's own erotic needs, it can truly be said that his perspectives of the world immediately around him are "wrong"—for him, "delightfully" (literally, "deliciously") so: "For the first time in my life I am happy!" He is living in a fool's paradise. The "wrong perspectives" of his dining room (food = sex) furnish the background of the stage setting as they do the background of the tragedy itself, since his wrong perspective will issue in despair and suicide.

As has been noted parenthetically above, the reason for the scene's being laid in the dining room is clear enough if not only the traditional

[90] See Harold Wentworth and Stuart Berg Flexner, *Dictionary of American Slang.*

associations between food and sex are recalled, but also Freud's remark in *Dreams* that "tables, [and] tables laid for a meal . . . stand for women."[91] Lorca says that the painted objects should look like a *cena primitiva*, which has been translated as "primitive Last Supper,"[92] but it is doubtful that the impression made in the theater would evoke precisely this notion (Last Supper) in the mind of the spectator. It is true that Lorca himself may be making some association between the Last Supper and the tragic climax of the play, since an important fantasy idea underlying Perlimplín's suicide is no doubt that of grandiose self-sacrifice; but why does Lorca call for a primitive style (i.e., in the style of Early Christian art prior to the application of the rules of perspective)? No doubt it is because Perlimplín's sexual treatment of Belisa is regressive or "primitive."

Marcolfa and Perlimplín are conversing. She is mortified because he has evidently been dishonored on his wedding night: five men, she says, "representatives of the five races of the earth," entered the bedroom and had sexual intercourse with Belisa. The critics have taken this episode at face value, which seems remarkable, considering that it is absurd—that is, taken at face value it has no meaning, in exactly the manner noted in the discussion of the dwarf. The "manifest content" of the wedding night is absolutely lacking in verisimilitude, and it is not sufficient to excuse this on the grounds that *Perlimplín* "is a farce, after all." A farce is an exaggeration of and a comment on possible behavior or possible circumstances, not an arbitrary concoction of impossibilities. Clearly this material has a latent content that must be dealt with as such, but to date the manifest content has been treated critically as if it involved no difficulties.

Certainly one cannot believe that on the wedding night five strangers (of five different races) literally entered the room, each by a different window, and had sexual intercourse with Belisa, unbeknown to Perlimplín, and that each of them left a hat at the bottom of "his" ladder. How is it possible that the bride would—or could—make five assignations with five different men in the double bed shared by her husband? Further, there is the question of how Marcolfa could know the intimate

[91] Freud, *The Interpretation of Dreams*, p. 355.
[92] García Lorca, *Five Plays*, p. 120.

details of the wedding night, and of how she might inform her master of them as if he were ignorant of the episode. Obviously this episode is impossible to implement literally, but in this it is no different from the absurdity of much dream material.

According to Freud in his chapter "Absurd Dreams," not only do the symbols in dreams have a latent meaning but also, when the manifest content appears as inherently absurd, this absurdity itself has a source and a meaning. That is to say, a logically contradictory dream situation may be the oneiric representation of contradictory (ambivalent) emotional attitudes.[93] Certainly feelings do not develop and evolve in accordance with the laws of logic, and the dream is concerned with one's affective life.

If Lorca is presenting a dramatic absurdity, it must be because something forced him to do it; there was no other way to represent what he had in mind, just as the dream work is forced to represent the idea or psychic presence of self-contradiction by means of an absurd situation. Five "strangers" entered the bed of bride and groom and had intercourse with the bride. When Marcolfa tearfully recalls in his presence this monstrous situation, Perlimplín does not react appropriately: "That's of no importance," he says!

And later, when he has arranged for Belisa to meet her admirer in the garden, he tells Marcolfa (nor is he being ironic), "Tonight my lady Belisa's new and unknown lover will come. What should I do but sing?" Whereupon he suits the action to the word and bursts into song: "Perlimplín has no honor! He has no honor!"

All this bears a curious resemblance to the well-known oneiric gap between situation and emotional reaction. This gap is discussed by Freud in his chapter "Affects in Dreams": "It has always been a matter for surprise that in dreams the ideational content is not accompanied by the affective consequences that we should regard as inevitable in waking thought. . . . In a dream I may be in a horrible, dangerous and disgusting situation without feeling any fear or repulsion; while another time . . . I may be terrified at something harmless and delighted at something childish."[94] The underlying principle, as analy-

---

[93] Freud, *The Interpretation of Dreams*, p. 431.
[94] Ibid., p. 460.

sis shows, says Freud, is that "the ideational material has undergone displacements and substitutions, whereas the affects have remained unaltered."[95] Which is to say that interpretation of the dream situation requires looking to the affect for the latent content; the manifest content tells nothing by itself. The affect has been displaced from its true psychical cause, and another, "innocent" cause has been substituted. Thus the manifest content of the five strangers is affectively a matter of indifference to Perlimplín (he didn't "wake up," he was not even aware that such an episode took place). Here the substitute idea (five strangers) is manifestly not "innocent," but it temporarily protects Perlimplín, by displacement, from despair and suicide. The morning after the wedding night he wakes up wearing huge golden horns, but he is unaware of their presence. And later, when Marcolfa confronts him with the fact of his alleged dishonor, he replies indifferently, "That is of no importance." He arranges for Belisa to meet a lover, and then sings, "Perlimplín has no honor!" The affect is contrary to what it must certainly be in external reality.

His bizarre reaction can be interpreted in one of two ways: (*a*) an attempt can be made to explain why he enjoys being dishonored, in which case the manifest content is being taken at face value; or (*b*) the manifest content can be treated as a substitute for some other, latent event. In the face of absurdity it seems that the second alternative is the necessary one.

In analyzing the dream as a kind of internal symbolic drama, Freud saw that it was generally needful to distinguish between the argument, or "plot" of the dream, and the method of representation. This latter is what he called the dream work. Here Freud is not simply distinguishing between form and content, since the distinction is impossible to apply. What he distinguishes is the manifest content—the gross action of the oneiric drama—on the one hand, and the problems involved in the nonverbal elaboration of significant latent ideas, on the other. In discussing the dream work he describes the devices of condensation, displacement, the problem of representability, and secondary revision ("secondary elaboration"). Since the dream as a whole is symbolic, it is useful to recognize the two groupings of dream ele-

[95] Ibid.

ments as belonging to either the symbolic action or the symbolic mode. These latter are not always easily distinguished in specific cases, nor is it always of crucial significance to do so, since the goal, after all, is to interpret the meaning of the dream rather than label the elements. The value of labeling the elements springs from the original intuition whereby Freud recognized the difference between manifest and latent contents.

We have seen how *Perlimplín*, as symbolic theater, bears a good deal of similarity to the dream, precisely by virtue of its being symbolic—involved with images relating to the dynamic interplay of conscious and unconscious life. Until the time of Freud, no one had hit upon any fertile method for interpreting dreams, because all previous attempts were centered upon the manifest content. And this problem, it seems, has presented itself anew in the task of analyzing Lorca's symbolic drama. Criticism on *Perlimplín* deals solely with the manifest content and ignores the symbolic mode—the "dream work"; or, to put it another way, the critics have treated the action and the mode as if they were both the manifest content.

A simple example is furnished by the huge golden horns worn by Perlimplín on the morning following the wedding night. Are these horns part of the "action"? Everyone knows well enough their meaning, but what should the spectator's attitude toward them be? Are the horns actually "there," so to speak? Is Perlimplín "wearing" them in the same sense that he wears a shirt or a pair of trousers? They are conspicuous and grotesque, but their presence goes "unrecognized" by Perlimplín and Belisa.

Symbolically, their presence really offers no problem to the spectator. He simply accepts them as a symbol for cuckoldry; they are "just a symbol." If one were to dream that a bull gored him, the bull's horns would be part of the action; but if one were to dream this episode of *Perlimplín*, the horns would have to be recognized as part of the dream work; it would constitute a solution to what Freud called the problem of "representability." It is a symbolic mode.

A more complicated example of dream work is afforded by the episode of the *duendes*. What is their relationship to the rest of the play? Are they two more characters in the sense that Marcolfa is a character?

That is to say, are they part of the action? Or are they part of the symbolic mode, analogous not to the flesh-and-blood characters, but rather to the golden horns worn by Perlimplín?

The logic of symbols forces one to choose the second alternative. The sprites are a projection, or "objectification," of an element of Perlimplín's psyche, rather than two actual visitors to his house. At one point Perlimplín "has" horns; at another point he "has" *duendes*. Since Lorca was characteristically concerned with the problem of the unconscious and its "representability," he was frequently guided by the example of how dream work solves the same problem.

These considerations are of importance in approaching the problem posited by the episode of the five strangers—or rather the dialogue concerning them—since one must recognize the possibility that he may be dealing either with an "episode" (= action) or a symbolic mode (= dream work). Who are those five strangers? They enter the play only in the form of a dialogue concerning something that Perlimplín sees out the window. This occasions the dialogue quoted above that begins with his question "Why are the balconies open?" and it takes a ritual form. He asks the simpleton's questions and Belisa gives him evasive answers that he accepts without further suspicion. It is the sort of dialogue found sometimes in the fairy tale. The following questions and answers, for example, appear in "The Twelve Dancing Princesses":

Q. Who is pulling at my dress?
A. You have only caught it on a nail.
Q. What made that noise just now?
A. It was only someone firing a gun in the distance.
Q. Why is the boat so much harder to row tonight?
A. What should cause that, but the warm weather?[96]

No doubt the most famous example of this occurs in "Little Red Riding Hood" ("What big ears you have!" etc.); and the question arises: why does it seem so appropriate to the world of the fairy tale?

The answer, of course, lies in the fact that the fairy tale is a genre for children and typically concerns the adventures of children and of

[96] "The Twelve Dancing Princesses," in *Grimm's Fairy Tales* (Follett), pp. 365–372.

childlike people: naïve and weak, morally innocent persons who tend to triumph over sophisticated, strong, and wicked people. The dialogue of the fairy tale reflects the fantasy world of the child and the ignorance of the child with respect to the world of the grownups. Hence the naïve questions. "Evil" in the fairy tale very frequently means sophisticated deception; there is no situation more common in the fairy tale than that of the child's being taken advantage of by virtue of his gullibility.

Here it can be seen that *Perlimplín* has something in common with the fairy tale, particularly in the "episode" of the five strangers. Perlimplín has been deceived in some gross way; confronted by the most blatant evidence, he only suspects; and when he voices his suspicions they are easily allayed by devious answers.

This similarity to the fairy tale is inherent in the material being used by Lorca, since he is concerned with infantile material as a determining force in the behavior of an adult. Belisa has successfully "deceived" Perlimplín in some special way as yet to be discussed, and this deception is indicated by the golden horns.

Belisa obviously knows that the horns are there, but naturally enough she makes no reference to them. Perlimplín, on the other hand, does not know they are there. This is not mere supposition on the spectator's part, but rather it reflects the symbolic truth of the horned husband. Surely a significant reason for the use of horns, precisely, as an indication of cuckoldry resides in the fact that the husband is typically the "last to know" of his wife's infidelity. Others (at least two) know, and when they see the husband they have an image of him considerably different from his own self-image. Since horns always grow out of the head, they are the one physical characteristic found in the animal kingdom which the carrier himself cannot see. It is possibly for this reason that horns are used as a sign of the cuckold and have nothing to do with the symbolism underlying horn per se.

So the audience and Belisa "see" the horns, even though they are not literally "there." To see in this fashion is to sense the presence of a psychological quality (e.g., "You see him as an egotist, whereas I see him as a philanthropist"). Perlimplín's possession of horns indicates that he is supposed to be seen as a cuckold, and that he is not supposed to be aware of this; further, it is something that he needs to be incapable of raising to consciousness.

If an obvious point seems to be overemphasized, it is because the understanding of it will help toward understanding the ambiguous element of the five strangers. Do they belong to the action or to the mode? The same question may be asked of the hats and ladders, since these belong to the five strangers, and Perlimplín "sees" them. Now "to see" means one thing when applied to the action and something else when applied to the mode. In the first instance it means that a material event is taking place; in the second instance it means that a subjective circumstance has been raised to consciousness—whether understood or not. (Dreams regularly raise material to consciousness that is usually not understood.) If the five strangers belong to the mode and if the hats and ladders are the evidence left behind, it means that Perlimplín dimly "sees" these strangers without understanding them. Indeed he needs to repress them. Marcolfa herself eventually knows about the five strangers, and adds the datum that they are of five different races.

The use of five strangers must be considered. Much is made of this number in the play, since there are five balconies, hats, ladders, and strangers. Obviously there are five balconies because there are five strangers, and vice versa. Probably no one would dispute that the five balconies (like the golden horns) certainly belong to the mode, not the action, since they are part of the inert stage setting against which the action takes place. If each stranger has "his own" balcony, it must be concluded that the strangers are a symbolic extension of the balconies.

It has been noted that Perlimplín treats Belisa as a surrogate mother, as the recipient of his infantile sexuality. His image of her does not correspond to the "real" Belisa. Since it is a projection onto her of a fantasy, one may conclude that it too belongs to the symbolic mode of the play, and it is this that lays the groundwork for the action.

Lorca calls for the consummation of the marriage to take place in a bedroom with five balconies because five strangers are supposed to enter them, each by his own balcony. The next morning Perlimplín sees the evidence, but it is meaningless to him.

If "five men entering five balconies" means multiple coition (as it must, since this is a wedding night—the occasion *par excellence* for sexual enthusiasm) a solution to the problem begins to become clear. Freud has been cited to the effect that "balcony window" has a double meaning: female genitals (= entrance) and bosom (= balcony projection). Both of these meanings are basic elements in *Perlimplín* since the protagonist enjoys sexual intercourse with a surrogate mother.

Belisa herself belongs to the world of adult sexuality. Perlimplín, as an old-maid bachelor, remains in the stage of infantile sexuality (his sex life can never have gone beyond masturbation). Therefore, when Perlimplín has sexual intercourse with Belisa, he enters, via her body, into the world of adult sexuality *as a stranger*. His initiation into this world is part of the action (the scene "covered" by the phallic dwarfs); but to characterize him as a stranger (= someone unknown to him) is part of the mode. He is acting a role new to him; as a matter of fact one of the dwarfs even applies to him the description "new-born."

Thus the play is the depiction of a conflict between Perlimplín and Belisa arising over their differing attitudes toward sex. He practices infantile sexuality and she needs adult sexuality. For him a wife is the female who satisfies his needs, just as mother (or Marcolfa) did.

Still, the question of Marcolfa's special knowledge needs to be explained, and the answer lies in the five balconies that are the original determinants of the five strangers. Marcolfa knows that her master is "happy" since the wedding night; but she would obviously know also that Belisa is something less than happy. A man can possess a woman in basically two ways: "selfishly," and "unselfishly." As part of the domestic life, Marcolfa would not find it difficult to intuit which way her master handled the wedding-night challenge.

The reason for "five" seems to be indicated clearly enough in the text: "five" stands for universality. If Perlimplín treats Belisa as a mother, she in turn treats him in some way as Everyman. When Perlimplín asks her, "Why do the balconies have five ladders?" she answers, "Because that's the custom in my mother's country." The five strangers who entered that night represent the "five races" of the world (i.e., Everyman). Belisa's attitude is that the copulator is Everyman, and she says that such an attitude is the custom in her mother's country. Note must be taken here, then, of the primitive matriarchal (prepatriarchal) point of view toward the male: he is the phallus bearer, not an individual man: "The basic law of the matriarchate forbids individual relations with the man and acknowledges the male only as an anonymous power, representing the godhead."[97] It was not Perlimplín himself who possessed Belisa on the wedding night; it was the anonymous power of the dwarf. Thus does Belisa's insatiable thirst manifest itself.

This thirst of hers has yet another aspect. Belisa, as the obsessively sexual woman, is a type. In world literature she is represented by Circe, who turns the man into an animal (by "unmanning" him), the sorceress who turns the man away from his spiritual goals. Her most frightful proclivity is that of the siren, or woman in her negative aspect as the mortal peril of the masculine spirit.

But the man is not only turned into a symbolic animal. The seductress can "unman" him in another way, which is most convincingly illustrated by the history of the word *effeminate*. A brief consideration of this word will further clarify Belisa's role in *Perlimplín*.

The History of the Effeminate Male

It should be recalled that the word *effeminate*, long before its now normal association with homosexuality, meant only "soft," or "decadent." An effeminate man was formerly (and ironically enough) a heterosexual male who preferred the company of women to that of men—the don Juan Tenorio type of man who persistently sought to enjoy his virility in the form of making love to women. He is in dialectical opposition to the "man's man," or "Hemingway man," who expresses his virility in the form of male tasks and male competition— athletics, the outdoor life, roughing it, heavy gambling sessions, and so forth.

This is a useful dialectical distinction. The two types rarely appear in anything resembling the pure form, but such tendencies and preferences are familiar enough as dominant traits of character. It is important to the "he-man" to define his maleness in terms of other men and

[97] Erich Neumann, *Amor and Psyche*, p. 75.

in terms of all-male standards. The Tenorio defines himself in terms of women: he attaches obsessive importance to the role of woman awakener, and for him the "frigid" woman is a challenge, not a tribulation. The two of them are types of the so-called lower masculinity, and in real life they are frequently thought of as men who ought to "grow up."

This dialectical polarity is nowhere more neatly illustrated than in Torquato Tasso's *Jerusalem Delivered*, the poem of the First Crusade, of arms and the man. Rinaldo, the mighty knight, falls in love with the sorceress Armida. He deserts camp, and two knights are dispatched to bring him back. They find him dallying in the Fortunate Isles, Armida's paradise for lovers. They show him his reflection in the shining face of a shield, and the mighty warrior is brought to his senses:

> Upon the targe his looks amaz'd he bent,
>   And therein all his wanton habit spied,
> His civet, balm, and perfumes redolent,
>   How from his locks they smok'd and mantle wide;
> His sword, that many a Pagan stout had shent,
>   Bewrapt with flow'rs hung idly by his side,
> So nicely decked that it seem'd the knight
>   Wore it for fashion sake, but not for fight.[98]

Tasso literally describes the sword (*ferro*) as *dal troppo lusso effeminato*, that is, "made effeminate by too much luxury."

The meaning of "luxury" in Italian (*lussuria*) and in Spanish (*lujuria*) is "lewdness," "lust," "concupiscence." *Effeminato* (as *afeminado* in Spanish) is a past participle meaning "made into a *femina*" (L. "female"). The knight who gave himself over to eroticism by cultivating the company of women found himself frequenting decadent luxury (since that was associated with the refined and soft existence of the Renaissance noble class), and his life itself became "luxurious," that is, concupiscent. Only where there was an abundance of wealth could *luxus* ("extravagance") be possible, and where there was *luxus* there was *lussuria*. So Rinaldo, the greatest of Godfrey's warriors, delivered himself into the "luxurious" embraces of Armida.

---

[98] Torquato Tasso, *Jerusalem Delivered*, XVI, 30. Trans. Edward Fairfax (1600).

Like another Circe she unmanned him, made him an extension of the luxurious woman's world. He was the woman's plaything, no matter how successfully he played the role of lover. Indeed, the more successfully he played it, the farther away he fell from the goal of the higher masculinity. The fact that his sword "hung idly by his side," effeminately decked with flowers, is enough to suggest symbolically the humiliation of his phallic strength. Like his sword it is an *inutile ornamento*, not a *militar instrumento*.

Perlimplín certainly never had an image of himself as the warrior; but neither did he have the self-image of don Juan Tenorio. He thought of himself as an innocent bachelor living a peaceful fantasy life. He had his books. All this is changed overnight. He suddenly faces the challenge of having to transform himself into the Tenorio, of having to "effeminate" himself; for now he must define himself in terms of Belisa's erotic needs, in terms of her "vocation," so to speak, just as Rinaldo turned himself into the plaything of Armida, or just as in *La Celestina* the gallant Calixto, in love with the beautiful Melibea, begins to style himself *Melibeo*. This necessity to change involves a loss of previous identity, and the notion is suggested by Perlimplín's early anxiety-ridden remark that marriage might mean the strangulation of the husband by the wife. Perlimplín, because of his introverted way of life, has a minimal self-identity as it is (see how he obediently gets married at the command of Marcolfa). Belisa, on the other hand, by virtue of her blossoming sensuality, positively exudes confidence in her own self. Perlimplín's marriage to her precipitates an identity crisis as soon as he discovers that her sensuality is not an object to be possessed, but rather a complex instrument to be skillfully played. He cannot identify himself now as the possessor of Belisa's body; she is not a kind of mechanical phallic sheath. He must "effeminate" himself, become the skillful awakener of her sensuality. He must become a Beliso, as it were.

It is impossible, at the virginal age of fifty, suddenly to assume an aggressive erotic identity, if one has spent his life playing the role of the passive schlemiel. There lies the body of what Lorca calls in a poem "the reclining woman,"[99] waiting to be erotically aroused; and the

[99] García Lorca, "Casida de la mujer tendida," in *DT*, pp. 570–571.

secret of arousing it is a mystery that Perlimplín is incapable of solving. As he says hysterically, "I would never be able to decipher your body!!!" To "decipher" means to solve the mystery of its erotic arousal.

Perlimplín, the Enraptured Duckling

The five strangers have been interpreted as multiple coition, recalling Freud's rule (numerical multiplication = temporal repetition), because they cannot be understood literally. And so now must come a consideration of the strenuous burden that this sexual demand lays on Perlimplín.

The possibility of such a performance on the part of Perlimplín is not absolutely out of the question (as is the entrance of five strangers), and here it is reasonable to postulate a farcical exaggeration. Another denizen of the eighteenth century, James Boswell, has discussed this very point in his private *London Journal*, apropos of a night spent with his Louisa: "A more voluptuous night I never enjoyed. Five times was I fairly lost in supreme rapture. Louisa was madly fond of me; she declared I was a prodigy, and asked me if this was not extraordinary for human nature. I said twice as much might be, but this was not, although in my own mind I was somewhat proud of my performance."[100] Of course this is the young Boswell speaking, and Perlimplín is middle-aged. But at the very least there is something farcical, not impossible, in the idea of the virginal middle-aged man suddenly discovering sexual reality and glutting himself on multiple orgasms, quite oblivious to the crying needs of his disappointed and abused partner. In the beginning of the consummation scene Lorca makes it clear that Perlimplín is painfully awkward in approaching his bride: he asks her first off if he is "disturbing her." He asks her if she is sleepy. He then talks about the weather ("The night has turned a bit chilly"). After more of this beating about the bush, Belisa is prompted to say that it is bedtime, whereupon he asks her permission to take off his coat.

Given this inauspicious beginning, it is clear that Perlimplín is going to be innocent of any foreplay technique. Throughout the night he takes her as if possessed of satyriasis, but Belisa, unlike Boswell's

[100] James Boswell, *London Journal (1762–1763)*, p. 139.

Louisa, cannot be expected to be "madly fond" of her enthusiastic bedmate.

He "loses himself in rapture," like a little duckling swimming about in a pond. Belisa suffers it all and allows him to "lose himself" in a kind of instinctual madness that is the beginning of his loss of identity. For from the morrow on he will progressively find himself disoriented in the world of adult sexuality. Belisa is obviously not interested in reciprocating the mother-child relationship, for she demands a lover who gives as fully as he takes, who feeds her own vast sexual hunger. She would require this of any man, at the expense of his spiritual identity. A man should forget his other aims in life and should devote himself entirely to her as the tyrant of his sexuality.

Marcolfa could know nothing of the intimate details of the wedding night, but she can soon intuit that Belisa has no intention of taking over the role of caretaker-mother. She realizes that Perlimplín has married an exigent beauty who requires the full sexual devotion of the male.

Thus the five strangers have a double significance: they refer to Perlimplín's sexual activity itself, and they refer to what this activity does to him by turning him into Everyman. Belisa is going to destroy his identity, just as Marcolfa had always protected it.

His transformation is indicated by the golden horns. They are golden because he has performed to his own erotic satisfaction; they are horns because his activity did not, to Belisa, represent "Perlimplín" the individual, but Man. She has not cuckolded him as yet, but it is her attitude that foreshadows her infidelity. She will always seek the man—one after another—and so Perlimplín has married an archetypal "cuckoldress" with an insatiable thirst.

The Custom of the Cortejo

Shortly into the marriage Belisa begins to seek and enjoy the company of the young gallants whom she meets on her daily walks, and Perlimplín readily accepts this. His complacent reaction need not arouse Belisa's suspicions, however, because it is not entirely the bizarre result of his own secret scheming. It is true that he has a plan: he is going to invent a lover for her, arrange for an affair, and then disguise himself as the fictitious lover. But his willingness to be an accessory to her infidelity is in accordance with the customs of the time. He is attempting to take advantage of established usage in order to solve his own subjective problem.

The custom of the *cortejo*, "the cicisbeo or gallant who dangled after a married woman,"[101] is discussed at some length by Charles Kany in his heavily documented *Life and Manners in Madrid: 1750– 1800*. That scandalous custom is much mentioned in the literature of the time, for "each lady of fashion had at least one *cortejo*"[102] and frequently several. Kany adds that "if we may judge from contemporary comedies, however, a woman of any class and in any place might have a *cortejo*."[103] "Their affairs were in most cases carried on openly, and were condoned because of the moral laxity which, outraged conservatives declared, ran like wild fire, consuming in its path 'shame, decorum, decency, and modesty.' "[104]

Kany gives special emphasis to the loss of independent identity suffered by the *cortejo*, who was popularly called a *mueble* ("piece of furniture") "because, like a piece of furniture, he served as a decoration at the side of his lady, performing in the drawing room the office of a mirror or painting."[105] Kany quotes at length a satirical sketch of the terrible demands made by the lady upon her lover, who really had no life of his own. The woman who could trade her sexuality for this kind of slavish devotion has truly unmanned her lover, and this is the sort of woman Belisa is, who, in Scene Two, recalls with pleasure how she is surrounded by admirers (potential lovers) as she takes her walks. One of them sends her importunate letters, and so she and Perlimplín agree to adopt the odious custom of the *cortejo*.

José Cadalso, one of the best-known satirists of the period, wrote a piece on the *cortejo*, and in it he explains that it causes men to fall into an *abominable effeminacy*.[106] Cadalso, as a rational and high-minded moralist of the time, sees the custom quite clearly as an immoral proc-

[101] Charles E. Kany, *Life and Manners in Madrid*, p. 209.
[102] Ibid.
[103] Ibid.
[104] Ibid., p. 210.
[105] Ibid.
[106] José Cadalso, "Prólogo," in *Optica del cortejo*, p. 4.

ess whereby the soul of the man—his higher masculinity—is devoured by the demon of sexuality. To one gallant he says, "Though you are a visible part of the rational world, you have become effeminate."[107] He says that the *cortejos* have been "shipwrecked" in vileness: "Is it not a pity that a personage as beautiful as is Man, an Understanding so perfect in all things as is his, . . . a Work supreme among the Works of the hand of God Himself, should waste his time . . . in matters unworthy of his rationality? . . . And is it not a pity that Man, who has . . . no perfection more admirable than that of a beautiful soul endowed with a special understanding with which . . . he might check his appetites . . . should make that soul the vile slave of his passions? Oh that Man might know himself!"[108] If it is possible for Man to lose himself in this way, to forsake his higher masculinity for the pleasures of the lower, it is because Nature, in her guise of Terrible Mother, has so ordained it through her instrument, the sorceress: the Circe, the Armida, the siren—and the Belisa.

In the discussion of "Rumpelstiltskin" it was shown how the negative phallic aspect of the man can be depotentiated by the wife-mother, intent on protecting her own offspring. In that story the young queen saves her husband from his own dwarf. In another Grimm story— "Snow White and the Seven Dwarfs"—the woman is depicted as ideal spirituality (the Jungian anima figure). The prince finds her in the middle of a great forest, living amicably with seven dwarfs (= seven years? She joins them at the age of seven; when the prince finds her and makes her his bride she is presumably fourteen). "Snow White" tells of how the ideal woman mediates between the man and the negative aspect of his sexuality. She, as the carrier of a projection (the man's own feminine unconscious), does not depotentiate the dwarfs but rather transforms the power of the seven dwarfs. She raises it to a higher, noninstinctual potential. The celebrated example of this among twentieth-century Spanish poets is that of Juan Ramón Jiménez, whose wife Zenobia was the other half of a perfect union. The poetry of Juan Ramón is not really "his" work but "their" work. She was the

107 Ibid., p. 27.
108 Ibid., p. 51.

silent partner, as Juan Ramón himself always knew. If he himself actually "wrote" the poetry, a large part of it was her and could not have come into existence without her, since she was the incarnation of his own upward-striving unconscious.

Such a woman, as representative of the man's soul, is diametrically opposed to the type exemplified by Belisa. Belisa is a specialist in man devouring: she destroys the man's potential soul. She devotes herself to giving off signals, and the man who is the victim of his dwarf will be drawn to those signals like an insect to a Venus flytrap. For her the ultimate manifestation of the male is in the form of the subservient and obsequious *cortejo*.

It is curious that the letter that Belisa receives from one admirer sounds like a specific and hostile answer to Cadalso's attack on the "lascivious delights" to which the *cortejo* devotes himself; for Cadalso defended the "beautiful soul endowed with a special understanding," and denounced the custom of the *cortejo* as encouraging woman to take advantage of the soul of man. Belisa receives a letter from a fervent admirer who writes: "Why should I want your soul? The soul is the patrimony of the weak, of invalid heroes and of sickly people. Beautiful souls are always on the point of dying. . . . Belisa, it is not your soul that I desire, but your trembling, white and soft body!"

And what of Perlimplín? At first he was concerned only with reaping egotistically the benefits of being married to a young woman who allowed him to take her. Now he knows that she has nothing but contempt for him because he cannot "decipher" the enigma of her sexuality. If he cannot do this it is because (as has been noted before) he is an exemplary schlemiel; and it is now appropriate to consider why this eloquent Yiddish epithet is applied to Perlimplín.

Who Is the Schlemiel?

Leo Rosten, in his encyclopedic *The Joys of Yiddish*, defines the word *schlemiel* as follows: "A foolish person, a simpleton. . . . A consistently unlucky or unfortunate person . . . ; a born loser. . . . A clumsy, . . . gauche type. . . . A social misfit, . . . maladjusted. . . . A pipsqueak, a Caspar Milquetoast. . . . A naive, trusting, gullible customer.... Anyone who makes a foolish bargain.... This usage is wide in Europe."[109] It will be noted that every definition given here applies to Perlimplín in one way or another. There is one important aspect of the schlemiel, however, that Rosten ignores, possibly on purpose. Freud, himself Jewish, is of help here. In recounting "A Chemist's Dream" he says that the patient kept repeating in his dream "Phenyl, phenyl." The chemist told him, says Freud, that professionally "he had always been very fond of all these radicals ending in '-yl,' because they were so easy to use: benzyl, acetyl, etc. This explained nothing. But when I suggested '*Schlemihl*' to him as another radical in the series, he laughed heartily and told me that . . . he had read a book . . . which in fact included some remarks upon '*les Schlémiliés.*' When he read them he had said to himself: 'This is just what I'm like.' "[110]

Freud, as an outspoken man, was not one to indulge in euphemisms and disliked even the conventional hypocrisies of civilized social intercourse. Here he admits to telling his patient that he considers him to be a schlemiel (whereupon the schlemiel "laughed heartily," thereby giving one more corroboration of Freud's opinion!).

But Freud's introductory remark to "A Chemist's Dream" discloses the basic reason for his unkind opinion: "This was dreamt by a young man who was endeavouring to give up his habit of masturbating in favour of sexual relations with women."[111] Though the idea is commonly avoided, it ought to be recognized as obvious: the schlemiel is the masturbator, since that is the natural extent of his sex life, given his general inability to cope with social situations and to establish rapport with possible love objects.

The English equivalent of schlemiel is the American slang term of abuse, *jerk*. This is how Harold Wentworth and Stuart Flexner define *jerk* in their *Dictionary of American Slang*: "An ineffectual, foolish, or unknowingly dull youth or man, usu. applied contemptuously to one who is overfamiliar, unprepossessing, eccentric, stupid, . . . or careless." Now *jerk*, as Wentworth and Flexner point out, had originally a sexual meaning, for it is from "jerk off," and so was applied

---

[109] Leo Rosten, *The Joys of Yiddish*, p. 344.
[110] Freud, *The Interpretation of Dreams*, pp. 383–384.
[111] Ibid., p. 383.

to one who masturbates. The symbolic connotation of mixing milk shakes manually naturally suggested the name "soda jerk," since the soda jerk was typically an adolescent boy, and the adolescent is traditionally the one most involved with autoeroticism, given his stage of psychosexual development. When he mixed milk shakes he was portraying publicly his private sex life.

The jerk, like the schlemiel, has not the ability to establish friendships with women—attractive women, especially, which implies the need to overcome rivals—to the extent that these women would welcome his sexual overtures or even take him seriously. This inability is the problem of Perlimplín the schlemiel, the jerk. Of his own volition he would never have gotten married. He was pushed into marriage, and Belisa was, in effect, sold to him by her mother. And so the schlemiel finds himself "trembling" in the presence of a desirable and desiring woman who is waiting to be seduced—aroused and excited by skillful foreplay.

What is to be thought when, the following morning, the schlemiel enthusiastically informs his bride that "for the first time" in his life he is happy? If he lost his virginity last night, he was transformed into a new man; he was the "stranger" who entered, and like the typical jerk he is "unknowingly dull" as a lover. But it will finally sink in that Belisa has nothing but contempt for him, and then he will come to realize himself that he is indeed a schlemiel.

Lorca insists on Belisa's opinion of Perlimplín as being a schlemiel, principally by the use of the pejorative diminutive that she habitually uses when addressing him. Throughout the scene of the wedding night, and in the scene following, she uses malicious diminutives like Perlimplinito ("little Perlimplín"), *caballerito* ("little gentleman"), *maridito* ("little husband"), *hijito* ("sonny boy"), Perlimplín *chiquitito* ("itsy-bitsy Perlimplín"), and—the most amusing of all—Perlimplinpinito ("eensy-weensy Perlimplín").

Perlimplín, as the schlemiel, is the man who cannot master the reality principle and who has a faulty and too-limited perception of other personalities. His general consciousness of what is going on around him is so imperfect that he perceives only minimal signals from it. In fact "reality" to him is principally the inner reality of his own confusion, and he is forever acting the dunce because he has never developed a consistent persona, or social image. Instead of simply acting, he gets himself entangled in the perplexing problem of *how* he ought to act, which in itself compounds his embarrassment.

At the end of the play Perlimplín reviles himself for being a *monigote*, among other things. As he lies dying he says, "Ah, don Perlimplín! You dirty old man, you *monigote sin fuerza* . . . ," which is translated as "puny puppet." In popular usage a *monigote* is a stuffed doll with a grotesque appearance, a kind of golliwog. The word is a pejorative derived from the Latin *monachus*, "monk," and meant originally "lay brother." The "lay brother" was seen contemptuously as an innocuous fellow of no particular account (he was at the bottom of the hierarchy), and when the word *monigote* is applied to anyone as an insult it means, as the Royal Academy explains, "an ignorant or dull person with no social character or worth."[112] Perlimplín, then, reviles himself as a *monigote*, which is nothing else than a word in Spanish for schlemiel and jerk.

Popularly one does not make a point of explicitly recognizing the sexual implications of these epithets. But it is clear enough that the social misfit is bound to have his sex life restricted principally to autoeroticism. Sex to him is Aladdin's lamp; the reality principle is consistently displaced by the pleasure principle. All one's wishes are fulfilled automatically by means of the autoerotic fantasy; ecstatic happiness is at one's fingertips.

The key to understanding autoerotic ecstasy must be sought in its psychosomatic aspect. The jerk may think that he simply enjoys masturbating; but the meaning of the enjoyment lies in the accompanying fantasies. Thus autoeroticism can be viewed as the interplay between the genital activity of the hand and the images that accompany this. It is here that a symbological connection can be made with what Perlimplín says about Belisa's effect upon him. Toward the beginning of the last scene he raves enthusiastically to Marcolfa: "Before, I was unable to think about the extraordinary things there are in this world . . . I lived on the threshold . . . But now! Belisa's love has given me a precious treasure that I did not know. See? Now I close my eyes and . . . I see

---

[112] "Persona ignorante y ruda, de ninguna representación ni valer."

what I want to . . . For example . . . my mother when the local Fairies visited her. Oh! You know what the Fairies are like . . . , tiny. . . . It's marvelous, they can dance upon my little finger!" This material is highly symbolic, dealing as it does with "Fairies." Perlimplín says that Belisa's love has given him a treasure that he "did not know," but of course he means a treasure that he *rediscovered*, since he goes on to associate it with a childhood memory. He means that material long repressed has at last been recovered.

But then what follows bears an extraordinary resemblance to the autoerotic fantasy. He closes his eyes and surrenders himself to a lovely image; "for example," he says, suggesting free association. He shuts his eyes and imagines once more his mother as he saw her when he was a little child (i.e., when he still saw fairies).

Now the fairies are the complement of the dwarfs, diminutive figures representing the kindly aspect of the unconscious. (The fairy is diminutive because the ego-consciousness of the little child is diminutive; "kindly" unconscious impulses will not overwhelm him, but will remain "small," that is, assimilable. When the young man enters the phallic stage the anima figure is never diminutive. But the dwarf is always small because the phallus is small by comparison with the entire body.)

Perlimplín says that the fairies are tiny: "It's marvelous, they can dance upon my little finger!" He here associates fantasy happiness with "dancing"; the fantasy that brings him happiness dances upon his little finger. The dancing proclivities of all dwarfs should be recalled (as Rumpelstiltskin dancing triumphantly around a fire), as should the association of the phallic dwarf with the finger: the Greek Dactyls, or subterranean dwarf-gods (*daktylos*, "finger"), Tom Thumb, and the Priapic forefinger described by Delcourt. The phallic symbolism of the finger has long been popularly used. The middle finger is commonly held up as an ithyphallic insult, as is the thumb in the sign of the fig. The ancient Romans called the middle finger *impudicus*, "lewd."[113] Thus, when Perlimplín speaks of infantile fantasy happiness as fairies dancing upon his little finger, this is reasonably understood to mean his "infantile [little boy's] penis."

[113] Theodore Thass-Thienemann, *Symbolic Behavior*, p. 217.

Here again Lorca is deep into Freudian theory, since Perlimplín is speaking of fantasy happiness in terms of his infantile mother image. His childhood autoerotic activity was Oedipal. When he masturbated as a little boy the good fairies danced upon his "little finger," which is to say, the realization of magic fantasies came about ithyphallically, and so that was the moment when the splendid fairies "visited" his mother. His mother was a "fairy vision" realized as an autoerotic fantasy. His secret happiness then culminated in the delicious return to Mother— and this reversion is what Belisa has awakened in him. When he was little his autoeroticism was accompanied by fantasies of mother's giving, and Belisa has renewed these fantasies. When he possessed her body on the wedding night his activity, long conditioned by auto-eroticism, was suddenly a fantasy made real, and he saw his dear mother as he saw her when he was a little boy. His confession that for the "first time" in his life he is happy really means for the second time—or for the first time in his adult life. Such is the sex life of the schlemiel.

Perlimplín as the Maniac

From Scene Two on, till the end of the play, Perlimplín shows growing signs of manic exaltation. As it turns out, he is plotting insanely, and his scheme will end in violent suicide, supposedly in order to realize an obscure and confused fantasy. Perlimplín's suicide is really the part of the play most resistant to analysis, for the same reason that suicide itself is the least understood of all human acts; an attempt to understand it will have to be based on a careful consideration of the mental state that immediately precedes it.

Perlimplín's insane plan begins to take shape in Scene Two, when he agrees to lend a helping hand in Belisa's incipient love affair. He claims altruistic motives: "Since I am an old man," he says to her, "I will sacrifice myself for your sake." But such declarations of willingness to sacrifice oneself cannot be taken at face value. Further, Perlimplín goes on to say, "No one ever did what I am doing. But I am now beyond the world and beyond the ridiculous morality of people." This is a key statement, for Perlimplín here admits to feelings of alienation. He says that he is now (*ya*) beyond the world, which means that he has crossed a threshold.

The crucial event underlying Perlimplín's behavior has already been described: in the erotic confrontation with Belisa he has lost his life-long identity and has found nothing with which to replace it. He has been impoverished. By all rights he should fall into a depression, but Lorca does not portray this reaction. He does portray instead what Freud called "the most remarkable characteristic" of depression (melancholia): "its tendency to change round into mania—a state which is the opposite of it in its symptoms."[114] And so it should be noted how Scene Two ends: Perlimplín, having announced his intention to sacrifice himself, starts to leave. Belisa asks him where he is going, and he exclaims grandiosely (*grandioso*), "You will know all later! Later!"

At the beginning of Scene Three, set in the garden, he is asking the grieving Marcolfa if she has followed his instructions concerning Belisa's rendezvous with her mysterious lover. Marcolfa misses the good old days when she took care of Perlimplín; but Perlimplín's attention is at present entirely devoted to his inner drama, now at a manic pitch of intensity. His plan, as noted, is to arouse Belisa erotically in a devious manner. He, the schlemiel, is incapable of doing this in his own identity, so he will present himself disguised as someone else whom Belisa can take seriously as a potential lover. Thus "he," Perlimplín, will successfully play the role of seducer and so achieve his current goal in life. Of course this "seduction" cannot lead to an erotic consummation, but that is the least of it, since Perlimplín clearly has another motive, to be discussed presently. For now, one should note the manic pleasure he takes in knowing that "he" has managed to excite his wife erotically. He interrogates Marcolfa closely concerning Belisa's reaction to the delivered instructions. Marcolfa says that they elicited an impassioned response. Perlimplín grows gleefully "enthusiastic" and states "vibrantly" that Belisa's passion for "that young man" is exactly what he needs. Marcolfa reprimands him tearfully for his in-

---

[114] Sigmund Freud, "Mourning and Melancholia," p. 253.

difference to his own dishonor, but he bursts into a gay, spontaneous song: "Don Perlimplín has no honor! He has no honor!"

He slips into the garden and finds Belisa excitedly awaiting the arrival of her Tenorio. He asks her "lewdly" (*concupiscente*), "Are you still waiting for him?" She admits that she feels "more ardor than ever." Perlimplín catechizes her further: he exclaims "strongly" (*fuerte*), "Why?" "Because I love him," she answers. Perlimplín clearly needs to lack no assurance that he is accomplishing his first aim: to seduce Belisa as successfully as the next man, even though the seduction depends upon a ruse.

Belisa waxes passionate: "I love him! Perlimplín, I love him! I am like a new woman!" She is thoroughly aroused. The plan has succeeded, and Perlimplín says with satisfaction, "That is my triumph." "What triumph?" asks Belisa. "The triumph of my imagination."

Now the time has arrived to implement the second, terrible part of the plan, which, needless to say, has nothing to do with self-sacrifice but rather is concerned with an insane revenge. He tells the expectant Belisa that he is about to murder the man she is waiting for! He has built her hopes to a climactic point and is now about to dash them viciously, even though it will cost him his life. "When your lover is dead," says Perlimplín, "you will be able to caress him always in your bed. He will be so lovely and spruced up [*peripuesto*], and you'll never have to fear that he will stop loving you. He will love you with the infinite love of the dead." And here Perlimplín clarifies with tragic and manic lucidity the circumstances that have been tearing him to pieces: "He will love you with the infinite love of the dead, and I will be free of this dark nightmare of your magnificent body . . . Your body! That I would never be able to decipher!!!" Perlimplín's outcry is the heart of one of Lorca's most poignant and compelling dramatic scenes. Those three exclamation marks betray a rare intensity, for they evoke the limitless despair of a broken old man who has lost not only his love object, but also his own ego-identity. What he needed most— Belisa's excited interest in him—could be gotten only by ceasing to exist, by pretending to be somebody else.

Perlimplín dashes off, and the horrified Belisa stands screaming bloody murder. He stabs himself in the breast and returns stumbling, muffled in his immense floor-length cape. He shows his face to Belisa and says: "Your husband has just killed me with this emerald dagger. (*He shows the dagger in his breast*) . . . He killed me because he knew that I loved you more than anyone else. While he stabbed me he cried, 'Now Belisa has a soul!' " Here Lorca reintroduces the manikin motif in the form of the *monigote*: "Perlimplín killed me . . . Ah, don Perlimplín! You dirty old man, you puny puppet, you could not enjoy Belisa's body . . . The body of Belisa was for young muscles and burning lips." Belisa, overcome with shock and dismay, gasps, "What have you done?" But Perlimplín continues: "Do you understand? I am my soul and you are your body. Let me . . . die embracing it." Belisa draws near to him "half naked" and embraces him. This is not a sign of affection, for she has not recovered from the traumatic state induced by the shocking event. In a daze she says, "Yes . . . but what about the young man? Why did you deceive me?" Perlimplín dies, asking absently, "The young man?"

Perlimplín's self-accusation ("puny puppet") could easily refer to impotence. Belisa has nothing but contempt for his way of playing the lover on their wedding night, and he soon becomes aware of this. His awareness of her opinion would certainly suffice not only to render him impotent, but also to cause a general withdrawal of erotic libido. A massive withdrawal of this kind leads to depression, and the depression eventually turns into mania. The manic stage as Lorca portrays it has been shown, and now must come a consideration of the dynamics of this whole psychic transformation and how it leads to suicide.

"Why" Do People Kill Themselves?

Alfred Alvarez, in his recent study of suicide (*The Savage God*), observes that "the processes which lead a man to take his own life are at least as complex and difficult as those by which he continues to live."[115] A cursory examination of the literature on suicide—works written not only by suicidologists but also by philosophers and poets—readily confirms this statement. The possible categories of voluntary death are no more limited than are the possible categories of life itself.

---

[115] Alfred Alvarez, *The Savage God*, p. 121.

It is frequently impossible even to distinguish between the "accidental" (or "subintentioned") suicide and the fully intentioned act. All suicidologists agree that the *means* may sometimes be more important than the resultant death; that is to say, the victim consciously attached more significance to the spectacle of his death than he did to ceasing to live. In fact it is not always certain that the victim is fully convinced that he will cease to exist. The significance of the gesture is, of course, always to be considered when the suicide is particularly violent or ghastly—what Alvarez calls the "operatic" suicide: "In each instance the suicidal gesture seems to have mattered more than its outcome. People try to die in such operatic ways only when they are obsessed more by the means than by the end, just as a sexual fetishist gets more satisfaction from his rituals than from the orgasm to which they lead."[116]

This point is of especial importance in *Perlimplín*; for while all critics who praise the "sublimity" of Perlimplín's final act find in it a noble altruism—self-sacrifice—(and this is by far the commonest critical reaction), they do not discuss the means. What motivation is suggested by that violent gesture—especially when the dying Perlimplín raves about how Belisa will forever afterward be confronted with the memory of that young lover whom she never got to embrace? As Alvarez says, ". . . it is as though the suicide believes, despite all the evidence to the contrary, that he will finally have his posthumous way, provided his death is sufficiently terrible."[117]

What are the psychodynamics of suicide—that is, the more commonly recognized "reasons" for killing oneself? The best-known theories of the psychodynamics of suicide are those of Emile Durkheim who, in his pioneer study on the subject, postulated three types—egoistic, altruistic, and anomic.[118] Consideration of these may be omitted, however, since Durkheim's study is that of a sociologist, and *Perlimplín* is not about a man vis-à-vis society at large. Nevertheless, it should be mentioned in connection with Durkheim that the notion of Perlimplín's suicide as altruistic, or sacrificial, must be discounten-

[116] Ibid., p. 123.
[117] Ibid., n. 50.
[118] Emile Durkheim, *Suicide*. Originally published in 1897.

anced because it is irrelevant to the play (though not to the victim himself). One always has to distinguish between self-sacrifice as a "crazy idea," and self-sacrifice as a realistic and deliberate assessment of the relationship between one's life and one's death. What is recognized as the bona fide sacrificial suicide is voluntary death seen as a final, validating act (cf. Jesus, Socrates, Codrus). Here the suicides realistically see "their concluding acts as the natural outcome of their convictions."[119] They validate their life because by ending it voluntarily they enforce and extend the basic meaning of what they have lived for. Contrariwise, if they did not die at the right moment, their life would be invalidated. If Socrates had not drunk the hemlock, he would thereby have accepted the court's verdict in order to escape alive, thus invalidating his life as the seeker of truth, by admitting that he was wrong.[120] And obviously the acceptance by Jesus of crucifixion was necessary to what he taught. An attempt to avoid it would have invalidated his role on earth. As George Kelly puts it: "To seek to die well is an object of the full life, and those who fail to live well never succeed in finding anything worth dying for. Thus life and death can be made to fit together, each as the validator of the other."[121]

Sacrificial suicide is thus seen as the uncommon suicide, for it rarely occurs and must be the expression of the necessary alternative. When by a confused assessment of the circumstances it is clear that the victim only *claims* a crucial state of emergency to exist, he has a neurotically inflated notion of the importance of his suicide and what he thinks it will accomplish.

Sacrificial suicide is regarded as an act of selfless dedication. It is not born of despair or hatred of life. Thus the heroic suicide, such as that of one who dies to save another in a mortal emergency, is usually not even thought of as suicide at all. In the pressure of the moment the hero may not have assessed the danger as necessarily fatal; but if he did, he clearly saw that his own voluntary death was the necessary course—that there was no alternative but to die on the spot in order to save the life of another.

[119] George A. Kelly, "Suicide: The Personal Construct Point of View," in *The Cry for Help*, ed. Norman Farberow and Edwin Shneidman, p. 258.
[120] Ibid.
[121] Ibid., p. 259.

It should be noted that all "intentioned" suicides are dictated by the victim's own belief that the act is necessary in some way or other. In most cases, when one reads of such deaths, he feels that they were unnecessary and that, had he been in the same circumstances, he would have sought a different solution. But this attitude is due to ignorance of the circumstances, especially the inner, psychic circumstances of the victim himself. As Kelly puts it, "the suicide makes *his* choice, not *ours.*"[122]

And so the burden of proof falls upon anyone who would call Perlimplín's death a sacrificial suicide in any other than a neurotic sense. How can it be demonstrated that Belisa would have been somehow "destroyed" unless he killed himself? And it cannot be shown that Perlimplín's death validates anything, since his life itself was never the attempt to validate anything. His death, like most suicides, is an escape from uncertainty. It is a negation of life, not an affirmation of it.

Now as to the possible motivations for suicide: a cursory survey of the more accessible literature on the subject immediately suggests that a multitude of explanations is available, some of which are relevant to *Perlimplín*.

Suicide may represent the attempt to escape from an *identification conflict*. This is the kind of suicide that Charles Wahl has called "other-directed." Here the victim has a weak sense of self. In his own eyes his worth vitally depends upon the opinion of others. It appears impossible to gain their esteem, and so the "unworthy" self is liquidated.[123] This notion of suicide could easily form the basis for a study of *Perlimplín*.

The other-directed suicide may stem not only from an identification conflict, but also from invidious *feelings of inadequacy, created by dependency*. Neurotic individuals have developed tendencies through being "dependent upon the achievements and support of others,"[124] as Perlimplín was "supported" all his life by Marcolfa. Marcolfa, in an

---

[122] Ibid.
[123] Charles William Wahl, "Suicide as a Magical Act," in *Clues to Suicide*, ed. Norman Farberow and Edwin Shneidman, pp. 23–24.
[124] Heinz L. Ansbacher, "Suicide: The Adlerian Point of View," in *The Cry for Help*, ed. Farberow and Shneidman, p. 207.

effort to transfer Perlimplín's dependency, chooses a wife-mother whose erotic achievement is so high that it creates an intolerable anxiety. Marcolfa made a terrible mistake here, for she brought to her master's bed a bride in the same way that she always brought him his breakfast—but the meal proved to be fatally indigestible.

Related to the dependency situation that creates a terrorizing sense of inadequacy is the suicide as the result of one's *self-hatred*: the individual is so ineffective a person by comparison with the person he lives with that his failure to live up to his existential commitments engenders self-disgust.[125] Perlimplín seems to be an exemplary case of this.

Similarly suicide can result from a general *fear of the life situation* itself. The challenge of sudden, alien circumstances may occasion such anxiety that the individual puts an end to his life. Others might run away or retreat into psychosis or construct a neurotic fantasy world.[126] Perlimplín tries the latter, but it puts him into a cul-de-sac that terminates in a confrontation with reality; ultimately he must show that he and the fictitious young lover are the same, at which point fantasy and reality reach a stalemate.

The dependency situation has elsewhere been described as *loss of security*, producing a *symbolic escape*.[127] A neurotic like Perlimplín lives his life as far as possible as a security-plus situation. Perlimplín was cared for and lived a minimally involved, introverted life. Suddenly extraordinary demands are made upon him to become intimately involved in life with another person—in what is the most "dangerous" form: erotic love.

The above is a form of *alienation* from one's known life style or (what is the same thing, really) alienation from one's self-image. One constructs a "sufficient" self-image, which allows him to believe that he is living adequately the challenge of life: "Detachment and living in imagination eliminate awareness of any failure of superiority by

---

[125] Herbert Hendin, "The Psychodynamics of Suicide," in Durkheim, *Suicide*, p. 143.
[126] Elizabeth Kilpatrick, "A Psychoanalytic Understanding of Suicide," in Durkheim, *Suicide*, pp. 151–154.
[127] Ibid., p. 153.

pushing reality into the background."[128] But if occasion arises when it becomes impossible not to judge the wretchedness of one's performance as a liver of life, one may be overwhelmed by a flood of alienation —that is, the new circumstances "prove" that one is a nobody—a schlemiel.

Suicide sometimes represents an attempt to escape from *expected suffering*: "It is well known to psychiatrists that the schizophrenic patient having terrific fear of what he can most accurately describe as disintegration, will be driven to any step to avoid it: psychosis or suicide."[129] Again, this explanation suggests Perlimplín, who has, by his invention of another image, already begun a process of disintegration. By the end of the play he has no identity to which he can turn. He clearly cannot persist in his masquerade of the young lover, nor can he retreat to his old Perlimplín identity.

To exterminate oneself in order to avoid disintegration is obviously self-defeating and is not consciously recognized as a motivation by the victim, though it may be clear enough to the victim's psychiatrist. The victim may consciously attempt to construe his suicide as an affirmative act (cf. the sacrificial suicide), but Kelly points out the clear difference in the economics of the act: ". . . everything seems so utterly unpredictable that the only definite thing one can do is abandon the scene altogether. [Sacrificial suicide] is one where realism has been carried to its ultimate conclusion: fatalism. [Fear of disintegration] is the condition of total anxiety, and the suicidal attempt . . . is a desperate bid for some kind, any kind, of certainty."[130] A Socrates dies with "the sense of knowing everything worth knowing," whereas the "common" suicide dies "knowing nothing worth knowing."[131]

That need for certainty—"some kind, any kind, of certainty"—is the need expressed by Perlimplín, who cries out that by killing himself he has found *freedom from a nightmare*. This is the terrible chaos of his life (with the challenge of Belisa's erotic libido at its center) that he would never be able to "decipher"; an intolerable anxiety from which his death will liberate him.

128 Ibid., p. 155.
129 Ibid., p. 163.
130 Kelly, in *The Cry for Help*, ed. Farberow and Shneidman, p. 260.
131 Ibid.

If one is to judge from the notes left by suicides, their deaths are frequently seen as *capital punishment*, self-inflicted. The unconscious does not distinguish between fantasies and actual deeds. If unconsciously a person wishes another dead, then unconsciously he has murdered that other and deserves to be punished.[132] The survivor, also, frequently blames himself for the beloved's suicide, thereby activating a recognition of unconscious hostility. In this sense the suicide can have a post mortem control over the survivor's sense of guilt. With respect to Perlimplín, it is not hard to show that he has reasons for hating Belisa, since she is the central object in a new, nightmarish world into which he has been cast in spite of himself.

Why, indeed, should he not hate her? She has been responsible for awakening in him *feelings of depletion and impoverishment*, and one who does this easily becomes the target of the victim's hostility. Belisa's arrival on the scene shows Perlimplín the spiritual impoverishment of the life he has been leading. She revives the "old infantile feelings of futility and helplessness."[133] Like the case history discussed by Maurice Green, Perlimplín is "a dutiful mama's boy," who obediently marries because it is decided that he should. Green's example barely survived "the subtle strangulation by his mother"[134]—and it should be noted that to Perlimplín a wife is like a mother (= giver) but at the same time represents the possibility of "strangulation."

Suicide is sometimes rationalized in suicide notes as an act of *self-glorification*. Elizabeth Kilpatrick recalls one such note left by a rejected lover: "My death will be so wonderful I will be admired by you."[135] This is how Marcolfa sees her master's suicide, and she says that Belisa is now "clothed in the glorious blood of my master." This attitude is related to suicide seen as the result of a *power fantasy*.[136] By one's voluntary death, one believes that he will control the spiritual destiny of another. Evidence for this is not lacking in the last scene of *Perlimplín*, which indeed is usually interpreted in exactly this way. But

---

[132] Wahl, in *Clues to Suicide*, ed. Farberow and Shneidman, p. 26.
[133] Maurice R. Green, "Suicide: The Sullivanian Point of View," in *The Cry for Help*, ed. Farberow and Shneidman, p. 232.
[134] Ibid., p. 231.
[135] Kilpatrick, in Durkheim, *Suicide*, p. 162.
[136] Louis E. De Rosis, "Suicide: The Horney Point of View," in *The Cry for Help*, ed. Farberow and Shneidman, pp. 238, 241.

the suicidal power fantasy is based on a false assessment of the extent of one's post mortem control over someone else. And, like the neurotic self-sacrifice, it represents a price all out of proportion to the alleged value to be gained.

Overlapping with the above is the suicide as an *act of aggression*: the suicide's death is a terrible act of punishment because another will suffer tremendous remorse ("you'll be sorry when I'm gone"). It is an *act of abandonment*, seen as a "fit punishment."[137] This is an aspect of suicide as the expression of *vindictiveness* and appears in an especially obvious form in the cases of violent suicide. When the suicide is not violent (i.e., "passive," as with sleeping pills or gas) it may be that the victim only sought respite—a long sleep. But the "operatic" gesture suggests far more than the mere desire to die. Perlimplín's bloody self-murder is an angry expression of the *demand for restitution*—an imperious demand for justice—among other things.[138]

Freud's Theory of the Mechanism of Suicide

The motivations for suicide that have been cited all apply with equal force and relevance to Perlimplín. It is perfectly reasonable to discuss his suicide as the outcome of an identification conflict, or as the striving to implement a power fantasy. His behavior can certainly be seen as other directed, as the result of feeling that he has to struggle with erotic forces raised to consciousness by Belisa. And his death is that of an impoverished spirit who no longer has anything to live for, nor can it revert to its old ways. He seeks freedom from a "dark nightmare."

But his self-destruction can justifiably be seen as a substitute murder of Belisa, since the manner in which he arranges it is fraught with hostility—and, in any case, there is common agreement that *introverted murder* is nearly always an aspect of suicide that has to be taken into account. And what doubt is there that a life situation has been created that represents the total loss of security with a resultant alienation? Further, the manic intensity of Perlimplín's behavior toward the end of the play may surely be taken as a sign that his suicide is for him not only

[137] See Hendin, in Durkheim, *Suicide*, pp. 139–141.
[138] De Rosis, in *The Cry for Help*, ed. Farberow and Shneidman, p. 251.

a release, but a glorious release. Consequently, Perlimplín's suicide could be motivated by all these considerations simultaneously or by one or any combination. At the same time it is not possible to credit Perlimplín with a sacrificial suicide except by using a neurotic rationalization of the term.

Apart from all those specific motivations, however, the matter should be explored from another point of view, which is to say, the mechanism involved. A given psychic phenomenon may be motivated variously; different people kill themselves for different reasons and for different combinations of reasons. But is it not possible to describe the act of suicide in a generic way so as to gain some theoretical understanding of the psychic mechanism which determines it? This is what Freud set out to do in his essay "Mourning and Melancholia." And since the concern here is with *Perlimplín* as a play produced in an atmosphere of psychoanalytic theory, it is now appropriate to consider Freud's theoretical explanation of the dynamics of suicide.

Two preliminary observations must be made however. First, it must be pointed out that the notion central to Freud's theory of suicide is that of the *psychic split*: a man does not kill "himself"; rather, one part of the psyche attacks another part of the psyche (for whatever reason). One part of the psyche is viewed as an object that ought to be exterminated (for whatever reason). And this is the characteristic aspect of Perlimplín's death: he splits his psyche into two parts, one of which is the "old" Perlimplín and the other of which is the young stranger; and then the old one kills the young one as a separate object. Thus the principal point of departure for Freud's theory of suicide is the most striking dramatic aspect of Perlimplín's death. The second general observation is this: sexuality lies at the heart of all psychoanalytic theory. A quantum of sexual libido is not directly assimilable to conscious life and so reappears either constructively (= "sublimation") or destructively (as neurosis, psychosis, or suicide). Similarly, the second characteristic aspect of Perlimplín's suicide is the symbolic sexual form it takes, for it is a destructive *phallic gesture*.

Keeping in mind these two phenomena that define the Perlimplinesque suicide, the following discussion is a detailed consideration of Freud's theory of the destructive psychic mechanism as he saw it.

"Mourning and Melancholia" (1917) is an inquiry into the dynamics of psychological depression and its connection with suicide. According to Freud the distinguishing features of melancholia are "a profoundly painful dejection, cessation of interest in the outside world, loss of the capacity to love, inhibition of all activity, and a lowering of the self-regarding feelings to a degree that finds utterance in self-reproaches and self-revilings, and culminates in a delusional expectation of punishment."[139] All this is relevant to the mental state of Perlimplín, with the exception of "inhibition of all activity"—which is the directly destructive side of the depressive state (hence the old label "manic-depressive").

Freud finds some striking analogies between the depression of mourning and other types of depression. Mourning is a normal form of depression caused by the death of a loved object. There are other cases of depression, however, that involve not the death of the loved object, but abandonment by it.

When a woman leaves one man for another, the first man may experience a profound depression, which he naturally explains by the loss of his beloved. But Freud sees that psychologically this is really no explanation at all, as well he might. Indeed, he must, since love itself is so complex. What does it mean to say "I love her"? Inevitably the beloved carries a projection of some kind; why does one love that person in particular? The beloved always represents some thing or things of unconscious importance to the lover. When large amounts of libido are attached to an object (cf. "dog lovers" and "cat lovers"—or haters) it is because the object symbolizes elements of the personality.

And so when the lover is abandoned by his beloved he may account for his consequent depression by saying that he has lost "her." But, says Freud, he may be aware of the loss that has given rise to his melancholia, but "only in the sense that he knows whom he has lost but not what he has lost in him."[140] That is the basis of the problem, and that is why Freud sees in depression a psychic split occurring: "one part of the ego sets itself over against the other, judges it critically, and, as it

[139] Freud, "Mourning and Melancholia," p. 244.
[140] Ibid., p. 245.

were, takes it as its object."[141] This is the self-reviling of Perlimplín. "In the clinical picture of melancholia," says Freud, "dissatisfaction with the ego on moral grounds is the most outstanding feature."[142]

Further, Freud finds that the self-criticism typical of depression inevitably applies first to someone the person loves. "Every time one examines the facts this conjecture is confirmed. So we find the key to the clinical picture: we perceive that the self-reproaches are reproaches against a loved object which have been shifted away from it on to the patient's own ego."[143] When Perlimplín reproaches himself as a "dirty old man" (*viejo verde*) ostensibly he is voicing the traditionally held belief that it is somehow indecent for old people to have a sex life; he should not have tried to establish a sexual relationship with young Belisa ("young enough to be his daughter"). But if one looks at this self-criticism in terms of what Freud calls "the key to the clinical picture" he can see that Perlimplín's self-reproach applies with equal force to Belisa. The avid interest in sex that is her outstanding characteristic has been displaced and shifted onto Perlimplín's own ego. He is repudiating an activity because this activity is the basis for Belisa's repudiation of him.

Freud reconstructs the process as he sees it: "An object-choice, an attachment of the libido to a particular person [viz., Belisa], had at one time existed; then, owing to a . . . disappointment coming from this loved person, the object-relationship was shattered. The result was not the normal one of a withdrawal of the libido from this object and a displacement of it on to a new one, but something different. . . . The object-cathexis [Perlimplín's attachment to Belisa] proved to have little power of resistance and was brought to an end. But the free libido was not displaced on to another object; it was withdrawn into the ego."[144] So Perlimplín loved Belisa in a weak way; she was a substitute mother, and when she refused to play the role of female giver, Perlimplín was sorely disappointed. Nevertheless, given his timid and

---

[141] Ibid., p. 247.
[142] Ibid., pp. 247–248.
[143] Ibid., p. 248.
[144] Ibid., p. 249.

inexperienced character, it does not occur to him to seek a mistress, as it does to many disappointed husbands.

The wedding night was "successful" in that it awakened in Perlimplín all the libido that once he had attached to his first love object, mother; as he says, Belisa's "love" has allowed him to see mother again as he did when he was a little child. A confession of this nature makes very doubtful the charge of impotence on the wedding night. He discharged great quantities of libido in a way that he had not done since childhood. And again, the object was a woman (i.e., the return of the mother image).

Subsequently, however, Belisa extricates herself from the role attributed to her by Perlimplín. The little boy believes that Mommy exists for only one purpose, to be his slave. But Belisa has ambitions of her own and concentrates her attention on the task of finding a *cortejo*. She means to have a lover who will be her slave.

Thus Perlimplín is left with a large amount of awakened libido that has no object to which it can be attached. And, having been aroused, it cannot be "forgotten" (repressed); it is withdrawn into the ego. Freud points out, in agreement with Rank, that "the object-choice [Belisa] has been effected on a narcissistic basis, so that the object-cathexis, when obstacles come in its way, can regress to narcissism."[145]

Such a regression has been implied throughout these pages, of course, particularly in connection with the malice of the phallic dwarf. Perlimplín was arrested in the narcissistic stage, and only too late in life does he come to face the challenge of the phallic stage. The crisis with Belisa brings about the result: "The narcissistic identification with the object then becomes a substitute for the erotic cathexis."[146] Perlimplín cannot "cathect" libido erotically and yet tells his bride after the wedding night, "For the first time in my life I am happy." But Belisa refuses any longer to gratify his regressive tendencies; she refuses to settle down into that kind of sexual relationship with a schlemiel, a *monigote*.

Freud finds it remarkable that depression could terminate in suicide. He sees the problem as similar to that raised by the depression of the

145 Ibid.
146 Ibid.

abandoned lover: the lover knows whom he has lost, but not what he has lost in himself. By the same token, when a person commits suicide, it is said that "he killed himself." But again, the psychological problem is very complex; for he did not simply kill "himself"; rather one part of him killed something in himself. Considering the normal strength of the will to survive, Freud believes that only the mechanism of the psychic split will theoretically explain how the ego "can consent to its own destruction."[147]

Thus the unattached (abandoned) love feelings turn back hostilely onto the ego. Ego "directs against itself the hostility which relates to an object [Belisa] and which represents the ego's original reaction to objects in the external world [= 'love' for Belisa]."[148] Perlimplín's suicide is the necessary choice among possibilities: he cannot repress the awakened libido; he cannot attach it to another person; he cannot murder Belisa for any number of reasons, the principal one being that he cannot murder the woman who carried his projection of the mother image. Furthermore her withdrawal in search of an ideal lover-seducer occasions powerful feelings of worthlessness. Previous to his marriage he had a self-identity of sorts, though it was hedged in by the maternal atmosphere established by his life style. When Marcolfa thrust him into a "new world" the task presented itself of seeking a new identity. At the beginning, he thought he had found it. Then Belisa withdrew. And so a fatal circumstance is prepared: he feels worthless, and he has available a large quantity of unattached libido. The outcome of a case like this is inevitable: the unattached libido, like a demon, seeks out the first object at hand; if a new love object is not available ("love on the rebound"), the "worthless" self-identity becomes the object of a manic attack; it is put out of its misery.

In discussing the manic interludes characteristic of melancholia, Freud describes the mania in Perlimplinesque terms: "joy, exultation . . . , triumph." Perlimplín himself speaks of his "triumph," and he exults in the success of his ruse. Freud accounts for this sudden manic outbreak as follows: "What has happened here is that, as a result of some influence, a large expenditure of psychical energy, long main-

147 Ibid., p. 252.
148 Ibid.

tained or habitually occurring, has at last become unnecessary, so that it is available for numerous applications and possibilities of discharge."[149]

"As a result of some influence," says Freud. This influence in Perlimplín's case is the resolution taken by Belisa to busy herself in finding a lover. Instead of sitting sulkily at home, she actively seeks admirers. Now Perlimplín is faced with the problem of arousing Belisa, of interesting her in him as a sexual male. His grappling with this problem represents the "large expenditure of psychical energy . . . habitually occurring"; Belisa's interest in the men outside her home relieves him of the immediate need to "save" her from a sexually sterile life. At the same time it shows him a "solution." For if Belisa intends to be an unfaithful wife, then Perlimplín, by means of disguise, can himself excite her interest. It appears, then, that *Perlimplín* affords a classic illustration of the manic dynamics of suicide as described by Freud.

The Critics' Appraisal of Perlimplín's Suicide

"You think you are [committing suicide] to punish your wife and actually you are freeing her. It's better not to see that. Besides the fact that you might hear the reasons they give for your action. As far as I am concerned, I can hear them now: 'He killed himself because. . . .' "

(Albert Camus, *The Fall*, p. 75)

Most of the critical commentaries on *Perlimplín* consist of short syntheses (as in the manual of literature) in which the critic cannot afford himself the luxury of anything like analytical detail; consequently, they are generally limited to dealing evaluatively with the manifest content taken at face value.

This content seems to manifest itself varyingly to different critics, but the favored interpretation by far is that which sees Perlimplín as an altruistic suicide. His love for Belisa "is so selfless that he has created the image by which she can discover love. . . . he gives his life so that she will learn the meaning of love."[150] Perlimplín, "through his suicide . . . has achieved the triumph of his imagination: he has given the

---

[149] Ibid., p. 254.
[150] Allan Lewis, *The Contemporary Theatre*, p. 248.

warm Belisa a soul."[151] "Perlimplín . . . kills himself so that Belisa may understand love and live a worthwhile life in the knowledge."[152] "Devoted to the redemption of a human spirit and apart from any taint as it transcends the normal values of everyday life, [*Perlimplín*] reaches the heights of magnificence."[153] Perlimplín kills himself so that Belisa "may love him through her memory of the lover whom Perlimplín disguised himself as."[154] Perlimplín, "married to a voluptuous girl, invents a lover for her and kills himself for her, in order to teach her the meaning of love."[155] "[In *Perlimplín*] love is viewed as the conflict of the flesh and the spirit, with the soul triumphant over the body through sacrifice and death."[156]

It will be noted that these commentaries all imply a high-minded morality to be the guiding force of the play. The tendency to treat Perlimplín's suicide as a sacrificial death places Perlimplín on the level of a Socrates or a Codrus. Further, it implies that Lorca was primarily interested in imparting a moral lesson—in showing how people ought to act. In the present pages this analysis assumes that the play is about how people actually do act, which is consistent with Lorca's approach in his other works. He is characteristically concerned with the complexities of the human psyche and not with the simplicities of any moralistic clichés.

The tenor of the critical evaluations quoted above is by no means necessitated by the text. The favorite critical view emphasizes the nobility of the play, but one critic, though supposing Perlimplín's suicide to be "noble," also sees it as being perfectly useless with respect to Belisa: his final confession of love "is lost on her, whose heart has not yielded to spilt blood, and remains unchanged."[157] This conclusion contrasts strangely with the belief that Perlimplín finally achieves a "triumph," giving "the warm Belisa a soul."[158] At the least

[151] Edwin Honig, *García Lorca*, p. 129.
[152] Robert Lima, *The Theatre of García Lorca*, p. 143.
[153] Ibid., p. 155.
[154] Ofelia Machado Bonet, *Federico García Lorca*, p. 62.
[155] John Gassner, *Masters of Drama*, p. 224.
[156] Francisco García Lorca, Introduction to *Five Plays*, by García Lorca, p. 8.
[157] Jean-Louis Schonberg, *Federico García Lorca*, p. 280.
[158] Honig, *García Lorca*, p. 129.

this variation in viewpoints indicates the ambiguity of the text and perhaps the futility of seeking in it elevated moral lessons.

At least one critic has found it impossible to recognize in Perlimplín's suicide the sublimity so readily noted by others: when Perlimplín invents the fictitious lover, he himself, in the eyes of Belisa, becomes a zero; "he cancels himself out by his own double," so entering the first phase of his suicide.[159] Here can be noted a recognition of the insignificance of the *monigote*.

Psychologically this self-cancellation precedes the act of suicide. As Menninger notes, "When to the ego the only appropriate behavior seems to be the initiation of a series of events expected to end in self-extermination, the ego has already virtually died."[160] And Perlimplín's suicide is not the result of a sudden decision made moments before it happens; it is the consequence of careful planning typical of manic behavior as described by Alvarez—who, in recounting the final days of a suicide known personally by him, observes that "she had learned that despair must be counterpoised by an almost obsessional attention to detail and disguise."[161] Perlimplín carries this "obsessional" planning out literally, with respect to the disguise. Despair grows out of a virtually dead ego, and what libido is available is invested not in constructive egoistic designs, but in the implementation of a complex and desperate piece of single-minded maniacal aggression.

If one observes the other mature tragedies of Lorca he can see a clear theme of aggression running through them: in *Blood Wedding* the two rivals kill each other; in *Yerma* the protagonist strangles her husband; in *Bernarda Alba* the youngest daughter hangs herself when she believes her lover has been killed. This fatal aggression is the upshot of what happens to people. It does not show how people implement noble ideals. And so, if only by simple analogy, it should not be supposed that Perlimplín's death is the illustration of any ideal, but rather one more example of spiritual "dyscontrol" resulting in a need to bring a situation to an abrupt end by fatally aggressive means.

It will be recalled that a feeling of omnipotence is frequently at-

[159] François Nourissier, *F. García Lorca*, p. 64.
[160] Menninger, *The Vital Balance*, p. 265.
[161] Alvarez, *The Savage God*, p. 35.

tributed to suicides who believe in their post mortem capacity to affect the lives of their survivors. Now nothing at all can be known or even surmised about what happened to Belisa after the end of the play. There is no such datum. To discuss her future would be like surmising whether Perlimplín went to heaven or to hell. But Perlimplín's belief in the effect of his suicide is indicated by his declaration that after his death Belisa will have her young lover *in perpetuum* as a (frustrated) memory, "so lovely and spruced up" in her bed—which suggests that he imagines her reduced forever to a nocturnal fantasy embittered by the suicide that she witnessed. He will inspire in her a very satisfying survivor guilt.

One of the most detailed discussions of Perlimplín's suicide is that of William Oliver, who says that Perlimplín "dies with his eyes open," which is to say that this is a fully conscious form of suicide. "Belisa, in turn, is shocked into an awareness of the human condition. Henceforth she will live or struggle, as did Perlimplín, within the tension of the human dialectic. . . . Only in *Perlimplín* do we find the hard-bitten courage to assess life, to despair of it, and then *to go on living.*"[162] This last cannot apply to Perlimplín, since he does not "go on living." Nor can it apply to Belisa, because it implies that the play has an aftermath that it does not have. Though Oliver says that Belisa "henceforth . . . will live or struggle," one cannot accept as a datum of critical analysis what Belisa might or might not do "henceforth"—because there is no "henceforth." The play ends when it ends; and that is where the data end. And with respect to Belisa, her last words are textually, "But where is the young man with the red cape? Oh God: where is he?"

These final words of hers do not suggest in any way that she is now ready to face a brave, new, and noble future. Perlimplín has, in effect, carried out a savage attack not only against himself but also against Belisa. He has led her to expect a future filled with erotic gratification and then attempted to traumatize her with the "ultimate horror." At the end of the play she stands asking where her young lover is. She appears to be in a state of shock, for it still does not sink in that there

---

162 William Oliver, "The Trouble with Lorca," *Modern Drama* 7 (1964): 14.

never was any young lover. So Perlimplín is dead—but where is the young man with the red cape?

William Oliver also tells us that Perlimplín dies "finding fulfillment in fulfilling Belisa's nature."[163] His explanation involves a use of the term *fulfillment* that is difficult of application. Applied to Perlimplín the term obviously means that his suicide was a sacrificial, validating act (= fulfillment). But it has already been seen that this interpretation is not possible, since his suicide is not the necessary alternative to remaining alive. His life would not be invalidated by remaining alive, since his life was never the attempt to validate anything in the first place. Certainly Perlimplín thinks the act is justified, since he carries it out. But no one else is required to share his possibly unrealistic assessment of what is "necessary." Lorca's depiction of the behavior of an unbalanced mind does not require one to take sides with its "distorted perspectives."

As for Belisa's "fulfillment": this notion evidently is based on the statement that "*Belisa ya tiene un alma*," "Now Belisa has a soul." But what can this having a soul mean, after all? The point should be clear to all, for it is not possible to believe that a man would kill himself with gratuitous violence for the vague purpose of "fulfilling" the nature of another person. There is no evidence anywhere—particularly in the literature on suicide—that such a motivation could ever be anything more than the neurotic rationalization of an act determined by nonaltruistic reasons.

What of the exhibitionism of Perlimplín's suicide? As a gesture it is (as has been noted) a phallic suicide. Perlimplín leads Belisa to expect the arrival of the seductive phallus bearer and then exhibitionistically shows himself to be the bloody victim of the phallus, and that is exactly what he is. The power of the dwarf has driven the "precious dagger" into his heart.

Belisa is said to be "shocked into an awareness of the human condition"—but is it possible that a man would commit bloody, fatal violence upon his own person in order to proselytize another person existentially? Self-destruction in the hope of initiating someone else into life knowledge seems to be a nonexistent phenomenon. But even

[163] Ibid.

as a postulate it still says nothing about the manner of the act—its significance as a gesture of the dwarf, whose power has overwhelmed the ego, so that the victim dies raving about escaping from the dark nightmare of a woman's body.

Two critics have attached importance to the connection in *Perlimplín* between love and death, and one of them has concluded that the theme of the play is "mystic" love: Perlimplín, by killing himself, removes the corpus and enables Belisa to love him *in absentia*, which makes it "mystic" love.[164] But this is a negative description of mysticism, which is to say no mysticism at all, or at best a weak metaphor that does not go far toward unraveling the complexities of the play, especially because once again it depends for its validity upon nonexistent events occurring after the final curtain falls.

The second critic to relate love and death in this play speaks of the "love-death theme,"[165] which is surely misleading, since the "love-death theme" normally refers to the ultimate union of the two lovers on the same plane. This critic connects the "love-death theme" with the notion of mysticism (cf. the Cathari) and so *Perlimplín* is supposed to show Belisa's initiation into "love's mystery."

But these moralistic conclusions are all subjectively determined by a highly selective treatment of the text. If one takes into account all details and not only a felicitous selection, he will be driven to describe the play in terms of its psychological determinants and not in terms of its potential for moral sublimity.

"¡Belisa ya tiene un alma!"

Much has been made of the dying Perlimplín's utterance that "Belisa has a soul now." His words are taken literally (when mentioned) in every critical discussion of the play that I have read, and are supposed to mean that Perlimplín, when he says this, is voicing Lorca's own idea of the meaning of the play. But this assumption is not necessarily accurate. The remark may (and probably does) reflect Perlimplín's own confused state of mind, not Lorca's detached consideration

[164] Marcelle Auclair, *Enfances et mort de García Lorca*, p. 250.
[165] Francis Fergusson, "*Don Perlimplín*: Lorca's Theater-Poetry," in *The Human Image in Dramatic Literature*, p. 89.

of what the play is about. As such the statement must be given a psychological value, not a moral one. Without trying to read into the play moral elements that are hardly there, one can account for the statement "now she has a soul" with the general psychology of "survivorship."

When a person kills himself he forces a transformation upon "the other person" in his life: he creates a "wound in the order of being" that the other person is absolutely powerless to ignore. It is one of the thoughts foremost in the revenge aspect of suicide ("you'll be sorry when I'm gone") because suicide creates a survivor, who finds himself at the mercy of guilt feelings. Even when there is no evidence that the suicide consciously sought revenge, whenever there is an immediate survivor one may observe that a form of "mental blackmail" has been used, "having the unconscious design of punishing because of a disappointing relationship."[166]

Throughout the play Belisa has been virtually without character, almost without an individual personality. She has the kind of "personality" granted characters in hardcore pornography and carries on ecstatically about her genital heat. Her lack of character and her expostulations of limitless erotic appetite recall the sexual orientation of pornographic literature: "Characteristically, pornography, while dreary and repulsive to one part of the normal (most usual) personality, is also seductive to another: it severs sex from its human context . . . , reduces the world to orifices and organs, the action to their combinations. Sex rages in an empty world as people use each other as its anonymous bearers or vessels, bereaved of love and hate, thought and feeling, . . . existing only in (and for) incessant copulations without apprehension, conflict or relationship."[167] "Anonymous bearers or vessels" of sex: so does Belisa characterize herself in the first scene when she describes her erotic thirst as limitlessly receiving the unending phallic stream that pours forever into the fountain that she is. "He who seeks me with ardor will find me," she says. The center of her self is her sexual libido, "raging sex."

[166] Joost A. M. Meerloo, *Suicide and Mass Suicide*, p. 97.
[167] Ernest van den Haag, "The Case for Pornography Is the Case for Censorship and Vice Versa," *Esquire*, May 1967, p. 135.

Belisa's demanding sexuality is opposed to what has been noted as Perlimplín's "misfortune"—his ignorance of erotic behavior ("ardor"), that is to say, sexual virtuosity. The sexual antagonism of these two people results in the withdrawal of Belisa and the consequent suicide of Perlimplín, partly as the culmination of his aggressive "practical joke" (cf. the trickster dwarf) and partly as a piece of aggression in itself: for he makes Belisa a widow under the most distressing and ghastly circumstances. He leads her to believe that he is preparing the way for her entry into an erotically satisfying union with another man —and then, with total unexpectedness and shocking savagery, he exposes her to the "ultimate horror": he plunges a dagger into his breast and then exhibits the results to her. It is a form of perverse exhibitionism with a vengeance. Whether these horrors will bother Belisa "later on" is irrelevant to this analysis, since there is no "later on"; nevertheless, Perlimplín exposes her to the "ultimate horror," and the hostility behind the act is apparent.

By "ultimate horror" is meant the basis for guilt feelings as described by Robert Lifton in his specialized study of the subject: "A type of memory which epitomizes the relationship of death to guilt appears in what I have called the *ultimate horror*—a specific image of the dead or dying with which the survivor strongly identifies himself, and which evokes in him particularly intense feelings of pity and self-condemnation."[168] An evaluation of Perlimplín's final act cannot avoid the question of why he so arranges it that Belisa will observe his death as a bloody horror. The intention is all too clear: "look what you have brought me to!" It is an attempt to induce "particularly intense feelings of pity and self-condemnation" by making her witness a "specific image of the . . . dying": her own husband.

The high specificity of this suicide requires a consideration of its psychological implications, for a strong suspension of disbelief is necessary indeed in order to accept the act uncritically as the expression of a vague ideal. Anyone at all familiar with the work of Lorca knows that he thought a great deal about violent death and dismemberment— that at times they were a fascination. An early prose piece is entitled "The Beheading of John the Baptist"; another, "The Beheading of

---

[168] Robert Jay Lifton, *Death in Life*, p. 48.

the Innocents." "Saint Lucy and Saint Lazarus" describes the sadism of the martyrdom of Saint Lucy. His "Martyrdom of Saint Eulalia" is particularly cruel, while *Poet in New York* is a veritable compendium of death and destruction. The *Lament for Ignacio Sánchez Mejías* involves a horrified obsession with the gory death of the bullfighter. And of course the dramatic trilogy—*Yerma, Blood Wedding*, and *Bernarda Alba*—concerns three cases of violence: two rivals who kill each other with knives, a murder by strangulation, and a suicide by hanging. All three cases curiously recall Perlimplín, for whom marriage meant the possibility of strangulation, and who killed himself with a dagger.

Lorca's fascination with the psyche and its relationship to death makes it difficult to treat *Perlimplín* in a context of high morality. Indeed, to treat it this way is to see it as a drama from the mid-nineteenth century. In discussing the plays of Lorca one will always get a much higher yield from the psychological point of view than from the moral or the ethical.

And so the intention behind Perlimplín's act—to confront Belisa with the ultimate horror—implies his belief in the resulting efficacy of suicide. He believes that he can successfully traumatize Belisa through confrontation with the death encounter, which means he believes that the meaning of her life will shift radically from "pornographic" matter to attempting to formulate the meaning of the death encounter. She will have to give herself over to trying to comprehend how her own being is related to the horrifying and absurd experience of seeing a presumptive lover suddenly turn into her husband with a dagger in his breast. The act easily reveals the intention behind it. And Perlimplín clearly believes that he has succeeded: for if Belisa is indeed traumatized (spiritually "wounded") she will turn from "body" into "soul"—that is, individuate as a survivor of the ultimate horror.

Marcolfa herself seeks the "noble" explanation, but Belisa evidently is psychically numbed; for the moment she does not change from the erotically oriented young woman of before. In the final moments of the play there is no evidence that Perlimplín's belief in the magic efficacy of his transforming act is in any way well founded. Just after Perlimplín dies Belisa exclaims weeping, "*¡Nunca creí que fuese tan compli-*

cado!" which may mean "I never thought he was so complicated!" or
"I never thought it was so complicated!" The translation by Graham-
Lujan and O'Connell reads "I never thought he was so devious,"[169]
which is perhaps a devious rendering. Preference here is to read the
remark as alluding to the entire situation: "I never thought it was so
complicated!" The erotic confrontation is complicated, not simple. As
previously noted, Belisa is characterized as "pornographically" simple,
with her "raging" erotic thirst depicted in terms of the insatiable
"vessel"—the fountain. If the erotic confrontation is not simple, as
pornographic stories present it, it is because it has psychosomatic determinants. To realize this is to inject a spiritual complication into the
sexual encounter.

The person who enjoys reading pornographic literature looks for
sexual fantasies that can be enjoyed simply, without any admixture of
"spiritual" complications. Sometimes it would seem as if "ideal sex"
would be precisely simple sex, which is to say purely physical—physically pure—with none of the complexities supplied by "impure"
worries, guilt, moral responsibilities, and so forth. But only the animal,
apparently, can have this irreducibly simple approach to sex. Men and
women have spirits, and these make sexual matters "complicated."

For Belisa, sex is largely animalistic (or so she is characterized in the
beginning of the play), and she happily and mindlessly goes forth to
enjoy an erotic encounter with an illicit lover, believing naïvely that
her husband would be indifferent, or even approving. But Perlimplín
has planned to shock her out of this pornographically simple approach
to sex. It is true, of course, that he in turn has a madman's belief in the
"simplicity" of spiritual matters. Certainly he is confused about what
he is doing, as his last words sufficiently imply. First he says, "Belisa
has a soul now," and then shortly afterward "explains" how matters
stand: "Do you understand? I am my soul and you are your body."
There is no reason to believe that his "explanations" show insight
rather than rationalizations. He needs to believe that his desperate act
will signify a restitution; that it will traumatize Belisa and therefore
bring her, despite herself, to an appreciation of how "complicated"
sex is. But his is a Pyrrhic victory and has any number of possible un-

[169] García Lorca, *Five Plays*, p. 130.

conscious determinants, some of which Lorca implies through his use of Freudian material.

Those who take Perlimplín's "soul" statement at face value are seeing the play in a simple way, in spite of the fact that they might take Belisa's last words as an admonishment. She, for one, knows at least that "it is complicated," even if the spectators want to make it nobly "simple."

Perlimplín *and the Fairy Tale*

That it is analytically necessary to elucidate the fairy-tale and mythic material in *Perlimplín* indicates that the play itself ultimately stems from Lorca's interest in dramatizing folk fantasy. His earliest play, *The Butterfly's Curse*, was written for children and represents a dramatic variant of themes treated in a narrative poem of 1918, "The Encounters of an Adventurous Snail."

The Butterfly's Curse and "The Adventurous Snail" involve the anthropomorphic world of insects and beasties and reflect that animistic aspect of folk material frequently associated with the name of Hans Christian Andersen. Lorca's attraction to the magic animism of the child's imagination shows itself at first in a way that promises to make of him another Andersen; and the following applies substantially to the early Lorca: ". . . when Hans Andersen looked back on his childhood home through the coloured spectacles of memory it was enhanced in beauty. It was the circle of his childhood dreams. Here he played with the marionette theatre which his father had made for him. He made costumes for the puppets himself, and on the ideas from the theatre posters which were given to him, he wrote the plays."[170]

By the late twenties *Perlimplín* was finished, and by then also Lorca had transcended the limited appeal of the animistic tale that eventually begins to tell on the patience of the Andersen reader: for Andersen extends the principle from anthropomorphic insects to living, articulate toys, flowers, vegetables, domestic furnishings—anything at all, as a matter of fact; and he tends to pass from the magic of animism to sentimentality and light satire. Animism is, after all, only a device of the fairy tale, not an end in itself; and Lorca leaves it behind with his

---

[170] Svend Larsen, in Hans Christian Andersen, *Fairy Tales*, p. 22.

early works, to pass on to the broader aspects of traditional symbolic narratives. For the fairy tale, at bottom, is always the story of initiation, as is *Perlimplín*.

Perlimplín has lived a virginal fantasy life protected from the outside world. When the play begins he is a man-child, and he is being urged into his initiation into the adult world—and this initiation lies at the very heart of the fairy tale. Lorca explicitly plays on the initiatory theme as being a passage into a new world, for Perlimplín exclaims, "Oh, Marcolfa! What world is this that you're getting me into?"

The fairy tale commonly represents the initiatory motif in terms of threshold symbolism, playing on the theme of childish sexual curiosity. Sexual knowledge is the secret chamber forbidden to the hero. Knowledge of the contents of the room is always dangerous, and a common motif of this knowledge is that of the sleeping princess, the personification of the benevolent feminine unconscious—the anima. In the Norwegian story "The Golden Castle that Hung in the Air" the hero, Ash Lad, finds "his" picture of the anima hanging on a tree deep in a forest. The girl portrayed lies sleeping alone in a chamber in the recesses of a castle far off, guarded by "all the wild animals in the world." When he finds the chamber he rests beside the princess, sleeping except "for a moment" around midnight. The result is a son.[171]

This story is an unusually explicit example of the meaning of the forbidden room, the room that adults forbid to children. Perlimplín himself, who had never crossed the threshold, tells us after his initiation with Belisa, "Before, I was unable to think about the extraordinary things there are in this world . . . I lived on the threshold [literally, 'I would stand in the doorway'] . . . But now!" And the motif of the forbidden room appears literally when the old bachelor confesses that he spied upon his bride through the keyhole while she was dressing for the wedding.

The grotesque fact about the story of Perlimplín is his age—fifty years. The comparative age of the sibling characters in the fairy tale is always significant, and Perlimplín's advanced age puts him in the position of the "elder brothers"—the ones who always fail to establish

[171] Peter Christian Asbjørnsen and Jørgen Moe, *Norwegian Folktales*, pp. 139–149.

proper communication with instinctual forces. It is the youngest brother or sister who succeeds, protected by a flexible ability to co-operate with the "helpful animals." Belisa herself clearly represents the force of sexual libido invading the life of Perlimplín, and he is not equipped to approach it safely, for his character has long since crystal-lized and is brittle. So it has been many years since Perlimplín qualified for the role of "youngest brother" (or young "only son"), and yet in his virginal ignorance he must confront powerful forces of instinct. He must enter into the lower regions with no hope of aid. Belisa reigns supreme in the chthonic darkness of her own world, and, like the many sleeping beauties of the fairy tale, she easily brings about the death of any man who would try to reach her side. He who can do this is a hero, and he always succeeds with help from friendly animals or fantastic beings. But in *Perlimplín* the animals—Belisa's cats—are dangerous, not helpful, as one of the dwarfs recalls. They threaten the death of the phallic hero—which is what Perlimplín fears for himself. And rightly so, since his fear of sexuality is in itself a kind of guarantee that it will be the death of him.

Most commonly the fairy tale represents instinctual regions as a great forest, a subterranean world, or as a world hidden beneath a lake or sea. In *Perlimplín* Lorca takes his cue from the latter. As in the fairy tale the seekers often discover the beloved in a world beneath the ocean, so in *Perlimplín*, since Belisa, on the wedding night, is to the protagonist none other than a personification of the sea—the frighten-ing sea of his childhood.

W. A. Clouston, in his turn-of-the-century theoretical work, *Popular Tales and Fictions*, discusses this motif in his chapter "Subaqueous Fairy Halls; Forbidden Rooms; Cupid and Psyche Legends."[172] The danger of entry into these worlds, as his examples show, is the danger of fascination with unconscious forces, much as has been noted apropos of *Jerusalem Delivered* where, in the Fortunate Isles of Armida, the higher masculinity, the upward striving, is sacrificed to the phallicism of the lower masculinity. Clouston's principal example comes from Irish lore and tells of a lake "in which many young men were drowned," corresponding to Perlimplín's expressed fear of the sea,

---

172 Clouston, *Popular Tales and Fictions*, I, 192–214.

and of Belisa-as-ocean. The hero descended into the world lying underneath this lake, and there is found the same world as that which ensnared the victims of Armida; for when the hero gazed upon this submarine world, "what should he see but all the young men that were drowned, working away in the pleasure-grounds as if nothing had ever happened to them."[173] These drowned men, then, are all engaged in symbolic gardening, and they, like Rinaldo, have been destroyed by fascination. They have succumbed to the power of Fascinus.

Here one should note that the destruction is spiritual, for the victims are arrested at the "effeminate" stage. But the garden of *Perlimplín* is planted with orange trees and cypresses. The orange (= chthonic sun) is a prime symbol in Lorca (as everywhere else, perhaps) for sensuality (certainly it is frequently the "golden apple" of the fairy tale, the magic cure for illness, unhappiness, and sexual anesthesia). But the cypress is the tree of the cemetery, and when Perlimplín enters the garden of the orange trees he simultaneously enters the realm of death—not simply spiritual death, but physical death.

Since Belisa's raging sexuality is the ocean realm so feared by Perlimplín, she is consistently equated with the water motif. Her erotic song describes the bridal bath in which the sun becomes a fish in the water between her thighs (consciousness descended into instinctual waters). Her thirst (not "hunger") is unending and she would be a fountain eternally flowing. After the marriage contract is made Perlimplín himself feels a new thirst and asks Marcolfa for a glass of water. It appears that she explains to him the symbolic meaning of his thirst and how it will be slaked. In his excitement just before his sexual initiation, he modestly compares his libidinal stirrings to "water growing warm in glasses." But those glasses of water are met head-on by the ocean itself in the image of Belisa who, dressed in her lacy negligee, looks like a foamy ocean wave. And finally, during the initiation, the dwarfs compare the spirit of Perlimplín to a happy little duck.

These motifs all appear in a Hungarian fairy tale, "Lovely Ilonka," in which the hero finds his beloved in the form of a bulrush. He plucks it from the water, opens it, and a lovely maiden springs forth. She declares that they belong to each other and asks for a drink of water: "My

[173] Ibid., p. 194.

heart's love, I am yours and you are mine; do give me a glass of water."
With the glass of water their love is sealed: ". . . the water was ready
and . . . she and the prince promised to love each other always."[174] But
a villain throws the girl back into the waters (a well), where she remains lost until the hero himself feels thirsty. He sends a servant to
draw water, and "in the bucket he pulled up a pretty little duck was
swimming." The duck turns into the maiden again (who then turns
out to be a magic spinner, of the kind who defeated Rumpelstiltskin).[175]

The dangerous waters of the fairy tale always represent a test for the
young hero, and they show how his commitment to instinct is eventually transformed into a viable adult spirit. But *Perlimplín* is typically
Lorcan in that it shows how the passage through the dangerous waters
fails because the victim was alienated from instinct to begin with. In
the end, the only specific consciousness that Perlimplín develops is the
knowledge that he can take his own life—which, though it can be a
piece of higher consciousness, is for Perlimplín self-defeating.

Lorca and Duende

It has just been noted that the knowledge that one can take his own
life "can be a piece of higher consciousness." With respect to the world
view of Lorca this is a commonplace truth, as any reader knows who is
familiar with Lorca's lecture on the concept of *duende*, "The Theory
and Practice of [the] *Duende*."[176] And because the *duende* is of major
importance in *Perlimplín*, no study of this play can be complete without an examination of Lorca's own ideas on the subject. What is the
relationship between Lorca's explicit formulation of the meaning of
duende and his use of *duendes* in *Perlimplín*?

In Spanish the primary meaning of *duende* (from L. *domitus*, "tam-
ing," hence "domestication") is "familiar spirit," or "sprite." But in
Andalusia the expression "to have *duende*" is used with reference to
inspired artists and performers. The peculiar thing about this expression is that it does not seem to call forth the image of a "sprite," any

---

[174] "Lovely Ilonka," in *Crimson Fairy Book*, ed. Andrew Lang, p. 4.
[175] Ibid., pp. 1–6.
[176] García Lorca, "Teoría y juego del duende," in *OC*, pp. 109–121.

more than the word *inspiration* suggests the conscious notion of breathing whenever it is used. "To have *duende*" is just an expression, and popularly refers to a kind of inspiration. And Lorca, in his famous lecture, does not even attempt to relate *duende* to dwarfs. His talk is a kind of essay in definition in which he seeks to explain what Andalusians (Gypsies in particular) think of as "real inspiration." *Duende* is not dissimilar to what the American Negro means when he speaks of "having soul," and it is applied to almost any activity where there is a successful realization of vitality or instinctual energy.

Lorca's lecture is not concerned with the analogy between the dwarf and that special inspiration which is the subject of his talk; but it may be of symbological value to indicate how they are related: how it is possible that the word meaning "dwarf" could also come to mean a certain kind of inspiration. Lorca quotes a flamenco guitarist to the effect that the singer who has *duende* does not have it "in his throat": "it comes up inside from the soles of his feet."[177] Which is to say that it is not finally a question of ability or skill or technique; it is the "spirit of the earth," a "Dionysiac scream."[178] To judge by what Lorca says, it is a mortal power that knows its own mortality. It is the struggle to realize one's own mortality in an immortal way. What is sensed, for example, in the late quartets of Beethoven involves more than complicated composing, more than the complex treatment of thematic material. A man's spirit is locked into a struggle with vast forces, and he leaves his impress upon them before they carry him under. It is creative energy that the listener not only hears, but also absorbs.

Lorca explains that *duende* is not "enlightenment" or sudden inspiration of the kind that seems to flood one's intelligence as from a light above; it is a visceral motion, a gathering of power for action. *Duende* is not the genial synthesis or the self-conscious dawning, but rather the driving impulse that gives one's achievement its vital character as a struggling tension.

A famed medium of our time, Eileen Garrett, described this quality as it appeared in her own person, and her testimony is of special interest because of her vocation, summed up in a complete commitment

[177] Ibid., p. 110.
[178] Ibid.

to the "other side"—unconscious forces struggling toward consciousness. Garrett's "inspiration" is raw in its final form, by contrast to the
esthetic creativity that uses inspiration as the foundation of a structure
consciously erected. Garrett's "inspired" feelings, then, are for her an
earth knowledge (cf. "the soles of the feet") that awakens in the
solar plexus:

> In the human constitution there is a point of focus that is the physical
> seat of the psychic faculties. It is the solar plexus, the great ganglion of
> nerves that lies behind the stomach. . . . it thinks differently from the brain
> —for it is a brain itself. When, in a situation of silent danger, a twig snaps,
> it is in the solar plexus that one first *feels* the effect. That the ear hears and
> the brain registers the sound are incidental facts, remote from the center at
> which life is then concentrated. . . .
> How rarely we are thus animated in the daily round of our routines!
> We lose the tension of a vital alertness that is native to us, and spend our
> energies casually along the lines of least resistance. . . .
> It is at the level of the solar plexus that human nature makes its deepest
> concessions to Nature.[179]

One senses a relationship between Lorca's *duende*, Garrett's vital alertness "native to us" and centered in the solar plexus, and the vital center (navel) of power wherein the yogin transforms his mortality into
immortality.

Lorca discusses at length the relationship between *duende* and
death, for "to have *duende*" is to take life seriously in the ultimate
way, as the one chance to confront death. One psychologist, speaking
of suicide, has doubted "whether anyone takes his life with full seriousness until he realizes that it is entirely within his power to commit
suicide."[180] Most people live as if they were immortal ("Yes, I will die
—but not tomorrow"), whereas the Spaniard (says Lorca) easily sees
life as a confrontation with death—hence the traditional Spanish fascination with the bullfight. There have been American bullfighters, and
it may be that these are seekers of the "subintentioned" suicide; but the
Andalusian *torero* can hardly be so indicted, unless the entire culture
is simply defined as "suicidal."

[179] Eileen J. Garrett, *Adventures in the Supernormal*, pp. 231–232.
[180] Robert E. Litman, "Psychotherapists' Orientations toward Suicide," in *Suicidal Behaviors*, ed. H. L. P. Resnik, p. 358. He is citing Rollo May.

In other countries, says Lorca, death is the occasion of odes and elegies.[181] By this one understands that elsewhere funeral rites are the renewed assertion of the collective life and the significance of the deceased's endeavors in the service of life. In the presence of death men draw together and close ranks against it. But not in Spain, the country where the expression of *duende*—mortal vitality—is popularly recognized as man's highest achievement.

This vital force is the transpersonal force of life that is ambivalent with respect to human beings: it makes the human manifestation possible, but it is also the incessant Becoming that swallows up everything that it makes possible. It is both one's creator and his executioner. Man is the only living creature who can raise this Becoming into consciousness, and by the same token he is the only living creature who can contemplate his ultimate end at the hands of the life force, and who can play with this force.

In *Perlimplín* the life force appears specifically in the form of the dwarf—phallic power—and as embodied in the "oceanic" Belisa. In his lecture on *duende* Lorca returns to the symbol of the ocean in order to explain its meaning. Each confrontation with *duende*—even as every bullfight—he says, is unique; it cannot be repeated and is therefore not susceptible to collective transmission. "*Duende* never repeats, just as the forms of the ocean in a tempest are never repeated."[182]

The man who raises himself from the phallic stage to the stage of the higher masculinity does so by wresting away the phallic power—*duende*—for noninstinctual ends. The bullfighter expresses what is to him the highest form of his own consciousness and self-discipline in an open challenging of a deadly brute force.

Those who find the bullfight an alien example have only to think of the high-wire acrobats of the circus. Here the terrible pervasiveness of *duende* can soon be felt: with a safety net under them, their act is an exciting display of discipline and timing; take the net away, and the performance enters into a new dimension—for the acrobats are now playing with death. When one watches high-wire acrobats working without a net, he can readily feel a galvanic "gut reaction" exploding

---

[181] García Lorca, "Teoría y juego del duende," in *OC*, p. 117.
[182] Ibid., p. 119.

in the solar plexus. That is his apprehension of *duende*. The sense of life itself as a chance to work with death paradoxically confers upon mortality the quality of immortality because what is meant by "mortality" includes the consciousness and the dread of it. To escape from this consciousness and dread is to work beyond it. Mortal energy annihilates mortal fear. Art with *duende* is art that takes this mortal striving as its theme. It is the "theme" of Beethoven's mature music, and it is the "theme" of the bullfight that for Lorca is "an authentic religious drama in which . . . one worships and sacrifices to a God."[183]

While Lorca does not discuss why the particular word *duende* happens to be the one used in the expression "to have *duende*," it is clear that the *duendes* of *Perlimplín* and the *duende* of his lecture are the same thing: the uprushing of instinctual energy in response to an alarming provocation. In *Perlimplín* this occurs on a phallic level; in the bullfight or in music on the level of the higher masculinity. The bullfighter works with it; the creative genius struggles to bring into manifest being his commitment to it; Perlimplín succumbs to it, flings himself desperately into the chasm. He worked without a net though he was ineligible to do so.

In the bullfight *duende* can, at any moment, rear up savagely and tear into the vitals of its victim, like one of those terrifying man-eating trolls that stalk the folk literature of Scandinavia; for even the magic talisman of disciplined skill does not always suffice. But Perlimplín never came close to considerations of discipline and preparation for self-realization. He was trapped in the cave of the smirking dwarfs, and in an agony of confusion he "gored" himself. The schlemiel committed the final, the ultimate "lonely act" of "self-abuse."

One can, like the ancient Romans, commit suicide for an ideal. But there are no ideals in the spirit of Perlimplín, the once-happy little duckling. And without ideals, "suicide is simply the most extreme and brutal way of making sure that you will not readily be forgotten."[184] Such is the extent of Perlimplín's accomplishment—the little accomplishment of a little man. At least one does not readily forget him.

[183] Ibid., p. 118. Lorca capitalizes here: "se sacrifica a un Dios."
[184] Alvarez, *The Savage God*, p. 108.

A Psychological Commentary on *Yerma*

DEAR ABBY: I just read the letter in your column about the husband who completely avoids sex. I was glad to learn I wasn't the only person in the world who feels this way about sex. I am a married woman, and thank heavens my husband isn't the type of man who makes unpleasant demands on me. . . .

What most people can't understand is that some people just don't care for sex that much. I personally find the very thought of it sickening. . . .

HAPPY WITHOUT SEX

DEAR HAPPY: If you are happy, and your husband is happy, then I am happy.

(*Arizona Daily Star*, March 22, 1972)

Yerma has received more critical attention, and a greater variety of it, than any other of Lorca's plays. This is no doubt due to the kind of human issues involved and particularly to the passionate Spanish reaction to them. The diversity of published interpretations means that the casual reader who seeks critical guidance to *Yerma* ought to be able to consult an anthology of commentaries knowledgeably compiled, but this does not exist; therefore, he must be content at best with a random perusal of the most accessible published analyses.

A comprehensive survey of the critical commentaries on *Yerma* reveals not only much contradiction, but also a consistent lack of communication among the critics, since they do not discuss the differences and contradictions that beset them. Hence this discussion of *Yerma* has a twofold purpose. First, a survey will be made of the basic issues involved according to the bulk of the "traditional," or conservative, criticism of the past three decades or so, which seeks to elucidate a moral conflict precipitated by defined causes. An assessment of this point of view will attempt to show why it is inadequate and even misleading.

Second, a new critique of *Yerma* will be set forth, which will include a résumé of the play and a review of the theoretical apparatus necessary to a relevant analysis. This review will involve a short presentation of the psychological concepts that clarify the conflicts suffered by the protagonist. These concepts include a consideration of the conflict between *unconscious goals* and *conscious goals*; the psychological concept of the *shadow*, and what is meant by the *assimilation of the shadow*; *emotion* as a psychological force; the theoretical meaning of *hysteria*; the spiritual significance of *singing*; and finally the theory of *psychosomatic sterility*.

This theoretical process is necessary if one is to have a broad but precise understanding of what Lorca actually achieved when he wrote *Yerma*. For too much criticism has dealt with the play in evaluative terms—generally the panegyric. But what does *Yerma* represent as a twentieth-century achievement? That is what these theoretical considerations are intended to show.

Lorca's "rural" tragedy *Yerma* and the extensive criticism on it go together in a way never envisioned by the critics; for, taken together, they illustrate how critics, en masse, may lag behind one creative mind for many years, apparently without anyone's becoming conscious of the fact.

Lorca had a dramatic idea fresh for the time (the thirties), and he worked it out as the basis for a tragedy; and for some thirty-five years now *Yerma* has been repeatedly analyzed and discussed, praised and faulted, without benefit of that idea. What the situation actually amounts to is this: *Yerma* belongs to the twentieth century in the most basic way possible, and yet it has been consistently examined and commented upon as if the traditional, "standard" critical point of view with respect to the tragedy were an adequate frame of reference.

To clarify the nature of this gap between the artist and his critics, one needs first to recall only the bare data of the play. Lorca created a woman character, Yerma ("Barren"), who is trapped in a childless marriage. Her one ambition in life is to become a mother, and she spends a good deal of her time throughout three acts lamenting her barrenness. Divorce is not an available solution; adoption will not suffice, because what Yerma craves is self-realization in the form of maternity, and not simply a child to care for; and she indignantly rejects the idea of adultery, affirming her belief in the sacrament of marriage. At the end of the play her husband tells her to resign herself to her circumstances; and when he approaches her lasciviously she strangles him in an access of rage and frustration.

What is to be made of this tragedy? What has been made of it critically down through the years? Out of three dozen or so critical discussions of *Yerma*, several typical reactions can be identified for study, and the following group of eight critics sharing a common point of view characterizes in particular the critical lag with which the present discussion is concerned.

In 1944 Alfredo de la Guardia published his book *García Lorca: Persona y creación* and in the chapter on *Yerma* describes what is to him the primary conflict: Yerma's elevated, spiritual need for motherhood ("good") vs. her husband Juan's ugly lust ("bad"). Juan cannot get Yerma with child, and yet he selfishly expects her to yield to his lewd desires. She, a "simple and good country woman,"[1] has lyrical visions of maternity that remind us of a Renaissance Madonna.[2] Juan, though he has sufficient proof of Yerma's wifely virtue, accuses her of infidelity. Worse, he gets drunk, waxes lascivious, tries to approach her; he embraces her and would kiss her: "This is not the mouth of husband and father-to-be; it is the mouth of the ineffectual male, of the hybrid mule, who wants only to satisfy a vile and momentary pleasure."[3] For this critic the primary conflict is the antithesis be-

[1] Alfredo de la Guardia, *García Lorca*, p. 300.
[2] Ibid.
[3] Ibid., p. 308.

tween *goce* (physical pleasure) and *gozo* (spiritual pleasure or joy, as when one speaks of the seven *gozos* of the Virgin Mary). Further, Yerma would never seek motherhood in adultery, because she needs a legitimate maternity consecrated by the sacrament of marriage. This is her "spiritual necessity," and she speaks of motherhood with a "religious tenderness."[4] This analysis suggests, finally, that *Yerma* is a case of justifiable homicide. She is "spiritual," and her husband's inability to rise above his lust understandably nauseates her.[5] Here then is a repetition of what was seen in the discussion of *Perlimplín*: the critical tendency to use morality as a tool of analysis; and *Yerma* in particular seems to elicit this tendency, perhaps because of the crucial and deeply emotional issue at stake.

Edwin Honig's book on Lorca, also of 1944, carries essentially the same critical reaction to *Yerma*. Yerma is one who cares about something fine—maternity—and she is a "richly poetic girl,"[6] while Juan does not seem to be able to transcend carnal love; and she therefore "chokes him for his impurity."[7]

In 1950 Roberto G. Sánchez, in his book-length study of Lorca's theater, emphasized Yerma's natural nobility. Like Honig, he believes that she is a poetic figure whose desire for motherhood (could any woman have a finer ambition?) carries her to an almost "mystical state," so that "for her, the world exists only when it is seen through the eyes of a mother."[8]

Motherhood is clearly a goal in life that it is not easy to denigrate successfully, though in the seventies the Women's Liberation movement is managing to do it. In 1951, at any rate, a woman critic, Ofelia Machado Bonet, fully agreed with the men who applauded Yerma's goal. In fact she is probably the most violent of all in her identification with Yerma's conscious attitude that leads to the murder of the husband: Juan does not even desire children and thus "condemns his wife to an undeserved sterility";[9] "[Juan] is the man who is purely

4 Ibid.
5 Ibid., p. 311.
6 Edwin Honig, *García Lorca*, p. 164.
7 Ibid., p. 176.
8 Roberto G. Sánchez, *García Lorca*, p. 58.
9 Ofelia Machado Bonet, *Federico García Lorca*, p. 129.

brutal and blind in his instinct; he is momentary pleasure, and not the sacred, grave, and fecund union. He is filth [*suciedad*], full of the slime [*lodo*] of the earth, and not pure, clear, and limpid maternity. She rejects him repugnantly."[10] At the end of the play, then, Juan evidently receives his just deserts.

A year later, in 1952, Juan Chabás, in his *History of Contemporary Spanish Literature*, concurs, and reinforces the notion of justifiable homicide by implying that Juan's lust at the climactic moment traumatizes the suffering wife, whose frustration reaches the breaking point: ". . . the lascivious and sterile mouth of the husband fills her with horror, and she struggles with his sterile caress to the point of strangling him."[11] This suggests a plea of temporary insanity.

Gustavo Correa, in his book on Lorca's "mythic poetry" (1957), emphasizes another aspect of the conflict: Yerma's need to recognize the sacrament of marriage in spite of her "ardent desire for motherhood"[12] lifts her to a truly heroic level. In her are refined the social and ethical norms of virtue, caste, duty, morality. Heroically she remains faithful to her husband.[13]

Similarly, Vázquez Ocaña, writing in 1962, sees Yerma as "sublime"; and "filled with anguish, and sure that the flower of her being cannot expect from Juan the sweet little life to which she had a right, she wildly defends herself against his caresses, and she kills him because, dry and withered, she is a field that will not tolerate the offense of a fruitless irrigation. But when she kills, her purity—the purity of a virtuous woman—is elevated to the sublime."[14]

And finally, in 1965, Delfín Carbonell Basset bestows upon Yerma one final touch of glory by pointing out that the killing of Juan is a kind of suicide: for he was her only hope. "And when she realizes that Juan will never give children to her, she decides to put an end to the farce. It is a heroic act, this; it is like dying and continuing to live; it is like living in death."[15]

[10] Ibid., p. 135.

[11] Juan Chabás, *Historia de la literatura española contemporánea*, p. 482.

[12] Gustavo Correa, *La poesía mítica de Federico García Lorca*, p. 85.

[13] Ibid.

[14] Fernando Vázquez Ocaña, *García Lorca*, p. 319.

[15] Delfín Carbonell Basset, "Tres dramas existenciales de Federico García Lorca," *Cuadernos Hispanoamericanos* 64 (1965): 129–130.

All the above critics, then, see in *Yerma* a dialectic between lust and motherhood. They see that a married woman has the right to expect children and when all means to this end are closed off, it is clearly adding insult to injury to expect her, at the high point of frustration, to enter into conjugal relations. And while Yerma may be a murderess, she did not kill with malice aforethought. It is a case of temporary insanity induced by an unbearable frustration and the presence of a selfish, unfeeling husband indifferent to any but his own erotic desires. The critical quotes show a willingness to argue the point with righteous indignation.

A second group of critical opinions is concerned more specifically with Yerma's virtue, her integrity, and her rectitude. It is true that she ends by killing her husband, but this is clearly the act of a shattered woman and so does not reflect upon her basic character throughout five long years of marriage.

Much has been made of Yerma's morality, or virtue (*honra*), because, after all, in the course of the play it is made clear that once, before her marriage, she felt her heart go out to a shepherd, Víctor, toward whom she still feels no little attraction. And, in the last act, an old lady suggests that her own son would make a better husband for Yerma because he is not sterile. Yerma, however, consistently rejects the idea of adultery or of abandoning her husband, because she has a profound respect for the marriage sacrament. A number of critics emphasize this point. Enrique Díez-Canedo, writing in the mid-thirties, characterizes the play as the "tragedy of yearning for maternity," and says that, besides Nature's denial of her, Yerma faces the denial of "moral constancy which her own spirit sets up."[16] And de la Guardia, who has already been quoted at some length, states that Yerma's *honra* is "of capital importance, because without it the conflict would be resolved."[17] It is her rectitude that makes adultery impossible.[18]

Guillermo Díaz-Plaja, in 1954, contrasts, *Yerma* to Lorca's famous poem, "The Unfaithful Wife" (*La casada infiel*); he says that *Yerma* is Lorca's "faithful wife."[19]

[16] Enrique Díez-Canedo, *Artículos de crítica teatral*, p. 141.
[17] Guardia, *García Lorca*, p. 300.
[18] Ibid., p. 311.
[19] Guillermo Díaz-Plaja, *Federico García Lorca*, p. 209.

Robert Lima, in his *The Theatre of García Lorca* (1963), states the conflict succinctly: "The choice is clear—life with Juan without fulfillment of her maternal needs or unsanctioned gratification outside of marriage."[20] He gives a negative value to Yerma's obedience to a moral code when he says that there are "two undeniable forces in conflict—the natural need of motherhood as opposed to a rigid morality which prevents satisfaction."[21]

In his *History of Spanish Literature* (1967) James Stamm simply applauds Yerma's sense of honor and personal integrity.[22] A year later Clemente Fusero tells us that Yerma's virtue, or moral integrity (*l'onore*), is of "essential importance" in the tragedy.[23]

Allan Lewis, in *The Contemporary Theatre* (1971), contrasts "a woman's anguished need for motherhood" to the fact that Yerma "is dutiful to the code of honor."[24] And in the same year, on the occasion of a performance of Villa-Lobos' operatic version of *Yerma* ("based virtually word-for-word on the play"), a publicity release states that Yerma "is doomed to be faithful to a man she hates, since, for the same traditional reason that she desires a son, she also desires to maintain her family honor."[25]

So far then, there are two compatible critical viewpoints: (*a*) Yerma is a noble woman who lives committed to one of the highest ideals that a wife can entertain, and will sooner destroy her life than give up that ideal by resigning herself to any kind of life without it; certainly she will not prostitute herself to a futile eroticism. (*b*) Yerma is a virtuous woman who, in spite of her deeply rooted need for maternity, will not compromise it by any immoral act (viz., adultery), even if such an act could give her the gift of motherhood. The end would never justify the means.

Three critics place a different (though sympathetic) interpretation upon this moral code, for they characterize Yerma as the victim of what Lima above calls a "rigid morality." Emphasizing the rigidity of

---

[20] Robert Lima, *The Theatre of García Lorca*, p. 220.
[21] Ibid., pp. 218–219.
[22] James R. Stamm, *A Short History of Spanish Literature*, p. 213.
[23] Clemente Fusero, *García Lorca*, p. 401.
[24] Allan Lewis, *The Contemporary Theatre*, p. 256.
[25] *Arizona Daily Star*, August 8, 1971.

this code, one can see Yerma as a victim of society. Anthony Aratari, for example, writing in *Commonweal* (1955), says that even though Yerma's "desire for children is really pure," she suffers from an "indifferent morality which has cut her off from fulfillment as a woman."[26] "Any solution of her conflict not based on an honor which is moral as well as physical is ignominy and slavery."[27] Arturo Barea, in his book on Lorca (1956), makes the issues even more clearly sociological: "Yerma's obsession is not only her own individual problem; it is the tragic result of a society which distorts, defiles, or throttles the spontaneous feelings of young women."[28] In Spanish society the "oppressive weight of frustration" falls upon the women.[29] And finally, Rafael Martínez Nadal, in 1970, writes that *Yerma* allows one to "infer a kind of silent denunciation, a protest against social conventions, the final cause underlying the betrayal of the sure instinct of the flesh."[30]

At least one critic, Francisco Umbral, strongly emphasizes the negative aspect of the moral issue in *Yerma*. Writing in 1968, he says that Yerma is essentially a deviant and therefore is forced to live beyond the pale of the collective morality; hence her deviance is the "curse of freedom," and her own being is destroyed in the process.[31]

In the opening remarks it was suggested that the mass of criticism on *Yerma* involved irrelevant considerations because Lorca was concerned with a new idea, whereas the criticism is based on traditionally accepted ideas and the use of morality in the attempt to get critical leverage. The examples of this have been seen, so the discussion will proceed in an attempt to show the irrelevance of such an approach.

Perhaps the very idea of "tragedy" suggests the need for an analysis grounded in morality. Lorca himself called *Yerma* a "tragic poem," which does not seem to be very far from calling it a tragedy. The ancient Greek tragedy, the Shakespearean tragedy, the Racinian tragedy—are these not, after all, concerned with moral conflicts? When

---

[26] Anthony Aratari, "The Tragedies of García Lorca," *Commonweal*, August 12, 1955, p. 474.
[27] Ibid.
[28] Arturo Barea, *Lorca, el poeta y su pueblo*, p. 48.
[29] Ibid., p. 55.
[30] Rafael Martínez Nadal, *El público*, p. 174.
[31] Francisco Umbral, *Lorca, poeta maldito*, pp. 217–218.

one discusses the issues at stake in a tragedy, does he not inevitably get involved with ethical questions?

The twentieth century has seen a general shift in attitude from morality to amorality, to a region beyond good and evil, not only in the arts but also in philosophy and psychology. In Spanish letters the nineteenth-century dramatists were characteristically concerned with the ethical conflict ("love vs. duty"), which really means a conflict in loyalties. Love, since it belongs to one's affective life, obviously has important determinants that are not conscious, that is, not known to ego. But the unknown determinants are obscured by prominent conscious aims that elicit the proud loyalty of ego. It is this loyalty to "naïve" consciousness that is commonly dramatized in nineteenth-century theater.

Lorca was one of the new writers of the early twentieth century who turned away from the conflict centered in consciousness in order to employ a different dramatic premise, just as the early depth psychologists were employing a new psychological premise for the treatment of neurosis: the concept of the unconscious goal. Hence it is no accident that the neurotic appears with some frequency in Lorca's theater.

The earliest insights of depth psychology came out of the experimental work of J.-M. Charcot, Josef Breuer, and Freud—work based on a common interest in hypnosis and hysteria. The important elementary insight as the basis for a system of psychology was, of course, the view that the unconscious part of the psyche is just as much an element of the individual human being as the conscious part. It follows from this that the deepest inner struggles threatening the psychic balance of every human being are those that arise from an incompatibility between what is sought consciously and what is needed unconsciously.

Because this conclusion seems so obvious in the latter half of the twentieth century, one tends to forget that Freud's contemporaries were far from taking it as a truism. In 1910 T. Sharper Knowlson, a reasonably well educated folklorist, was able to write: "In our dreams we are the same Egos as in our waking moments; and we see the same people we know in daily life, and recognize them; *proving* that there is an exercise of the same memory centres as in conscious life."[32] This

[32] T. Sharper Knowlson, *The Origins of Popular Superstitions and Customs*, p. 119. My italics.

author, like most of his contemporaries, is entirely innocent of the notion that dreams may be interpreted in terms of a conflict between conscious and unconscious goals, and so he believes that the solution to the "problem" of dream interpretation lies in explaining dreams as a "psi" phenomenon: "The direction in which we are likely to find the truth is telepathy."[33]

The defining of neurosis, or psychic "dyscontrol" (characteristic of dream life) as rooted in the conflict between conscious and unconscious goals, is basic to the modern view of the human psyche, and it is this approach that characterizes Lorca.

Lorca was gifted with great psychological penetration, and he was basically interested in how psychical disturbances are created by the conflict that is being discussed—the "hysterical" conflict. He knew that one all-important psychic component, the symbol, has its origin in the unconscious (he discusses it at length in his public lectures).[34] Therefore, no commentary on his theater can leave out of the reckoning his conscious recognition of the dynamics of psychic imbalance (and their manifestation by symbol) that lie at the root of depth psychology.

The recognition of a possible conflict between conscious and unconscious goals placed morality in a new perspective, since unconscious goals are amoral. To treat the neurotic with sermons on ethics is pointless, since the use of ethics is a rational activity, whereas the unconscious goal sought by the neurotic is nonrational. By the same token it appears useless for the critic to discuss the morality or ethics of Yerma's behavior, because the play is not about that. It is about a neurotic conflict. Thus the moral evaluation of her final, murderous act is irrelevant because such an evaluation assumes the act to express the pursuit of conscious goals (rational or not).

Nor can it be the task of the descriptive critic to define the unconscious goal of a neurotic character. To do this would be to "psychoanalyze" the character; it would be to seek explanatory data in infantile experiences that are not in the play. In *Perlimplín* these do make a

---

[33] Ibid.
[34] See especially Lorca's lectures "La imagen poética de Góngora" (*OC*, pp. 62–85) and "Las nanas infantiles" (*OC*, pp. 91–108).

brief, tentative appearance as a kind of "screen memory." But Lorca knew that it was unconvincing and artificial for the dramatist to pretend to possess an omniscient case-history knowledge of his characters' unconscious goals. Barring deep analysis (which is the search for such goals) unconscious aims are known only by their effects. When these effects are constructive it is pointless to use them as material for dramatic treatment, and certainly they cannot be used as the basis for tragedy, since by definition constructive effects cannot lead to tragic consequences. But the dramatic treatment of the neurotic conflict in terms of its effects is a speciality of Lorca, and the critic must avoid the temptation to analyze such conflicts into their ethical components. The moralistic point of view ultimately requires data not supplied by the play.

The criticism on *Yerma* that has been cited so far occasionally appears to take into consideration the perspective that has been outlined here. Díaz-Plaja, for example, writes that "from the psychiatric point of view, *Yerma* presents a well-known form of feminine hysteria, which has as its motive the obsession of maternity."[35] But this is a casual use of "psychiatric" terms that Díaz-Plaja employs in a simple descriptive way and not for the purpose of analyzing the dynamics of Yerma's conflict. It is a more-or-less technical way of stating that Yerma is crazy.

The general tendency to use a pre-twentieth-century ethical point of view is encouraged by the critical desire to relate Lorca to a pre-twentieth-century Spanish tradition. A number of critics (de la Guardia and Correa, for example) point out that Lorca represents a new birth of seventeenth-century Golden Age drama, especially that of Lope de Vega. This in itself is enough to lead one astray critically if one tries to make much of Lorca's debt to the seventeenth century. For if one thinks of Lorca as a modern Lope he may seek similar dramatic premises—which brings him right back to the issue of morality and "good guys" and "bad guys" (who are consistently absent from Lorca's mature drama in spite of the critical lambasting dealt out to Yerma's "lascivious" husband).

The point of view of this discussion is going to be that *Yerma* is a

[35] Díaz-Plaja, *Federico García Lorca*, p. 208.

prime example of psychological conflicts as created in dramatic form by a twentieth-century imagination. If Racine, for example, was a great moralist, then may one not say that Lorca was a great psychologist, in the sense that he belongs as much to the twentieth century as Racine does to the seventeenth? This means that he knew how to exploit dramatically the neurotic conflict, just as the depth psychologist knows how to go about helping the neurotic to bring order out of chaos.

The critics' concern with the morality of Yerma's behavior centers on the old question of a conflict between loyalties: Yerma's yearning for motherhood (love of, constancy to, an ideal) vs. her duty as a wife. She wants one thing and constantly talks about it; on the other hand, she realizes that she must be a virtuous wife though the marriage be barren. This is a good, conservative conflict of the sort that has been a staple of dramatic tragedy for over two thousand years. But it will not work when applied to *Yerma* because it leaves too many things unaccounted for—things that a few critics simply discount as "poetry" and therefore inaccessible to analysis: ". . . for Lorca [Yerma] was always a creature of poetry, never a case of clinical psychology."[36]

Yerma, seen as a conflict between two conscious goals—moral issues collectively recognized—must be analyzed in terms of "evidence" supplied by Yerma's own words. She suffers, and she knows "why" she suffers. But Yerma's self-analysis of her sufferings can be shown to consist of confused and inconsistent rationalizings. She "explains" to herself the effects of repressed material.

Critics commonly refer to Yerma's "frustrations," but by this they do not mean the kind of frustration that leads to repression. Yerma's "frustration" is commonly seen as conscious disappointment. She knows consciously that her desire for maternity is frustrated, but this only means she can't have what she consciously wants. But Yerma is also repressed, and the whole play is concerned with telling this to the audience and to her. But mainly to the audience.

Lorca knew that telling a person he is repressed—as various characters tell Yerma—cannot possibly remove the repression; and so naturally when the characters in the play sing the praises of spontaneity, the message is for the audience, not for Yerma. She cannot be cured by

[36] Sánchez, *García Lorca*, p. 59.

all the sermons and chants in the world, but these can enable the spectators to see the direction in which the play is going to go.

The treatment of *Yerma* as the tragedy of conscious conflict has given rise to a rather extraordinary set of answers to a pseudo-puzzle with which nearly every Lorca critic has concerned himself, to wit: why can't Yerma have a child? Even though the critics have studiously avoided getting into "clinical" questions, they have nearly all felt that any explication of *Yerma* as a moral conflict was bound to be somehow incomplete unless one could account for Yerma's barrenness. The need to seek a "cause" grows out of the need to place the "blame" for a moral conflict; for how can one evaluate an ethical problem without knowledge of its determinants?

Since there has always existed the desire to avoid "psychoanalyzing" the characters, this search for the "cause" has most often produced by way of explanation an efficient cause, as the reader will see. This discussion, on the other hand, intends to adduce a formal cause, that is, an aetiology to be found in the internal structure of Yerma's own psyche; a cause that can be documented by evidence in the text.

Why Can't Yerma Have a Child?

Here will be considered forty-two published critical commentaries, analyses, and reviews of *Yerma*. Twenty of these appear as separate chapters or as detailed discussions in books on Lorca; four of them are articles on *Yerma* that have appeared in learned journals; five of them are articles on some aspect of Lorca, and these too have appeared in learned journals. Nine are taken from discussions of Lorca's drama in manuals of literature, while the remaining items are journalistic.

The problem is to see how critics have answered the question of why the marriage of Yerma and Juan is barren. Of the forty-two critical commentaries consulted, five are noncommittal, and three involve analyses of the situation that transcend considerations of efficient causes. Of the thirty-four remaining critical interpretations, then, ten clearly "blame" the wife, and twenty-four clearly "blame" the husband. The "causes" may be tabulated as follows:[37]

---

[37] These opinions are distributed as follows (see bibliography for further information): *Yerma is sterile*: Babín, Borel, Descola, Díaz-Plaja, Díez-Canedo, Martínez

Yerma is sterile   10
Juan is sterile   13
Juan is "frigid"   4
Juan is "selfish"   7

Of these causes the first two are self-explanatory. The third is under-standable, even though in English the term is misapplied to a man. It is used here because the critics themselves use it. The fourth—the "selfish Juan" theory—is more puzzling and will have to be discussed in some detail. Similarly the whole question of terminology will have to be included in the discussion, since key words like *frigid, impotent, sterile,* and *barren* are consistently used without benefit of definition and are occasionally used interchangeably without apparent justification.

It is possible to account for each of the four theories cited above in terms of what might be argued as being internal evidence. Those who believe that Yerma's barrenness is caused by her own sterility take the title of the play—that is to say, the "name" of the protagonist (more about this anon)—as a *fait primitif.* For these critics the word *yerma* evidently means simultaneously "barren woman," and "sterile wo-man." Thus, for Jean Descola, *Yerma* is "the drama of the sterile woman."[38] For Mora Guarnido, Yerma is one of "those lean and sterile women."[39] Díaz-Plaja tells us that Yerma "lives the tragedy of her sterility."[40] Robert Skloot, more than any other critic, puts especial emphasis on the negative condition of Yerma: ". . . we must see that Yerma *was born to be barren,* as her name indicates. . . . She is . . . marked from birth, and her fate is announced every time her name is mentioned."[41]

Nadal, Mora Guarnido, Schonberg, Skloot, Williams; *Juan is sterile:* Auclair, Chabás, Chandler and Schwartz, Cobb, Correa, Elizalde, Nourissier, Stamm, Vázquez Ocaña, Valbuena Prat, Zdenek, *Time's* review of *Yerma* (December 16, 1966), and the publicity release for Villa-Lobos' *Yerma* (*Arizona Daily Star,* August 8, 1971); *Juan is "frigid":* Fusero, Honig, Lott, Río; *Juan is selfish:* Barea, Cannon, Carbonell Basset, Gassner, Lewis, Lima, Machado Bonet.

[38] Jean Descola, *Historia literaria de España,* p. 323.
[39] José Mora Guarnido, *Federico García Lorca y su mundo,* p. 172.
[40] Díaz-Plaja, *Federico García Lorca,* p. 207.
[41] Robert Skloot, "Theme and Image in Lorca's *Yerma,*" *Drama Survey* 5 (1966): 157.

The critics who espouse the "frigid Juan" theory can point for evidence to Yerma's remark toward the end of the play where she says that whenever she and Juan have conjugal relations she always notes his *cintura fría*, which translates freely as "cold loins." At any rate the application to Juan of the word *frío* no doubt accounts for the misuse in English of the cognate "frigid."

Seven critics conclude that Yerma is childless because her husband is "selfish"; and no matter how one thinks this ought to be interpreted, the evidence for it lies in Yerma's remark to Dolores and the Old Lady (Act Three, Part One) that Juan does not long for children, "and since he doesn't long for them, he doesn't give them to me."

And finally, as evidence for the "sterile Juan" theory, one need only recall the indictment voiced by the Old Lady in Act One, Part Two, who, in sympathizing with Yerma, curses all men (i.e., such as Juan) of "blighted seed" (*simiente podrida*). Tabulation shows that more critics agree with this diagnosis than with any other.

Not the least remarkable fact to emerge from a study of the criticism on *Yerma* is this: though four different theories are used to explain Yerma's barrenness, none of the critics ever suggests that there is, or could be, any disagreement on the matter, or that his own theory is less than a self-evident fact. Here are characteristic statements by those who believe Juan to be sterile: ". . . now she knows: it is not she who is sterile, it is Juan";[42] ". . . the sterile and lascivious mouth of the husband fills her with horror";[43] "[Yerma] discovers that it is her husband who is unwilling and *unable* to have a child";[44] "Gradually Yerma has been coming to realize that it is he who is to blame. . . . Juan represents the weed with blighted seed which interrupts the cycle of Earth's perpetuation";[45] "[Yerma] is in complete despair on learning that her husband . . . cannot give her children";[46] "It is her hus-

---

[42] Marcelle Auclair, *Enfances et mort de García Lorca*, p. 324.
[43] Chabás, *Historia de la literatura española contemporánea*, p. 482.
[44] Richard Chandler and Kessel Schwartz, *A New History of Spanish Literature*, p. 137. My italics.
[45] Correa, *La poesía mítica*, p. 84.
[46] Stamm, *A Short History of Spanish Literature*, p. 213.

band Juan . . . who is sterile";[47] "[Yerma] joyously married the man her parents chose for her, only to find him to be sterile."[48]

The "sterile Juan" theory is possibly the one that has gained widest currency among students of Spanish literature because it is the one set forth by Valbuena Prat in his popular *History of Spanish Literature*. Professor Carl Cobb, in his survey of Lorca's work for the Twayne World Authors Series, considers Valbuena's opinion sufficiently important to be singled out: "Dr. Valbuena has suggested that the play should actually be named *Yermo*, since Juan is the barren one."[49]

The sterility theory, whether applied to Juan or to Yerma, is untenable, in spite of the fact that it dominates critical thought on the play. It is untenable for the simple reason that sterility, as a fact, cannot be known except by means of empirical tests. Known sterility is a phenomenon of the modern, technologically advanced society—a piece of "city knowledge." People nowadays can conveniently find out their blood type; they can know whether their cholesterol level is too high, whether or not they suffer from low basal metabolism; and, if childless, they can know whether sterility is the cause. Such are the blessings of technology.

But could one suppose, for example, that Lorca might have written a "primitive," "rural" play about a couple facing the tragedy of the Rh factor? What if one were to say that Juan's principal complaint was low blood sugar?

That hypothesis would be unsatisfactory; and it is equally unsatisfactory to state that Juan (or Yerma) suffers from organic sterility. Barring a visit to a metropolitan clinic, there is no possible way that such a fact could be a dramatic premise, much less eventually be "realized" by anyone in the play. Not even the dramatist himself could snatch a hidden fact like this out of thin air. If knowledge of a fact depends upon scientific research, it is useless to pretend that it does not, useless to pretend that the fact is known, "anyway."

It is not difficult to explain why a plurality of critics would interpret the play as concerning a barren woman married to a sterile man. The

[47] *Time*, December 16, 1966, p. 87.
[48] *Arizona Daily Star*, August 8, 1971.
[49] Carl W. Cobb, *Federico García Lorca*, p. 136.

reason is to be found in a felt necessity for such a theory. This arises from the fact of Yerma's honor. As was earlier pointed out, critics have commonly taken this to be a tragedy based on a moral conflict between Yerma's anguished desire for motherhood and her need to remain true to her marriage vows. The possibilities of adultery and separation both present themselves in the play, but Yerma rejects them as inacceptable. The critical reasoning evidently goes like this: Yerma shows her virtue and her integrity by remaining faithful to her husband, even though he is sterile. If she herself were sterile she would have no good "practical" reason to reject adultery as a possible solution to her problem.

Known sterility cannot be a datum of the play, however, and so both the "sterile Yerma" and the "sterile Juan" theories must be discarded. This leaves two other theories to be examined, the "frigid Juan" theory and the "selfish Juan" theory.

Four critics state, with varying degree of emphasis, that Yerma is childless because Juan is "frigid." None of them defines this term or suggests how such "frigidity" could be a cause of barrenness. Honig refers to Yerma's "fear of Juan's frigidity" but elsewhere says that Juan is impotent. He evidently has second thoughts about this, however, for subsequently he says that Juan has never "been troubled about [Yerma's] desire for a child—his own impotence admitted or not."[50]

The failure to explain how an undefined "frigidity" on the part of the husband could result in a childless marriage means that the use of the term merely begs the question: "[Yerma's] only remaining hope for salvation lies in having a child by her frigid husband";[51] Yerma's barrenness is the "simple consequence of the husband's frigidity";[52] Juan is the *varón frígido*, the "frigid male."[53] Certainly "frigid" cannot mean "impotent" in the sense that Juan is unable to engage in intercourse, since Yerma admits to the material fact that they have periodic conjugal relations. In Act Three, Part One, she says to Dolores, "When he covers me he fulfills his duty." At the same time she complains of

[50] Honig, *García Lorca*, p. 175.
[51] Robert Lott, "*Yerma*," *Modern Drama* 8 (1965): 21.
[52] Fusero, *García Lorca*, p. 398.
[53] Guardia, *García Lorca*, p. 310.

Juan's "cold loins"; but the fact that she finds her husband "cold" is not a simple, empirical datum concerning Juan. Rather, it means that she and Juan engage in loveless sex, in sex without passion.

Nevertheless, in the final scene of the play Juan becomes passionately aroused, and some critics have preferred to take this, rather than Yerma's accusation, as evidence for Juan's marital behavior. The "cold" Juan disappears, to be replaced by the "hot" Juan. He is the "purely brutal [man] and blind in his instinct; he is momentary pleasure."[54] Díaz-Plaja uses even stronger language: Juan is "the man who desires [his wife] with the passion of the strong male, who sees in her only the female who satiates him."[55] According to de la Guardia, Juan's mouth is filthy with lust.[56] Thus, from this point of view, it is not Juan's "coldness" that finally exasperates Yerma, but rather his lust: ". . . the lascivious and sterile mouth of the husband fills her with horror, and she struggles with his sterile caress."[57]

If the sterility theories must be discarded because they are inadmissible, the "frigid Juan" theory must be rejected either as meaningless or as inoperative. It cannot mean "impotent" (this contradicts the text), and if it means "unenthusiastic" the quality of the seed would not be affected.

The fourth theory noted above is the "selfish Juan" theory, evidently based on Yerma's remark to the effect that, since Juan does not long for children, he therefore does not give them to her. At least one critic understands this in such a way as to suggest that sexual abstinence is meant: "[Juan's] real dryness is that he does not want to give Yerma a child, that he wills to deny her the fructifying water. . . . We may wonder if Yerma is aware of the irony—that Juan passes the nights bringing water to his fields instead of satisfying her more compelling thirst."[58] But it has already been noted that, according to the text, abstinence is not involved in Yerma's problem ("When he covers me he fulfills his duty"). Nor could Juan's alleged denial be a reference to

---

[54] Machado Bonet, *Federico García Lorca*, p. 135.
[55] Díaz-Plaja, *Federico García Lorca*, p. 208.
[56] Guardia, *García Lorca*, p. 308.
[57] Chabás, *Historia de la literatura española contemporánea*, p. 482.
[58] Calvin Cannon, "The Imagery of Lorca's *Yerma*," *Modern Language Quarterly* 21 (1960): 127.

coitus interruptus ("he fulfills his duty"). Therefore Yerma's accusation ("since he doesn't long for children he doesn't give them to me") appears to be an irrational notion. She and Juan have normal intercourse, but the union is infertile. Why? Because Juan is "selfish."

And the idea has been championed by critics. *Yerma* is about "a woman consumed with the craving for fertility while her husband persists in denying her a child."[59] The very meaning of Yerma's life lies in "the perpetuation of her being in offspring, but her husband denies them to her."[60] Yerma suffers from a "need for motherhood, which her husband fails to supply, not that he is impotent, but that he enjoys her physically without wanting children."[61] Yerma is "a woman deprived through the selfishness of her husband." "Through a selfish contradiction of his marital obligations, [Juan] denies Yerma the child of her innermost desire. It is because of this denial that the tragedy exists."[62] Yerma is "sterile," says Arturo Barea, "not because of a physical defect, but because . . . the seed has been denied her."[63] Richard Chandler and Kessel Schwartz state the matter somewhat evasively: "[Yerma] later discovers that it is her husband who is unwilling and unable to have a child."[64]

The theory of the "selfish Juan" is based on an implicit recognition of the psychosomatic determinants of barrenness, but there has never been any evidence to the effect that a man's attitude can sterilize his seed. What evidence has been adduced for psychosomatic sterility relates to the woman, not the man, and this shall be considered in due time. For the present, one should not accept Yerma's diagnosis uncritically; it cannot be the answer simply "because she says so," since she is speaking of matters in which she is so emotionally involved that her opinion gives not empirical knowledge about the actual situation, but rather insight into her own hysterical state. Yerma's "selfish Juan" remark can easily be seen as a hysterical rationalization whereby she

---

[59] John Gassner, *Masters of Drama*, p. 704.
[60] Carbonell Basset, "Tres dramas existenciales," p. 129.
[61] Lewis, *The Contemporary Theatre*, p. 255.
[62] Lima, *The Theatre of García Lorca*, pp. 218–219.
[63] Barea, *Lorca, el poeta y su pueblo*, pp. 46–47.
[64] Chandler and Schwartz, *A New History of Spanish Literature*, p. 137.

seeks to place the "blame" by adducing an efficient cause, originating elsewhere, for her own condition.

By the same token Yerma also decides that Juan is at fault because he is "cold." But, at the end of the play, when he approaches her lustfully, she criticizes his lust by killing him.

Thus, each one of Yerma's own negative beliefs about Juan ("cold," "selfish," "sterile," "lustful") has been used by several critics as the basis for an explanation of the play—to the exclusion of the remaining theories. But each of these theories is really only the reflection of Yerma's own shifting opinion. She does not finally "realize" anything at all about Juan, but rather about herself. What this is remains to be discussed in the light of textual evidence.

Résumé of Yerma

When the play begins, Yerma and Juan have been married for two years, and the action covers at least three more, during which the personality of Yerma progressively deteriorates as it becomes clear that her need for motherhood will never be realized. The plot is minimal. The play is episodic and is essentially a lyrical study of the protagonist.

In the opening scene Yerma sits alone dreaming of how a shepherd brings her a child dressed in white. She awakens and sings a cradle-song. Enter Juan. In the dialogue that follows Yerma voices her anxieties and suggests that perhaps he is lacking the requisite vigor:

Yerma. Won't you drink a glass of milk?
Juan. Why?
Yerma. You work hard and you're not built to do hard work. . . . Your face is pale, as if you never got any sun. . . . We've been married for two years and you get gloomier and leaner, as if you were growing backwards.
Juan. Are you finished?
Yerma. Don't take it amiss. If *I* were sick, I would want *you* to take care of me.

Juan leaves to work his farm, and María, a young friend of Yerma, comes to confide that she is pregnant after only five months of married life. Yerma's anxieties and self-doubts are stirred. She clutches the

girl and says, "When did it happen? Tell me. You weren't even thinking about it [literally, "You were *descuidada*," "off guard"]. And you
were probably singing, weren't you? I sing. You . . . tell me . . ." She
wants to know what kind of emotional relationship María and her
husband have, and María gives her to understand that her husband is a
passionate lover who arouses her. On their wedding night so passionately did he pour forth a litany of love phrases that it is almost as if
the child conceived is "a dove of light which he slipped into my ear."

The scene following takes place between Yerma and Víctor. Víctor
is a shepherd with whom Yerma thinks she almost fell in love once
long ago. It is given to understand that she makes invidious comparisons between her puny husband and the robust Víctor, a "mountain
of a man." He is an honest, straightforward fellow, who jovially
recommends that Yerma tell Juan to "try harder" if she wants children.

Here ends Part One of Act One. When the curtain rises on Part
Two the scene is outdoors. Yerma is taking Juan his midday meal, and
she meets the Old Lady, an uninhibited, festive personality who has
lived sensually, has borne nine sons, and who has a high opinion of
erotic activity. Yerma expresses her anxieties, and the Old Lady recommends enthusiasm. Lovers, she says, should "let our hair down and
give us to drink in their own mouth." To get pregnant you simply sing:
"I lay on my back and began to sing." Yerma confesses that she has
never enjoyed sensual pleasure, though once she was on the verge of
being awakened by Víctor; but she could not yield because she has
always had a sense of shame (". . . *es que yo he sido vergonzosa*"). She
says that while she and her husband continue to have sexual relations,
it is "never for the fun of it" ("*nunca por divertirme*"), and the Old
Lady diagnoses this as the root of the problem: "And so, you're barren
[*vacía*]!" It is her impression that Yerma's nervous condition pre-
cludes the giving of any rational advice ("I would talk to a calmer
woman").

Yerma meets next two young friends and engages one of them in a
conversation on her favorite topic. This Girl enjoys sex for the sake of
sex; the sacrament of marriage has nothing to do with it, and she freely
confesses to having enjoyed premarital relationships while engaged:
". . . one actually gets married long before going to the church."

"When we were engaged we did the same thing that we do now." What is a church wedding? "Foolish notions of the old folks."

A second conversation with Víctor follows, and Yerma's eerie intensity puts him ill at ease. She looks at Víctor hungrily, and he "slowly shifts his eyes away, as if afraid." The act ends with a brief, uncongenial conversation between Yerma and Juan.

Act Two opens with the scene of the Washwomen (i.e., village women doing their laundry at the river bank). They are gossiping, and they eventually begin to sing about married love as sensual intensity: "You have to groan in bed." "And you have to sing!" Sensual fury is the ideal: ". . . our bodies are furious branches of coral."

Part Two consists of a marital quarrel between Yerma and Juan, who has installed his two sisters in the house as chaperons; for, jealous of his honor, he objects to Yerma's willful restlessness. His work requires protracted absences, and people gossip. Yerma, on the other hand, feels herself wasting away in a living death; and now, as she bitterly tells María, it is "three against one."

One of the Girls appears briefly to make certain final secret arrangements with Yerma, for, as shall be learned, she is determined to pay a clandestine visit to Dolores, a local witch. Víctor stops by to say farewell; family obligations call him elsewhere. He remains impassive before Yerma's acrimonious generalities.

When Yerma is left alone she sneaks off to see Dolores. The theater is in total darkness. One of Juan's sisters comes onstage carrying a lamp. She calls softly, "Yerma!" followed by her sister, who calls more loudly. The first calls again, this time "imperiously," so that the effect is a crescendo that might be represented like this: "Yerma!" "Yerma!!" "Yerma!!!"

The last act begins at the house of Dolores, where Yerma seeks a magic cure for barrenness. She says that she and her husband continue to have intercourse but complains of Juan's "coldness." "And I," she says, "who have always been nauseated by hot women, should like to be like a mountain of fire at that instant. . . . I am not an indecent wife; but I know that children are born from man and woman. Ah, if I could have them by myself!" And it is here that she expresses the notion that their unions are not fertile because Juan does not long for children: "I can tell it in his glance, and since he doesn't long for them, he doesn't give them to me." She does not love him, she says, but nevertheless he is her only salvation, "for honor and family."

But Juan has traced her to the house of Dolores. There follows a violent scene of marital strife that ends with Yerma cursing her fate: "It's one thing to want something with your head, and something else that the body—body be damned!—will not respond."

Part Two begins with the Pilgrimage Scene, which culminates in a primitive fertility rite in a mountain hermitage. The scene is dominated by two masked figures, the Male and the Female. The stage direction reads that "they are by no means grotesque, but rather of great beauty, and convey a sense of pure earth." Here sensuality is apotheosized in a way quite like that of the singing Washwomen, with the addition of instrumental music and dancing. Just as the Washwomen sang of the impassioned wife who must "shine" erotically ("Let her shine! Again let her shine!"), so sings the Male: "Oh, how she shines!"

Yerma, of course, has joined the pilgrimage. She runs across the Old Lady, who has come to the spectacle. She tells Yerma that her barrenness is all the fault of Juan, who comes from a long line of weaklings. Yerma is evidently seeking a new mate, since she has joined the pilgrimage, for that is what the pilgrimage is all about: "Women come here to be with new men. And the Saint works the miracle. My son is waiting for you, behind the hermitage. My house needs a woman. Take up with him and the three of us will live together."

Yerma indignantly refuses ("What about my honor?"), whereupon the Old Lady exclaims angrily, "All right, have it your way, . . . *marchita* ['withered']." Yerma reacts powerfully (*fuerte*): "*Marchita*! Yes, I know! *Marchita*! You don't have to rub my face in it! . . . Ever since I got married I've been going over and over that word, but this is the first time I've heard it, the first time that it has been spoken to my face. The first time that I can see that it's true." Enter Juan, whose patience is at an end. He tells Yerma in so many words to be realistic, and she is shocked by his lack of understanding or even interest in her fate. He recommends resignation, but she exclaims "*Marchita*!" Juan grows conciliatory and embraces her—and with an extraordinarily poor sense of timing, tells her how beautiful she is by moonlight. He is aroused now and attempts to possess her ("Kiss me . . . like this").

"Never that," she replies, "never!" She screams, clutches him by the throat, and strangles him to death. When the act of murder is finished she says, "*Marchita, marchita,*" and adds, "but safe. Now I know it for certain." Bystanders approach while she screams, "I have killed my child, I myself have killed my child!"

Yerma and the Shadow

This discussion began by recalling the difference between a conflict between two conscious goals and one between a conscious and an unconscious goal. It was pointed out that the published criticism on *Yerma* is based on an unspoken assumption that the former holds true; all the critics who have been discussed reason on the grounds that Yerma's sudden and unexpected murder of Juan is an action that comes about *as the result of a sudden understanding.* The wording makes this clear: ". . . now she knows; it is not she who is sterile";[65] "Yerma discovers that it is her husband who is unwilling and unable";[66] "Gradually Yerma has been coming to realize that it is he who is to blame";[67] Yerma despairs "on learning that her husband . . . cannot give her children";[68] "The wife comes to learn that Juan's sap . . . is like stagnant water."[69] This places the emphasis upon the tragic climax as an event caused by the conscious comprehension of an impasse.

As has already been demonstrated, it is incorrect to assume that Yerma "comes to realize" that Juan is sterile, simply because there is no way in which she could possibly realize any such thing. But setting aside this objection, one must still consider the fact that Yerma is brought to her final, desperate act by way of an emotional conflict; therefore, special consideration must now be given to the psychological

[65] Auclair, *Enfances et mort*, p. 324.
[66] Chandler and Schwartz, *A New History of Spanish Literature*, p. 137.
[67] Correa, *La poesía mítica*, p. 83.
[68] Stamm, *A Short History of Spanish Literature*, p. 213.
[69] Vázquez Ocaña, *García Lorca*, p. 319.

dynamics of what passes for "emotional behavior." What assumption underlies the use of the word *emotion*?

To begin at the beginning, one must recognize that emotion itself is, by definition, unconsciously determined and, second, it is a fact that the individual is rare who, without special training in the dynamics of human behavior, can give even a tolerably relevant account of the intricacies of his own emotional outbursts. If he could, such a person would indeed be considered spiritually sophisticated in the ways of human beings. The father who, in an access of rage, beats his son unmercifully with a belt, could hardly know "why" he does this, if by "why" one refers to anything other than the immediate precipitating cause. Any other "reasons" he might give would have to be accounted rationalizations. This is a truism, since the kind of self-understanding being talked about would, ipso facto, preclude the possibility of uncontrollable rage, that is to say, emotional behavior greatly disproportionate to the immediate precipitating cause.

"Self-understanding" is used to refer to what the analytical psychologists (who have made this aspect of human behavior their special province) call the *assimilation of the shadow.*

The *shadow* is roughly similar to the Freudian subconscious. It represents those instinctual tendencies that are unassimilable per se to the conscious personality, or to the collective idea of tolerable morality. (This changes from age to age, of course. Among certain people cruel corporal punishment of children may constitute part of "tolerable morality"; among others, it is the sign of an unbalanced mind.) Tendencies that are intolerable are generally repressed in the process of growing up. When repressed they are nonexistent as far as the conscious personality is concerned. But of course they have not ceased to exist. They are characteristically projected upon another person and experienced objectively in the form of an enemy.[70] One then feels free to attack the enemy, even to annihilate him, with a "good conscience"; and when asked for reasons, one can give only reasons that belong to the conscious personality. Thus the witch hunter can explain "why" he burned a witch; but such regressive behavior automatically pre-

---

[70] See Erich Neumann, *Depth Psychology and a New Ethic*, pp. 39–40, 50.

cludes the possibility of his understanding that the witch carries a projection of the witch burner's own repressed dark side, or shadow.

In *Yerma* the reasons for the sudden, savage murder of Juan ("temporary insanity") cannot possibly be found in any episode explicitly set forth in the plot. Juan's general indifference and Yerma's mounting frustration at her barrenness can certainly be used to explain why Yerma should be something less than happy with her life; but they do not account for her murderous reaction, simply because, as has been noted, emotional outbursts can never be significantly accounted for by external and consciously known causes. This is not all "psychology"; it is partly a matter of dialectics, since behavior that is primarily motivated by consciously known factors is not called by the name of emotion.

Lorca is dealing with the most passionate levels of the human personality—the climax of *Yerma* shows this—which means that Yerma does not suddenly erupt into violence for reasons consciously known to her. Nevertheless, all the critics discussed above have tried to see Yerma's dilemma from her own consciously formulated point of view. The reasons they give for her murder of Juan are reasons with which she herself could readily agree. Thus, Juan insults her noble maternal ambition by approaching her erotically, knowing all the time that he cannot get her with child. He *knows* how important this is to her— hasn't she told him so clearly and passionately? And yet he has the gall to tell her, first, to resign herself to a barren life, and second, to yield herself to his lust. So "naturally" Yerma falls into a rage and murders him.

This kind of explanation implies that Yerma herself is aware of what she is doing. But awareness of what lies behind an emotional outburst, of what supplies the unexpected flood of destructive energy suddenly mobilized, means more than a knowledge of immediate causes. Primitive, regressive behavior in the form of sudden, savage aggression always has unconscious sources. For indeed, it is necessary to understand first that something has suddenly *surfaced*, whereas the critical commentaries that have been quoted speak of something that has been on the surface throughout the entire play: Yerma's consciously formulated conflict. Furthermore, the manner in which that emotion expresses itself must be accounted for. As noted in the discussion of Perlimplín's suicide, the form of the act, the act seen as a gesture, is as important as the consequences.

Yerma's final act would no doubt be defended in a court of law as the product of temporary insanity—which is a shorthand way of saying what has taken several paragraphs to say here. The increasingly common acceptance by judges and juries of the plea of temporary insanity means they recognize that the conscious personality (= "sanity") of a murderer was used by unconscious forces. A common and often infuriating answer by arraigned criminals to the question "Why?" is, "I don't know."[71] To the lay moralist it seems that a person who was aroused enough to commit murder ought to know "why" he did it. The answer "I don't know" seems like an outrageous piece of nonchalance, considering the fate of the victim. And yet the crime of passion appears to be a crime committed anonymously. It is not uncommon for the perpetrator of particularly vicious aggressive acts to have absolutely no recall of what he has done.

Generally speaking the individual possessed by rage cannot spontaneously know the why any more easily than the person possessed by passionate love. What answer could be expected to the question "Why did you fall in love with her?" And so if Yerma were asked "Why did you strangle your husband?" she obviously could give only the answers that the critics have given.

But one may suspect that Lorca wrote more deeply than that. *Yerma* is not a play about a woman who murders her husband because he is in some way at fault. Indeed, the whole question of who is at "fault" is really irrelevant to the drama, because this is not a kind of melodrama with a plot based on a simple material fact ("*Yerma*: the tragic story of a young wife married to a sterile husband"). Lorca's drama constitutes a statement by him concerning the dynamics of vital forces —which is to say that Yerma is childless for psychosomatic reasons that have nothing to do with fault or blame. The dynamics of unconscious vital forces create problems for all human beings and tragic conflicts for quite a large minority. Lorca is concerned with the struggle to reconcile these forces with human goals. A play by him typically

[71] Karl Menninger, *The Vital Balance*, p. 214.

constitutes a statement of this kind, and it is now the purpose of this discussion to clarify not the "cause" of the conflict, but rather the nature of it. Knowledge that such conflicts can be of a certain nature (i.e., that they can even exist at all) is the important knowledge here.

Critically the discussion will have to begin with the hypothesis that the drama is a unified whole; that the various elements, including the sequence of scenes and the nature of these scenes, have a common denominator. As a critic dealing with the work of a significant poet, one must necessarily begin with such an assumption, because of what heuristic value is it to state that a work of art is built upon certain principles, and then to conclude that it is defective because it contains elements that are irrelevant? Perhaps certain elements of the work only seem irrelevant because one's critical assumption is gratuitous.

The notion that *Yerma* is defective is put forth by two critics, Díaz-Plaja and Jean-Paul Borel. According to the first, the secondary characters hardly matter at all, for they are only there as a kind of "contrast." At times, as in the scene of the Washwomen, they serve a "purely scenographic purpose."[72] The "allegorical" scenes (i.e., of the Pilgrimage) "have no justification whatsoever, not only within the thematic unity of the work, but even within the profound sense of Yerma's sorrow." They "distract the spectator" and make him forget the "real sense of the tragedy."[73] Similarly, Borel asserts that all the secondary characters are part of the décor, and "are only there in order to illuminate all aspects of Yerma's personality."[74]

These are extraordinary critical statements, above all the former. If the "allegorical" scenes "have no justification whatsoever," this can only mean that they have no justification from that critic's point of view; this does not mean, though, that there might not be another point of view according to which the entire drama is indeed a unity.

Yerma's Hysteria

It has been noted that at least one critic brings up the question of Yerma's possibly hysterical condition, though he does not pursue the

---

[72] Díaz-Plaja, *Federico García Lorca*, p. 210.
[73] Ibid., p. 211.
[74] Jean-Paul Borel, *El teatro de lo imposible*, p. 54.

subject; he merely explains that "from the psychiatric point of view, *Yerma* presents a well-known form of feminine hysteria, which has as its motive the obsession of maternity," though he adds that it rarely leads to the tragic consequences seen in *Yerma*.[75] This is all he says on the subject, thereby equating "hysteria" with "obsession," without, however, suggesting what the dynamics of such an obsession might be. An explanation of those dynamics is, nevertheless, the primary desideratum at this point. The woman who, enraged, strangles her husband when he approaches her erotically and who cries "Never!" may be reasonably suspected of hysteria. But what, precisely, does hysteria mean?

Hysteria (from the Greek *hystera*, "uterus") was anciently believed to be a female condition attributable to disturbances of the uterus. The condition was characterized by a complete lack of control over one's emotions. Plato, in the *Timaeus*, describes it thusly: just as with men the organ of generation "seeks to gain absolute sway," so is it "with the so-called womb or matrix of women; the animal within them is desirous of procreating children, and when remaining unfruitful long beyond its proper time, gets discontented and angry, and wandering in every direction through the body, closes up the passages of the breath, and, by obstructing respiration, drives them to extremity, causing all varieties of disease."[76]

Plato's description of hysteria implicitly distinguishes between psyche and soma. The subject—the individual woman—carries within her an "animal" "desirous of procreating children." This is a somatic need—therefore instinctive—which, when frustrated, attacks the body entire and causes "all varieties of disease"—including the state commonly labeled "hysteria." Of course people today no longer think of hysteria as rooted in disturbances of the uterus, nor is the term even exclusively applied to women. Hysteria is seen as an inhibiting condition that produces functional disturbances—and in Yerma's case this means a disturbance of the uterus.

For hysteria should not be understood simply as a distressful symptom of barrenness itself (as Díaz-Plaja equates it with the "obsession

[75] Díaz-Plaja, *Federico García Lorca*, p. 208.
[76] Plato, *The Dialogues of Plato*, p. 67.

for motherhood"), but rather as a symptom of the psychosomatic condition that can or may lead to barrenness. Freudian thought considers hysteria to be a characteristic consequence of repressed sexuality, with which one may or may not agree in all cases. But in a specific instance in which a woman long barren murders her husband in an access of outrage when he approaches her erotically, one is rationally justified in examining the notion of hysteria as the result of repressed sexuality.

Such a woman is not simply outraged because she is barren. Rather (as the play reveals) her attitude toward sexuality creates, first, a functional disorder within her own instinct and, second, an uncontrolled reaction toward another intimately involved with her sexuality. She is barren because she is hysterical, not hysterical because she is barren. Her barrenness is a primary hysterical condition, and her uncontrolled emotional behavior (murder of a would-be lover) is a secondary manifestation of what is popularly known as "hysteria." Erotic behavior demanded by her circumstances means a challenge beyond her capacity to respond.

It has been seen that Yerma's behavior throughout the play cannot at any point be determined by her "knowledge" of her own sterility, or of Juan's, since this is a technological premise transcending the conditions of the play. It has also been shown that according to the text one may not say that Juan is either impotent or abstentious. For those who seek a "cause," this leaves only the "selfish Juan" theory. But in speaking of a functional disorder that militates against conception, it is hardly meant that the husband's attitude ("selfish Juan") somehow renders his seed sterile. What is meant at the very least is that the sexual relationship between man and wife produces somatic disturbances in the wife so that the union is infertile. Never mind whose "fault" it is (it is surely mutually determined); even if the husband is a wretched lover, even if the union takes the form of rape, the functional damage occurs in the body of the wife, where conception is supposed to occur.

If the functional disorder belongs to the husband, it takes place not in the form of sterilizing his seed, but rather it renders him impotent to engage in intercourse—or else produces premature ejaculation. Impotence is the male form of "frigidity," then, but the text says that

Juan "fulfills his duty." The unions are physiologically complete, and Yerma does not blame Juan for any kind of sexual inadequacy.

Further, Lorca's play is not about Juan; it is about Yerma. She has a problem, and the primary assumption here should be that the play concerns not whose "fault" it is, nor any conflict between good and evil, but rather the nature of Yerma's problem. One must assume that *Yerma*, as a lyrical play, constitutes an exploration of the protagonist's psyche.

Hysteria has been defined as the product of sexual repression. As such, it is understood to mean "frigidity," which does not mean, however, replacing an explanation by a label. Yerma's negative attitude toward sexuality inhibits conception. This involves no attempt to place the "blame" (it has been said that there are no frigid women, only poor lovers), but rather to clarify an idea of Lorca's concerning the creative act in general.

It has been noted that the play is about Yerma, not about Juan— but that is secondary in the world of Lorca. In the deepest sense *Yerma* is about the creative act and the conditions that may inhibit a fertile union, whether in a strictly biological sense or in the spiritual sense. But only the biological sense will be considered for now.

Yerma wonders why she is not pregnant. At the very beginning of the play her suspicions concern Juan's physical weakness: ". . . you're not built to do hard work. . . . Your face is pale. . . . you get gloomier and leaner, as if you were growing backward." Some critics take this as expository knowledge: from what Yerma says here, one is supposed to think that Juan is sterile. And the notion is evidently corroborated by what the Old Lady says in Act Three, Part Two, to the effect that Juan is to blame because he comes from a family of puny men.

But this is an old wives' tale, the belief that weak men have weak seed. It is a piece of primitive physiology, as is the idea that strong, virile men tend to have more boys than girls—or vice versa, by the "law of contraries": ". . . if a man is stronger than the woman, the children will be mostly girls; if the woman is greatly younger or stronger, the progeny will be chiefly boys. This bears out the old English proverb: 'Any weakling can make a boy, but it takes a man to make a girl.' "[77]

[77] Frank Harris, *My Life and Loves*, p. 135.

Primitive genetic beliefs also include the notion that the right testicle produces males, while the left produces females,[78] since the right side is the "strong" side.

The characterization of Juan as a relatively weak man has one obvious, prosaic justification, since it contributes to the verisimilitude of the last scene, when Yerma overcomes him physically. So far as it provides expository knowledge, however, Juan's puny physique has no significance except that it motivates Yerma to seek a primitive rationalization for her barrenness. She will offer several primitive notions of this kind throughout the course of the drama before she achieves fully conscious realization of the root of the problem.

The Creative Attitude

Critics who have granted much importance to placing the "blame" for Yerma's barrenness have sometimes found it difficult to justify the lyricism of the play. If the meaning of the play lies in external causes (such as Juan's sterility), then the "action," it seems, ought to be directed outwardly. A review in *Time* magazine relates that for two hours Yerma "yearns privately and publicly for a baby, leaving the spectator with the idea that that Spanish town could use an adoption agency."[79] But is that what "happens" in *Yerma*? The scenes with the Old Lady, the scene with the Girl, the one with María, the scenes of the Pilgrimage—are these mainly concerned with Yerma's "yearning publicly for a baby"? In constructing his drama Lorca has provided two series of confrontations, one of which reveals the problem and the other diagnoses it. The diagnostic scenes will now be examined in order to observe their unity of content.

The first is the scene between Yerma and her young friend María. María, pregnant after only five months of married life, is represented as enjoying a fulfilling erotic relationship with her husband. Yerma asks anxiously about the moment of conception: "When did it happen? Tell me. You weren't even thinking about it. And you were probably singing, weren't you?" The key expressions here are *estabas descuidada* ("you were off guard," "you weren't even thinking about it") and

[78] Pliny, *Natural History*, 8:176.
[79] *Time*, December 16, 1966, p. 87.

estarías cantando ("you were probably singing"). María affirms that she was indeed "off guard" (*"Sí, descuidada"*). When Yerma suggests further that María was "probably singing," she adds with some uncertainty, "I sing. You . . . tell me." But evidently the same kind of "singing" is not involved. There is something here that Yerma does not quite grasp, or else that she secretly fears to be true, and that she would like María to discuss. But María does not want to go into the intimate matter, and she changes the subject.

Subsequently Yerma talks with the Old Lady, the one who says that lovers should "let our hair down and give us to drink in their own mouth." To get pregnant she says, "I lay on my back and began to sing." Yerma confesses that sensual pleasure repels her, and the Old Lady concludes, "And so, you're barren!"

Yerma next meets the Girl who enthusiastically praises premarital sexual activity and scorns the marriage ceremony as a silly convention perpetuated by the old folks.

The long scene of the Washwomen culminates in a paean to the joys of the conjugal bed. One must "groan," one must "sing," one must "shine," and "shine again." This joyous singing is accompanied by the rhythmical washing motions of the women as they beat the clothes on the rocks.

The singing of the Washwomen is thematically repeated in the fertility rite of the Pilgrimage Scene, accompanied by music and dancing. It culminates in the sung praises of the "shining" and "burning" dance of life.

It is clear that the townspeople of this play all sense a causal relationship to exist between eroticism and fertility. This may or may not be a sociologically accurate portrait, but then, *Yerma* is not a sociological play. Lorca has set forth his own knowledge of the dynamics of the creative act, and in this dramatic poem collective opinion praises erotic freedom, just as in *Blood Wedding* collective opinion centers upon the procreative value of the sexual act.

Erotic enthusiasm is aptly called "love play," because creative acts must be preceded by free play—spontaneity, a relaxing of the will and of ego-intentions. One must give freely of one's energies in a full enjoyment of creative activity as its own end. It is a rite of passage, so to speak, which frees one to enter into a new world of relationships latent in the object of his love and unprejudiced by his own preconception of what the result "ought" to be: ". . . to play with something means to give oneself up to the object . . . ; one so to speak infuses one's own libido into the thing played with. . . . the play develops into a *magic action which conjures up life*. . . . To play means to bridge over the gap between phantasy and reality by the magical action of one's own libido; play is thus a *'rite d'entrée'* which prepares the way for adaptation to the real object."[80] This kind of play, then, has its original basis in playing with instinctual forces aimed at actual reproduction of the species. But in the artist it appears in "sublimated" form, as Lorca himself was well aware. Lorca was keenly interested in the dynamics of creativity, and that is why *Yerma* represents a symbolic return by him to the phenomenon of biological creativity as an "allegory" of what creation means within the psyche of the artist: 'Play is at the beginning of all creative activity, for it is only when we can adopt an attitude of purposelessness, and can do things for their own sake, freed of all end-gaining ambition, that something new can emerge which finds expression in sound, words, movement or paint. Through recreation we are re-created, and it is as if we have, like the kitten, to allow ourselves to be picked up and carried by something 'other.' "[81]

The attitude of playing is what Thoreau called "indifferency": "The artist," he wrote, "must work with indifferency. Too great interest vitiates his work."[82] For Thoreau this applies to any kind of productive labor: "I have no doubt that a good farmer, who, of course, loves his work, takes exactly the same kind of pleasure in draining a swamp, seeing the water flow out in his newly cut ditch, that a child does in its mud dikes and water-wheels. Both alike love to play with natural forces."[83]

Primitive people are known to believe in and to practice creative play, and this manifests itself in the form of *singing*: "The words of a song have considerable creative force; objects are created by 'singing'

[80] Gerhard Adler, *Studies in Analytical Psychology*, p. 97 n. My italics.
[81] Patricia Dale-Green, *Cult of the Cat*, p. 154.
[82] Henry David Thoreau, *Journal*, March 25, 1842, in *The Writings of Henry David Thoreau*, VII, 349.
[83] Ibid., November 8, 1857, in *The Writings*, XVI, 170.

the requisite words. Väinämöinen 'sings' a boat, i.e., he builds it by modulating a chant composed of magic words. . . . 'To make' something means knowing the magic formula which will allow it to be invented or to 'make it appear' spontaneously.''[84] This concentration on the activity itself is meant to allay fear concerning its outcome; for worry about the possible inefficacy of one's creative activity brings "bad luck": it interferes with the creative process, robbing it of needed energy. The ego-intention must be "forgotten," one must "work with indifferency," one must allow himself "to be picked up and carried by something 'other.' " Here is how Aldous Huxley has described it: "All that the conscious ego can do is to formulate wishes, which are then carried out by forces which it controls very little and understands not at all. When it does anything more—when it tries too hard, for example, when it worries, when it becomes apprehensive about the future—it lowers the effectiveness of those forces and may even cause the devitalized body to fall ill.''[85]

The "singing attitude" is the fertile attitude, and *Yerma* is an extrapolation by Lorca out of his own experience. It is the attitude recommended, praised, and practiced by the women of the village: María, who was *descuidada*, "off guard," or "indifferent" in the Thoreauvian sense, and singing; the Old Lady who says she always sang in bed; the Washwomen who sing of singing in bed. It is the singing attitude praised in the singing of the Pilgrimage.

Yerma's feelings, on the other hand, are characterized by a disgust for erotic play. True, she tells María that she too "sings," but in the general context of her anxieties about motherhood, her singing apparently does not go beyond consciously striking the attitude of the "successful" wives in order to see if it works—like the nonbeliever who imitates the behavior of the faithful in order to see whether faith can be induced.

While some of the critics have identified their attitude with that of Yerma ("Juan is lewd; he deserves to die") it should be noted that Lorca himself in his stage directions for the Pilgrimage Scene has stressed caution on this very point. He writes that the symbolic sex fig-

[84] Mircea Eliade, *The Forge and the Crucible*, pp. 101–102.
[85] Aldous Huxley, *The Doors of Perception*, p. 52.

ures of the Male and Female "are by no means grotesque, but rather of great beauty and conveying a sense of pure earth," a cautionary statement very likely intended to forestall any misguided stage production attempting to reflect Yerma's negative attitude in the presentation of the Male and Female. Might not the producer who believes in the "lewd Juan" theory see to it that the two sex figures appeared "grotesque"? Lorca clearly thought it needful to emphasize the point.

Lorca's idea of the creative attitude is reflected in his lifelong involvement with the child's world and with music: for the little child is the player *par excellence*, and music making is the perfect example of play as an end in itself. The musician's only "product" is the activity itself, to which uninhibited immersion is the precondition of success, nowhere more apparent than in the popular music forms—folk, jazz, and rock music in particular, famous for an excellence that derives from improvisational zeal.

Similarly, physiologists explain that there can exist a causal relationship between libidinal enthusiasm and fertility, which is to say that fertility is connected with psychosomatic factors. One reads, for example, in *The Consumers Union Report on Family Planning*, concerning the psychological reasons for infertility in some women, that besides organic factors "there may also be another cause: deep-rooted emotional conflicts that express themselves in body disturbances preventing pregnancy. . . . for other women the very struggle to achieve motherhood seems to reduce their fertility. Many women become pregnant, for example, only after they have 'given up' and arranged to adopt a child."[86] In other words, in a childless marriage where sexual intercourse takes place (and where there is no organic sterility) psychosomatic disturbances perforce manifest themselves in the body of the wife, not the husband—regardless of where the "fault" may lie. But if this realization, like known sterility, may be called a piece of technological knowledge derived from the modern theory of psychosomatic maladies, it is, nevertheless (because it is psychosomatic), intuited by primitives and explicitly expressed as a belief by the characters in *Yerma*—the offspring of Lorca's own imagination. And Lorca

[86] *The Consumers Union Report on Family Planning*, pp. 116–117.

knew by experience the theory of creative play, as does every person whose life is devoted to creative activity.

The world view of the preintellectual imagination is filled with beliefs in psychosomatic phenomena, and such beliefs characteristically operate as self-fulfilling prophecies. In some vague way Yerma intuits that her sexual impulses have not been destroyed, but repressed; that psychic energy is not destroyed, but transformed. Toward the beginning of the play she does not see it as repressed sexuality, but rather as frustrated maternity: "Every woman has blood for four or five children," she tells María, "and when she doesn't have them, it turns into poison, as will happen to me." She suspects that repressed creative force can reappear in destructive form—a matter of common knowledge among primitive people, as ethnologists are well aware: "All Mexican Indians know that illness can be caused by emotional disturbances, such as fear or anger. This discovery was made centuries before the advent of modern psychiatry. One of the most widespread illnesses in Mexico is *bilis*, an overflowing of bile produced by pent-up anger. In Tecospa, a man usually purges himself of the excess bile by fighting his enemy or beating his wife, but since women have no way to give vent to their anger they are more likely to suffer from *muina*, which is anger that has been bottled up."[87]

Throughout the course of the play, however, Yerma believes that her *bilis* is caused by frustrated motherhood. Maternity is, to be sure, a creative force once it has come into being. Until that moment, however, it is not strictly accurate to speak of it as frustrated creativity. What is frustrated in Yerma is not the creative force of maternity (by definition, since she is barren) but rather the creative force of eroticism. This is the nature of her problem, and not until the end of the play does she raise to consciousness a bitter realization of this fact. The most significant datum of the final scene is the repeated use of the word *marchita* ("withered").

This discussion has pointed out the difference in attitude toward eroticism as revealed by the collective attitude of the villagers in *Blood Wedding* and that of the villagers in *Yerma*, noting that this difference has no sociological explanation, but rather a dialectical one. This is an

[87] William and Claudia Madsen, *A Guide to Mexican Witchcraft*, p. 41.

important point to bear in mind if one is to avoid confusing issues. Yerma's acquaintances are erotically free, while she is repressed, and their freedom interacts dialectically with her repression. One critic, Barea, recognizes Yerma's sexual repression, only to draw a sociological conclusion, for "it is the tragic result of a society which distorts, soils, or strangles the spontaneous feelings of young ladies."[88] But this can hardly be the case, since Yerma is depicted as a social deviant who realizes the source of her deviance: she is *marchita*. And this ought not to be taken as a piece of criticism leveled by a lay social critic. It goes deeper than that.

Yerma finally accepts that her "name" is not "Yerma," but rather "Marchita," and she dwells on it throughout the final moments of the play, for it appears six times in just a few moments of dramatic action, and in the above résumé of the play it has been given the prominence that it requires ("*Marchita*! Yes, I know! *Marchita*!"). This is nothing less than a recognition scene, and Lorca gives it full emphasis. Yerma is at last transformed enough to realize that *yerma* describes the result of being *marchita*.

While *yermo* is an agricultural term applied to the land, *marchito* typically describes flowers—the sexual part of the plant. It means "withered," but this cannot be taken to mean simply "old," since Yerma is not old (past the childbearing years), and because she herself finally confesses that the word has always threatened her with self-knowledge, ever since her wedding day: "*Marchita*! Yes, I know! *Marchita*! You don't have to rub my face in it! . . . Ever since I got married I've been going over and over that word, but this is the first time I've heard it, the first time that it has been spoken to my face. The first time that I can see that it's true." No, *marchito* does not mean "old," but "nonfunctioning": the sexual flower within her withered away during adolescence—for whatever reason (one cannot know the unconscious goal that this implies). She could not function as a flower in sex play, just as she could not "shine," "sing," or moan spontaneously in the nuptial bed. For she herself says that this sort of thing disgusts her. At the beginning of the play she avers that she entered fearlessly into the conjugal relationship, but it is clear that her libidinal

[88] Barea, *Lorca, el poeta y su pueblo*, p. 48.

energies were principally occupied with her ego-intention—the will to pregnancy. And even when she feels her attraction to Víctor, she looks at him in such a way as to inspire a certain aversion ("he slowly shifts his eyes away, as if afraid").

The hysterical "Victorian" disgust that Yerma feels for the "hot" woman, together with the vague fear that this very disgust of hers is actually the root of her frustration, finds its most extreme expression in her confessions to Dolores (always excepting, of course, the final, psychotic manifestation): Juan is not a passionate lover, she complains, "and I, who have always been nauseated by hot women, should like to be like a mountain of fire at that instant." And here her disgust takes the most extravagant form possible: ah, if she could only have children by herself! This is the primitive notion of self-fertilization, here a dismissal of sensuality as an unnecessary evil.

At the end of the play Yerma, having raised to consciousness the realization that she is *marchita* (and so cannot "sing"), is thereupon confronted by an erotic challenge, and this quite unhinges her. Here one ought to consider why she kills Juan as she does. After all, Lorca could have arranged matters differently. He could have had Marchita seize a stone and strike down her husband; he could have arranged for the presence of a knife (as he does in *Perlimplín*); or (like the Duque de Rivas, writing *Don Alvaro*) he could have conceivably included a precipitous cliff in his final scenery. But he calls for Juan to be strangled, and so one must concede the gesture its full importance.

That strangling is the mode of execution called for ought to be explained within the context of the play; and can there really be any doubt that the way Juan dies is a retaliatory punishment for his "singing," a punishment by talion? The pickpocket gets a hand lopped off, the Peeping Tom is blinded—and the singer is strangled.

Yerma's act is not unprecedented. In the medieval *Golden Legend*, Jacobo de Voragine tells a story about St. Agnes. The governor put her in a house of prostitution; the son of the governor went with friends to see her; he approached her and was rejected. He became furious that she would not act the erotic role assigned her and flew at her, determined to have his will. But "when he tried to touch her, a great light enveloped him, and since he had refused to render homage to God, he

was then and there strangled by the devil and he died."[89] Eroticism is
a diabolic attitude, according to the puritan idea. Yerma clearly suffers
from this belief; she had wanted to circumvent this hard truth about
herself, but when, at last, she accepts the new image of herself as Marchita the nonsinger, and when Juan begins to sing, she throttles him.
She does not murder him because she hates him or because she "realizes" that he is sterile—and certainly not because he is "cold"! She
strangles him because he is "singing," and she cannot endure this terrible challenge to her fatal limitation, finally recognized openly.

Ironically enough the review in *Time* magazine ends with the following criticism of the actress playing the title role: "Her vocal range
tends to be loud, louder, loudest, and she has yet to learn that the seat
of passion is not the larynx."[90] But of course this is precisely what
Yerma *does* learn: that symbolically the seat of passion is indeed "the
larynx," as the instrument whereby one expresses his attitude toward
the creative activity. One "sings" a child.

Immediately after killing Juan, Yerma is made to say, "*Marchita,
marchita*, but safe. Now I know it for certain." Why "safe"? Previously she has used "honor" as a reason for avoiding a possible erotic
solution; but now, when Juan is ready and willing to sing, she says,
"Never that!" and murders him, which betrays her, finally: why "never
that"? Is not "that" the way to get pregnant? Here Juan is being lascivious, sensual, like nearly everyone else in the play. But the only
"singer" threatening her now is Juan—and with him out of the way
she will be safe—safe from the damnable threat of having to engage
in a disgusting duet. Unlike the woman whose letter is quoted at the
beginning of this chapter, Yerma is married to the "type of man who
makes unpleasant demands" on her. And it is clear that Yerma just
doesn't "care for sex that much," and that she personally finds "the
very thought of it sickening." The letter quoted goes on to explain:
"I am not an unloving person. . . . I just happen to feel that love can
be expressed in other ways. Besides there are too many people in the
world already." Clearly Yerma does not believe that there are "too

---

[89] Jacobo de Voragine, *La leyenda dorada*, I, 109. My translation of the Spanish
version.
[90] *Time*, December 16, 1966, p. 87.

many people in the world already," but she does believe that "love can be expressed in other ways"—as a mother, not as a lover.

So Yerma's problem was not childlessness after all; it was sensuality, the need for human couples to sing to each other. Do that, and fertility will take care of itself: as the Old Lady says, "Children come like water." Procreation is necessary to the continuation of the species, but the individual human being is not a species. The individual human being needs to sing, and without this he withers away. A familiar theme in Lorca is the spiritual difference between children and adults; the adult is the child who has lost his capacity for singing. The crisis of adolescence does this for some people, while others (like Lorca himself) learn to keep operative their singing abilities. It has been remarked more than once that Lorca had an amazing insight into the woman's spirit, but this is not so amazing if one remembers that Yerma herself is basically a symbol for the difficulties of creativity—conception, pregnancy, and birth—in the spirit of the poet. In his early poem "Presentiment," Lorca even draws a specific analogy between his own creativity and biological maternity. A "presentiment" is the intuition of an inspired idea that the poet feels vaguely stirring within, in inarticulate form. Deep in the unconscious lies a "secret"—secret knowledge, a new insight—and when it is born into the light of day, it will be manifestly new. At this point Lorca uses the image of motherhood and applies it equally to himself, in the form of the editorial "we":

> . . . the child to come
> will tell us a secret
> when he is playing in his bed
> of stars.
> And it is easy to deceive him;
> therefore
> let us offer him tenderly
> our breast.[91]

To "deceive" the new infant is to make him become part of one's psychic routine, to turn him into an obedient citizen of one's conscious microcosm, to cure him of his originality. But this must not be done;

[91] García Lorca, "Presentimiento," in *Libro*, pp. 213–215.

the infant must be suckled tenderly so that he will grow and bring transformation. Thus does the artist achieve spiritually what the woman does biologically; and so it was natural, not unusual, for Lorca to concern himself symbolically with the phenomenon of the woman's psyche. Like sex, art is ultimately the expression of our *movimientos naturales*, our "natural movements," as Lorca's fellow poet, Juan Ramón Jiménez, called them.

So one is quite mistaken to see Yerma as the embodiment of Mother Nature, frustrated by a sterile (or selfish or impotent) husband. Yerma is "out of phase" with Mother Nature and cannot accept the premise of procreation that Mother Nature has built into this planet ("I wish I could have children by myself"). Yerma is Lorca's portrait of repression, and to take her otherwise is to miss his idea of the need to sing in order to be fertile. In singing—instinctual spontaneity, the expression of "natural movements"—on Mother Earth's terms (which Yerma says "nauseates" her) lies the secret of survival as an individual human being, a creature with a spiritual life unknown to the brute animals.

What Is Yerma's Name?

What is the name of the protagonist of *Yerma*? In the theater journal *Drama Survey*, Robert Skloot writes of her: ". . . we must see that Yerma *was born to be barren*, as her name indicates. . . . She is . . . marked from birth, and her fate is announced every time her name is mentioned."[92]

Skloot is the only critic to make much of "Yerma" as a name. It is a mistake to do so, since the interpretation of "Yerma" as a name will not bear analysis. Aratari is right to point out that it is an "invented name,"[93] meaning, apparently, an ad hoc "name" bestowed by Lorca. On the whole, the critics are silent on the matter, though this too is as much of a mistake as Skloot's attempt to see "Yerma" as a name.

For *yermo*, after all, is a descriptive adjective, and when it is applied to the protagonist of this play, it functions primarily as an epithet. The reader of the play easily succumbs to the illusion that it is a "name"

---

[92] Skloot, "Theme and Image in Lorca's *Yerma*," p. 157.
[93] Aratari, "The Tragedies of García Lorca," p. 474.

through sheer repetition, since it appears constantly throughout the script. Whenever the protagonist has a line to deliver, naturally the word *Yerma* appears on the page. But the audience receives an entirely different impression; for the word *Yerma* does not even appear in the dialogue until the end of Act Two! And there it comes as the climactic end of the act:

> First Sister-in-law.   (*softly*)   Yerma!
> Second Sister-in-law.   (*louder*)   Yerma!
> First Sister-in-law.   (*in an imperious voice*)   Yerma!

This is the crescendo effect that was mentioned in the résumé. At this point the curtain falls, and the act ends dramatically with the repeated exclamation "Yerma!"—occurring for the first time. It seems clear that these sisters are not addressing the protagonist by name; after five years of childless marriage she has earned an epithet, which the sisters now hurl at her as such.

Otherwise one never learns what the protagonist's name is. The other characters in general address her as "Hey, you" (María calls her *"criatura"* ["child"]; the Old Lady once calls her *"muchacha"* ["girl"]). Toward the beginning of Act Three (i.e., right after the sisters have taunted the protagonist with the epithet) Dolores reacts to an impassioned speech of hers: "Yerma!" she cries. It is a simple exclamation and may now be understood as epithet-cum-nickname. These are the only instances in the entire drama where the word "yerma" appears, strange to say—a fact not suggested by the statement that "her fate is announced every time her name is mentioned." At the conclusion of the play *marchita* is substituted for *yerma* as an epithet. In a final episode of self-knowledge, the protagonist comes to realize that the "correct" epithet is "withered." In the last two episodes *marchita* not only occurs six times, but also is discussed as being the right epithet to sum up the meaning of the play. The epithet *Yerma* (it turns out) only describes the effect of being *marchita*. The protagonist (as she herself explains) had always tried to avoid recognizing this fact, but in the end she accepts it: *"Marchita!* Yes, I know! *Marchita!* You don't have to rub my face in it! . . . Ever since I got married I've been going over and over that word, but this is the first time I've heard it, the first time that it has been spoken to my face. The first time that I can see that it's true." As an auditory experience, so to speak, in an acted version of the play the epithet *Marchita* finally overwhelms the epithet *Yerma*, which has been given forth as the title of the play. But in the end one sees, along with "Yerma," that the "correct" title is *Marchita*. It seems that this is not an analytical subtlety, but rather a piece of irony built into the work (similar to the trick used in *Blood Wedding*, where Lorca introduces a character—Death—who does not appear in the dramatis personae).

The Safety of Solitude

The psychosomatic relationship between eroticism and procreation appears to be relatively late in the evolution of the human psyche. Certainly the most primitive dynamics of the procreative act find their model in the world of the brute animals. As Robert Briffault points out, modern notions about "love" among the animals are a kind of romantic anthropomorphism—an anthropomorphism made possible precisely by the final evolution of channeling instinctual lust into the realm of human love. In the animal world "the attraction between the sexes is not primarily or generally associated with the order of feelings which we denote as 'tender feelings,' affection, love. These have developed comparatively late in the course of organic evolution, and have arisen in relation to entirely different functions."[94] Briffault further explains that in the primitive forms of life the female does not seek out the male because she "loves" him, or even "desires" him; rather, she "requires the male as a substance necessary to her reproductive growth and nutrition, as an object of assimilation."[95] This is the rapacious look that Yerma directs at Víctor, causing him to shift his eyes away, "as if afraid." The ovum cell assimilates the sperm cell, and in like manner certain primitive female organisms (rotifers and spiders) devour the male. Here the male is not the "mate" in the human sense of the word, but rather the sacrificial victim needed by the species to complete the impregnation and growth of the female. As Briffault concludes, "It

[94] Robert Briffault, *The Mothers*, pp. 46–47.
[95] Ibid., p. 47.

would be more accurate to speak of the sexual impulse as pervading nature with a yell of cruelty than with a hymn of love."[96]

This pattern of procreation in the female is basically the primitive one, then. Higher up in the scale of evolution, but before love has come to dominate the phenomenon of procreation among human beings, there are instances in which copulation still proceeds on the idea that it may be dissociated from love (and, therefore, jealousy). In the primitive institutions of incubation and temple prostitution, the female is encouraged to seek impregnation, but with no thought of permanent union with her partner in this highly important act. As Ernest Jones points out: "Several different practices have been included under the designation Incubation. The most typical is the union of a person with a god or goddess during sleep in the sacellum of the temple. . . . It characteristically presents itself . . . as a device for remedying impotence or sterility. . . . the most renowned of all the Incubation cults [is] that of Aesculapius. Towards the end of its vogue his cult had spread from its source in Epidauros to some three hundred and twenty sites. The cure of sterility was one of the central features of this cult."[97] The successful treatment of "sterility" by incubation obviously means that a psychosomatic sterility has been relieved. The patient spends the night in the temple, "and the Saint works the miracle," as the Old Lady tells Yerma. The patient lies on the couch, or *kline* (hence "clinic"), and is transformed psychosomatically through contact with awakened unconscious forces. Thus does the modern psychotherapist trace his origins.

Naturally the sacred union "with a god or goddess" was accomplished by means of a surrogate, or vicar, such as priest or priestess, as Philip Waterman explains: ". . . at certain festivals of Siva the priest takes the place of the god and unites in loving union with those women whom Siva has not blessed with offspring through the instrumentality of their own husbands."[98] Nevertheless, this practice was not necessarily limited to union with a specified surrogate of the fertility god. What is called nowadays "temple prostitution" included a pilgrimage

[96] Ibid., pp. 47–48.
[97] Ernest Jones, *Nightmare, Witches, and Devils*, pp. 92–93.
[98] Philip F. Waterman, *The Story of Superstition*, p. 69.

to the temple of the deity in order to effect union in the sacred temenos: "The Babylonian Venus was known as Mylitta. According to the law in the land, it was the duty of every woman, once in her life, to go to the temple of the goddess and there to submit to the caress of the first stranger who tossed her a coin, pronouncing as he did so the formula: 'I invoke the goddess Mylitta.' "[99]

Hence the notion of a pilgrimage for sexual purposes to the sacred temple is of venerable antiquity. When Yerma joins the *romería* (literally a pilgrimage to Rome, but by extension any gathering at the shrine of a saint), one is given to understand that essential to the ritual is sexual union with a stranger, or casual mate, as a consequence of which "the Saint works the miracle." This remark of the Old Lady strikes one as a bit ironic, and rightly so, since European civilization has long since evolved beyond the practice of temple prostitution— though in the Middle Ages a "sublimated" Christian form of the practice was used in church ritual, as that surrounding the cult of St. Foutin, supposedly the first bishop of Lyons: ". . . his rites were suggestive. A jar was placed beneath his emblem [the phallus], to catch the wine with which it was regularly anointed. This wine was left to sour, and then it was known as 'holy vinegar.' The women drank it in order to be blessed with children."[100]

It should be noted that in the last act of *Yerma* an extraordinary contrast is presented between an ancient sexual rite (temple prostitution) and Lorca's more highly evolved singing "rite" of fertility, represented in the form of Juan's "singing"—the culminating manifestation of what all the secondary characters have been describing and recommending throughout the course of the drama. Yerma has learned nothing from these recommendations, since, instead of seeking to resolve her problem in terms of the recommended "singing," she regresses so far as to join a *romería*.

But then she discovers anew that even the ancient practice of temple prostitution depends upon "loving union" with the surrogate. It is indeed more primitive than the modern form of singing in bed, since this singing is supposed to occur exclusively with one's permanent

[99] Ibid., p. 52.
[100] Ibid., p. 70.

mate. The secondary characters in the play do not insist upon the legal question, of course; the connection between the sacrament of marriage and procreation has another function, a binding social function—but it has nothing to do per se with the efficacy of the sexual act. And so the secondary characters all know that Yerma is asking how to get pregnant, not how to get pregnant "decently" or "acceptably." There is absolutely no way out of this bind: Yerma must try something new, something she has not tried before. She attempts various solutions, but she is always faced with the primal need to sing. When, at the pilgrimage, she indignantly rejects the idea of "temple prostitution" after the choral and dancing sequence exalting the song of life, the dance of life, she is then faced with what for her is the only "acceptable" possibility—union with a singing husband (since she will not take a stranger). And so she exclaims "Never that!" and strangles the cursed throat that sings. Now she is "safe." Alone, to be sure, but safe.

PART THREE

A Symbological Commentary
on *Blood Wedding*

The symbolic interlude is no doubt a most characteristic feature of Lorca's theater. In *Perlimplín* we have seen it in the form of a dialogue between two *duendes*, and in *Yerma* as a fertility rite. Certainly it is at the center of Lorca's dramatic efforts, and in *As Soon as Five Years Pass* it ceases to be an "interlude" at all, for it dominates the "action" entirely.

In *Blood Wedding* the symbolic interludes of any density are two, a lullaby and a soliloquy. The others—the nuptial song, a sensual love scene, and the final lamentation—involve no symbolic ramifications of much complexity. The principal symbolic interest of the play is rooted in the lullaby and in the soliloquy.

Résumé of Blood Wedding

The opening of the play is set in the house of the young man known simply as *el Novio*, "the Groom," who lives alone with his mother.

The Mother bitterly mourns the violent death of her husband and a second son whose killers—members of the Félix clan—have been punished with nothing more severe than imprisonment.

Her son asks her to request formally in marriage his sweetheart's hand, and she accedes, though she senses that the match is inauspicious. They say that the girl (called *la Novia*, "the Bride") has had a previous suitor who subsequently married a cousin of hers; and now the Mother learns from a neighbor the identity of her son's predecessor: Leonardo, a member of the Félix clan. She overcomes her immediately hostile reaction, for (after all) Leonardo is guiltless; he was only a child of eight at the time of the feud.

The second scene takes place in the home of Leonardo. It is morning; Leonardo's wife and his mother sing a cradlesong of some length —it takes several minutes to stage—and it has a sinister, dramatic text like no lullaby the average person has ever heard. Enter the master of the house. The domestic atmosphere is tense; Leonardo appears to be leading a double life, since at dawn his horse is frequently discovered exhausted and covered with foam. Leonardo, silent and aggressive, dominates the scene and irritably refuses any explanation. It is clear, however, that his wife and her stepmother share the audience's suspicions; and one rightly senses that gossipy news of the approaching wedding will serve only to exacerbate Leonardo's sullen temper. He leaves abruptly, and the two saddened women take up anew the lyrics of the tragic lullaby.

The act ends with the formality of the wedding arrangements: the Groom and his mother call on the father of the Bride. There is mutual, if quietly grave, approval of the match. The scene is joyless, a piece of necessary business has been concluded. The Bride is responsive to the match only as to a duty, a social responsibility. In the last moments of the act the servant girl of the Félix household asks the Bride about the mysterious comings and goings of a night rider—Leonardo, as a matter of fact. The Bride hurls an angry denial:

> Bride.   That's a lie! What business does *he* have here?
> Servant girl. He was here.
> Bride.   Shut up! Damn your tongue!
>   (*Sounds of hoofbeats*)

Servant girl. (*At the window*)
Look, come to the window. Was it?
Bride. It was!

The first part of Act Two portrays the wedding day. The Bride's nerves are frayed, and she is hardly capable of entering into the spirited and festive simplicity of the folk celebration. Nor is one surprised when Leonardo manages to see the Bride alone before the ceremony. He is bitter and recriminatory, and it becomes clear that the passionate attachment that the two feel for each other will not be denied. When Bride and Groom go off to church she is trembling with passion for another man.

Scene Two is the wedding reception, and the guests are arriving. The atmosphere is dominated by the ill-concealed frustration of the Bride. A typical incident: the Groom, in a poorly timed effort at playfulness, steals up behind his bride and embraces her by surprise—prompting a startled reaction:

Bride. Get away!
Groom. Are you afraid of me?
Bride. Oh! It was you?

The embarrassing anguish of the Bride mounts by the minute. She pleads a sick headache and leaves to lie down. Very shortly it dawns on the guests that both Leonardo and the Bride are missing. Worse: someone saw them riding off on a horse at full gallop. Amid general consternation the Groom's mother gives orders for the formation of a posse: again blood must be spilled.

The final act opens at night in a gloomy forest, where the guilty couple are being hunted down. Three doom-saying woodcutters appear, and they discuss the episode fatalistically ("Blood will out"; "they had to follow their instincts"; "they will most certainly be slain"). Exeunt the woodcutters, to make way for the most powerfully sustained symbolic interlude that Lorca ever conceived.

The night forest is gloomy and still. Here it is up to the director's sense of timing to give the audience the weird impression that they have been "abandoned," as it were. In the double obscurity of auditorium and stage the audience waits for the spectacle to continue. There is a moment of uncertainty, of crossing a threshold into another world, the world of pure symbol. The knowledgeable director will carry the empty stage for as long as possible to the point where the audience begins to shift uneasily. And then, off to one side is perceived a faint blue luminosity that grows. It increases in intensity and, in among the densely grown trunks, one makes out a figure at the center of the unearthly aura: it is a young man—a woodcutter—with pasty white face. He is the Moon, and he moves with the detachment of the sleep-walker. He speaks to the world of the night forest: he is freezing and he seeks the warmth of new blood; his light will seal the doom of the hunted. When his soliloquy is finished he is joined by his collaborator, the figure of Death in the guise of an old beggar woman. The fate of Leonardo and his lover is certain.

The audience sees the two of them, resigned to their impending destruction. They recognize the necessity of their commitment to each other in a "violent" and "sensual" dialogue.

This climactic episode ends as once again the audience is confronted by the dark and empty forest. Again the blue light, as the thin music of two violins is heard, then two heart-rending screams. Absolute silence. The beggar woman suddenly looms up centerstage with her back toward the audience. As she slowly raises her arms to either side, her dark cape gives her the appearance of a great black bird. There is no sound as the curtain falls.

The final scene of the play is denouement, concerned principally with the lamentations of the women. Leonardo and the Bridegroom have killed each other and the Bride is an outcast.

The Cradlesong

In order to facilitate the comparison of the English and Spanish texts of the cradlesong, I have numbered the lines presented here, ignoring those that have been omitted.

> Lullaby, my child, lullaby
> about the big horse
> that would not drink the water.
> The water was black

5   among the branches.
When it reaches the bridge
it tarries and sings.
Who can say, my child,
what is wrong with the water
10   with its long tail
along its green hall?

Go to sleep, my carnation,
for the horse refuses to drink.

Go to sleep, my rosebush,
15   for the horse is starting to weep.
His hoofs wounded,
his mane frozen,
within his eyes
a silver dagger.
20   They were going down to the river.
Ay, how they went down!
The blood was running
stronger than the water.

Go to sleep, my carnation,
25   for the horse refuses to drink.

Go to sleep, my rosebush,
for the horse is starting to weep.

He would not touch
the wet river bank,
30   his hot muzzle
covered with silver flies.
He would only whinny
at the hard hills
with the river dead
35   upon his throat.
Ay, big horse
that would not drink the water!
Ay, sorrow of snow,
horse of the dawn!

40   Stay away! Stop,
close up the window

with branch of dreams
and dream of branches.

. . . .

Horse, my child
45   has a pillow.
His cradle of steel.
His coverlet of linen.

. . . .

Stay away, do not enter!
Go off to the mountain.
50   Through the gray valleys
where the mare is.

. . . .

Go to sleep, my carnation,
for the horse refuses to drink.
Go to sleep, my rosebush,
55   for the horse is starting to weep.

Nana, niño, nana
del caballo grande
que no quiso el agua.
El agua era negra
5   dentro de las ramas.
Cuando llega al puente
se detiene y canta.
¿Quién dirá, mi niño,
lo que tiene el agua
10   con su larga cola
por su verde sala?

Duérmete, clavel,
que el caballo no quiere beber.

Duérmete, rosal,
15   que el caballo se pone a llorar.
Las patas heridas,
las crines heladas,
dentro de los ojos
un puñal de plata.
20   Bajaban al río.
¡Ay, cómo bajaban!

La sangre corría
más fuerte que el agua.

Duérmete, clavel,
25   que el caballo no quiere beber.

Duérmete, rosal,
que el caballo se pone a llorar.

No quiso tocar
la orilla mojada,
30   su belfo caliente
con moscas de plata.
A los montes duros
sólo relinchaba
con el río muerto
35   sobre la garganta.
¡Ay, caballo grande
que no quiso el agua!
¡Ay, dolor de nieve,
caballo del alba!

40   ¡No vengas! Detente,
cierra la ventana
con rama de sueños
y sueño de ramas.

·   ·   ·   ·   ·   ·   ·

Caballo, mi niño
45   tiene una almohada.
Su cuna de acero.
Su colcha de holanda.

·   ·   ·   ·   ·   ·   ·

¡No vengas, no entres!
Vete a la montaña.
50   Por los valles grises
donde está la jaca.

·   ·   ·   ·   ·   ·   ·

Duérmete, clavel,
que el caballo no quiere beber.
Duérmete, rosal,
55   que el caballo se pone a llorar.

The River as a Symbol

The river and the bloodstream run parallel. The impulsion of flow-ing water bespeaks the *pulsus venarum*, the pulsing of the veins, and an artery is both waterway and bloodway:

> I was born upon thy bank, river,
> My blood flows in thy stream,
> And thou meanderest forever
> At the bottom of my dream.[1]

This is not mere allegory, not an intellectually derived comparison. Flowing water is libido out in the open. Rushing, pounding water—the demented convulsions of the rapids—directly seizes the fancy and dissolves it into a cataract. It is as much sensation as idea: "There is something more than association at the bottom of the excitement which the roar of a cataract produces. It is allied to the circulation in our veins. We have a waterfall which corresponds even to Niagara some-where in us."[2] When Thoreau wrote that, he had experienced for him-self an "idea" set forth in his own lifetime by more than one Romantic poet.

But that symbolic process itself is not Romantic any more than blood and rivers are Romantic. The most archaic eye of man sees as identical the macrocosm and the microcosm; rivers and blood have run parallel since first they were seen to run. Empirical knowledge of the circulatory system was preceded by an inner, looming sensation of *aion*, the lique-faction of the vital principle that drives the living body.[3]

Aion is not all excitement and turmoil. The lulling rill and shaded brook, the babbling arroyo that quiets the mind and hypnotizes with a monotonous purling—this is the idyllic stream of bucolic gentility, the rivulet of introversion and retirement within shady bowers at the hour of siesta—the Waters of *Il Penseroso*:

And when the Sun begins to fling

---

[1] Henry David Thoreau, *Journal*, in *The Writings of Henry David Thoreau*, VII, 438.

[2] Ibid., February 12, 1851, in *The Writings*, VIII, 155.

[3] See Richard B. Onians, *The Origins of European Thought*, pp. 205, 208–209, 254.

> His flaring beams, me Goddess bring
> To arched walk of twilight groves. . . .
> There in close covert by some Brook . . . ,
> Hide me from Day's garish eye, . . .
> And the Waters murmuring
> With such consort as they keep,
> Entice the dewy-feather'd Sleep.[4]

Those "twilight groves" and that "close covert by some Brook" are where the water was "black among the branches." "When the Sun begins to fling / His flaring beams" is when, exhausted, one seeks the murmuring Waters that "entice the dewy-feather'd Sleep." One falls into the Waters of Lethe, into what Lorca calls, in his lecture on the lullaby, "sleep and its tame river"[5]—the murmuring stream of the gently flowing Afton.

But Lorca's lullaby tells also of a weary horse that would not drink of the river. Why did he refuse to drink? What is wrong with the water? Does this refusal perhaps express the mutual exclusion of two opposing principles? Or is it a horse that refuses to refresh himself? "Who can say, my child?"

This horse is the *caballo del alba,* the "horse of the dawn," which means that he is the solar horse, the steed of the solar hero. He carries within him a raging torrent that cannot be reconciled with the gentle stream that ripples and sings around the pilings of a bridge. He cannot deliver himself up to a principle contrary to his own essence. The charger of the firmament is always at the pitch of excitement, for he symbolizes that very alertness and boundless energy characteristic of human libido at full tilt.

The flowing river knows all the seasons of the bloodstream: "the life in us is like the water in the river; it may rise this year higher than ever it was known to before and flood the uplands."[6] When it rages it is heroic, destructive, all-powerful, daemonic—anything one likes. When it flows gently it is melancholy, indolence, languor, and somnolence, and this is the stream into which the lullaby would entice the

---

[4] John Milton, *Paradise Regained, the Minor Poems, and Samson Agonistes,* p. 200.
[5] García Lorca, "Las nanas infantiles," in *OC,* p. 97.
[6] Thoreau, *Journal,* June 9, 1850, in *The Writings,* VIII, 33.

little child. Sleep is a "tame river," and the business of the lullaby, says Lorca, is to "tame the little horses that rear up excitedly in the eyes of the child."[7] The horse of the lullaby was exhausted, but would not drink, would not give himself up to the gentle stream that sings. Any parent who has ever crooned over a fretful child knows of what is spoken here.

To eat or to drink a substance is to incorporate its qualities. No rule is more widely recognized in symbolic ritual. For the ancients the analogy between river and bloodstream was more than "poetic": it was magic and so was acted upon. ". . . in early Greece . . . on attainment of puberty a lock at least of a youth's hair was cut off and offered to the neighbouring river. . . . At puberty the . . . [*aion*] of the body, the liquid that is life and that issues in new life, has been brought to fullness, thanks mainly to the local god of liquid, the lifegiving stream."[8] Anciently it was believed that the waters of the Nile were so fecund that a barren woman had but to drink them in order to be cured.[9] Egyptian livestock was supposed to be exceptionally fertile: ". . . there are Goats in Egypt that produce quintuplets, while most produce twins. The Nile is said to be the cause of this, as the water it provides is extremely progenitive."[10] The tranquil river from which the big horse would not drink is a magic substance that would transform him into itself. It is a river that rarely appears in Lorca, for whom the river is more often the amorphous counterpart of the steed or other great beast. The life energy of a powerful man is, he says, like a "river of lions";[11] it is an annihilating tide: "There is in your breast a torrent where I will drown," declares the voluptuous Fiancée of *Five Years* to the virile ithyphallic athlete she loves.[12] Walt Whitman, an enormous libido figure in *Poet in New York*, is like a sleeping river,[13] and the Poet within him is an inner river with the strength of a bull: "You were seeking a Nude who would be like a river, bull, and dream."[14]

[7] García Lorca, "Las nanas infantiles," in *OC*, p. 97.
[8] Onians, *The Origins of European Thought*, p. 299.
[9] Aelian, *On the Characteristics of Animals*, III, 33.
[10] Ibid.
[11] García Lorca, *Llanto por Ignacio Sánchez Mejías*, in *OC*, p. 541.
[12] García Lorca, *Así que pasen cinco años*, in *OC*, p. 1079.
[13] García Lorca, "Oda a Walt Whitman," in *NY*, p. 524.
[14] Ibid., p. 525.

The annual awakening of the bloodstream takes place in an infra-human river bed (*cauce inhumano*) where the blood "plaits rushes of springtime."[15]

The river as a symbol of fertility and of alert libido occurs several times in *Blood Wedding*. The nuptial song tells the Bride, "May the rivers of the world bear thy crown," a fertility wish comparable to Yerma's "I can be like the waters of a stream."[16] When it is supposed that the illicit couple have united in their own wedding of the blood, they are conjectured to be now like two emptied rivers. When the two rivals, Leonardo and the Groom, lie dead, they are like two torrents that have been finally stilled. The Bride herself compares Leonardo to a "dark river."

It is easy to see that Lorca is typically concerned with the river as a symbol of libidinal tension and discharge. And the same is true of the steed, a beast that can hardly move without expressing a power far in excess of that which emanates from even the most impressive hero.

The cradlesong about the weary horse and the singing stream carries a double role: it functions specifically as a lullaby to the infant child, but its meaning is symbolically related to the rest of the play. That this is so is suggested (if by nothing else) by the length of it and by the symbolic complexities of the words. These are drawn from the texts of actual Spanish cradlesongs cited by Lorca in his lecture on the Spanish lullaby. There he describes the sadness typical of the *nanas* (cradlesongs) of his country, pointing out that this sadness has something to do with the mother's attitude toward her own fate: "We should not forget that the cradlesong is invented (and their texts express it) by the poor women whose children are for them a burden, a heavy cross frequently impossible to bear. Each child, instead of being a joy, is a sorrow, and, naturally, they cannot help but sing to him, even in their love, of their disgust with life."[17] He further points out that the "fundamental object of the lullaby is to put to sleep a child who is not sleepy."[18] He speaks here of the *daytime songs* for the child who wants

[15] García Lorca, "A Carmela, la peruana," in *PS*, pp. 638–639.
[16] García Lorca, *Yerma*, p. 1319.
[17] García Lorca, "Las nanas infantiles," in *OC*, p. 95.
[18] Ibid., p. 97.

to play: "go to sleep, my child, / for I have work to do, / [I must] wash your clothes and sew."[19]

To put the child to sleep is to plunge him into the waters of the unconscious. When the child is old enough to understand the words of the song, the mother must take care not to stimulate him in the process of singing to him—or, as Lorca puts it, "the mother takes up a position off to one side over the water,"[20] when she becomes aware that the child is concentrating too consciously upon the words.

According to Lorca the most popular lullaby in Granada is the one about the man who did not water his horse: "he took his horse to the water / and left him unwatered [literally, 'without drinking']."[21] Another lullaby says, "I gave to my horse / little leaves of green lime / and he would not eat them."[22]

Mention has been made of the difference between the river and the horse as libido symbols—the amorphousness of the one and the clarity of form taken by the other. The degree of differentiation is always a characteristic of symbols determining the extent of their mystery and numinosity, since, in general, mystery is a correlate of amorphousness and numinosity grows from clarity of figure. In the lecture on the *nanas* Lorca alludes to this when he describes an imaginary horse as being a cross of these two qualities: "half nickel, half smoke."[23] In the *nana* about the man who did not water his horse the sleepy child hears how they "go off through the dark foliage toward the river," but he never sees them clearly. Conscious attention flags and he vaguely discerns in the penumbra of approaching sleep the man's dark clothing and the shining rump of the horse.[24] This vagueness of image is appropriate to the task of leading the sleepy fantasy down to the quietly flowing river. The shadowy figures must lead him into the dark regions of sleep, which is to say that they function as *psychopomps*. They lead the child to where "the water is deepest," to the "simplest quietude," says Lorca.[25]

19 Ibid.
20 Ibid.
21 Ibid., p. 100.
22 Ibid., p. 99.
23 Ibid., p. 101.
24 Ibid., p. 100.
25 Ibid.

The lullaby of *Blood Wedding* is being used as a daytime song. Lorca has explained that the object of the lullaby is to put to sleep a child who is not sleepy, and he singles out a daytime cradlesong. In *Blood Wedding* the exhausted horse that will not drink from the river is weary from traveling through the night, but cannot stop, for his energy is not spent. He whinnies at the hills, and is apostrophized to "go off to the mountains, / through the gray valleys." The singer asks that the sleeper be not disturbed, in a way reminiscent of "Sweet Afton." The horse is told not to enter, and to cover up the window with shadow:

> Stay away! Stop,
> close up the window
> with branch of dreams
> and dream of branches.

With his very light the solar horse will cast the shadows of sleep.

Sun as steed is undoubtedly the most common and universal use of the horse symbol. The solar horse is the great beast with shining coat, the hero's stallion that travels across the face of heaven with the swiftness of the wind. He is libido now seen not as the "Niagara somewhere in us," but as the omnipotent and searing ball of fire. Like the sun, the solar horse is the shining cosmic traveler who brings fertility in his train. Hence it is natural enough, in the morning lullaby, to ask him to pass by the child "who is not sleepy," and to beg that he cover the window with shadows of dark foliage, to make a bower for the child who must sleep. Adults work by day and sleep by night, since their routine is determined by the course of the sun. But let not the diurnal passage of the sun interfere with the sleeping of the baby.

The Solar Horse

We have noted that the lullaby of *Blood Wedding* has a double function, since it is related symbolically to Leonardo's role as the night rider.

In his talk on the *nanas* Lorca cites lullabies with twofold function, such as the song of the adulteress who uses the cradlesong as a pretext for signaling her lover:

> He who is at the door

must not come in now,
for father is at home . . .
He should come back tomorrow,
for the father of the child
[will be] in the mountain.[26]

In *Blood Wedding* Leonardo is the adulterous one. Both his wife and his mother-in-law are aware of this if only because of the circumstantial evidence furnished by the horse: his condition in the morning easily leads to the conclusion that he is being used hard at night. He is covered with sweat and his eyes are popping out "as if he had come from the ends of the earth." In other words, by dawn Leonardo's horse is in the same condition as the horse of the lullaby.

The horse—particularly the horse as a noble animal, not as the beast of burden, the nag—plays as large a part in the symbol-making activity of man as it has played in man's history. The steed is the kind of horse to which pertain all the admirable equine characteristics praised by man. Men have always idealized the steed as symbolic of the best in themselves, just as the rider on horseback tends to identify himself with the animal upon which he rides. And so does the horse appear in myth and folklore: as he carries a man, so is he symbolically the carrier of man's own biological libido in its most heroic and impressive manifestations.[27]

This means that the general significance of the horse as a symbol is related to the unconscious instinctual sphere, since it is this that supplies the inspiration and the drive that lie behind the noblest ambitions of man. The solar hero himself is the culture hero, the mythical figure symbolizing the collective drive toward human ways, the rising above the brute animal level. If the hero so frequently has a horse it is because his instinctive drives enhance his consciousness and empower him to implement his aims; the horse "carries" him and transforms him into a conqueror. Hero and steed together become a new creature, a semidivine animal.

In his *Symbols of Transformation* Jung describes at some length the appearance of unconscious powers in equine form: ". . . there are clair-

---

[26] Ibid., p. 106.
[27] Gerhard Adler, *Studies in Analytical Psychology*, p. 156.

voyant and clairaudient horses, path-finding horses who show the way when the wanderer is lost, horses with mantic powers. In the Iliad (XIX), the horse prophesies evil. They hear the words the corpse utters on its way to the grave—words which no human can hear. . . . Horses also see ghosts. All these things are typical manifestations of the unconscious."[28]

But of course the steed does not symbolize the unconscious in the way that a pale ghost might, for he is heightened vitality and irresistible energy. That is why he represents not only the unconscious, but also the unconscious as libido vigorously manifest. The horse is universally identified with the efficacy and fertility of all three volatile elements in their highest state: he is like the sun, the wind, and the ocean. More will be said about the solar horse, since this plays an especially important role in *Blood Wedding*. But at the same time one should remember that the steed easily identifies with the wind, just as the swift charger is commonly said to run like the wind, or to be a "drinker of the wind." In his poem "Otherwise" ("De otro modo") Lorca pictures the wind as an invisible horse when he says that the breeze "caracoles" about, using the term from equitation.[29]

The horse has often appeared as rising from water—rivers, founts, and the ocean. No doubt the ocean is most commonly thought of as a womb symbol, but this applies to all those characteristics that the womb and the ocean have in common: the one is a microcosmic pleroma, the other a macrocosmic pleroma. But the ocean-as-tide occupies another symbolic sphere. Here the powerful thrust of the tide is that of libidinal energy in irresistible form, and so the ocean tide is assimilated to every powerful, thrusting flow of water in motion; hence it is not only Helios who drives a chariot; so does Neptune, and those surging beasts that lug the chariot of the great sea god are personifications of the living impulse that travels ceaselessly across the expanses of the seven seas. The horse is always the traveler in motion, never at rest.

But there is also an Irish belief that the relatively still lakes and deep pools are inhabited not only by water spirits, but also by "mysterious white horses," who are charged especially with the protection

[28] Carl Jung, *Symbols of Transformation*, p. 277.
[29] García Lorca, "De otro modo," in *Canciones*, in *OC*, p. 414.

of the alder tree. This is because the alder, being one of the most water-resistant woods, was for many centuries a material essential to the ancient lake dwellers.[30] The lacustrine man is particularly aware of his exalted state above the deep waters, and so the wood that supports him and his home is protected by the animal that carries all men, the horse. Its whiteness is no doubt due to its benevolent aspect, since the black horse signifies the opposite—death, which is to say descent into the anonymous depths whence man came.

The horse as a fertility symbol is universal and appears frequently in connection with the phallic leg and hoof. The legendary origin of the Hippocrene ("horse-fountain") is a good example. The hoof of Pegasus struck the rock and a fountain gushed forth; the water from this spring inspires poets, and so the poet who "rides Pegasus" is doing exactly the same thing as the poet who drinks from the Hippocrene: they are both, like the mythological hero, using their instinctive drives in the form of enhanced libido as powerful as the stallion in order to conquer.

In the Grimm tale "The Two Travelers" the theme of the fertile "water-horse" crops up anew. The hero is given the task of creating a wellspring in the courtyard of the palace and so his horse "galloped as quick as lightning thrice round it, and at the third time it fell violently down. At the same instant, however, there was a terrific clap of thunder, a fragment of earth in the middle of the courtyard sprang like a cannon-ball into the air, and over the castle, and directly after it a jet of water rose as high as a man on horseback, and the water was as pure as crystal, and the sunbeams began to dance on it."[31] Here one notes the additional symbolic allusion to thunder, which links the terrestrial fertility horse to the solar horse in the form of lightning: "Lightning . . . is represented theriomorphically as a horse. . . . In accordance with the primitive idea that thunder fertilizes the earth, lightning and horses' hoofs both have a phallic meaning."[32]

One of the closest symbolic parallels between horse and river occurs in a Turkestan tale, "The Magic Horse," cited by Marie-Louise von

---

[30] Diarmuid MacManus, *Irish Earth Folk*, p. 47.
[31] *Grimm's Fairy Tales*, p. 495.
[32] Jung, *Symbols of Transformation*, p. 277.

Franz. As frequently happens the helpful animal, having performed the necessary tasks, requests the hero to dismember him so that he can be magically transformed into a higher state. In "The Magic Horse" the heroine obediently slaughters her horse and follows the instructions given her: "She threw the head aside, pointed the legs in four directions, threw away the entrails, and sat down with her children under the ribs. Then from the legs grew golden poplars with emerald leaves, from the entrails villages, fields, and wheat, and from the ribs a golden castle. But from the head sprang a silvery brooklet. In a word, the whole region was transformed into a true paradise."[33] That silvery brooklet from the head of a horse is indeed reminiscent of the Hippocrene, living proof of the efficacy of the horse as phallic power. To bestow fertility is to realize—make real—instinctual potential, bring it to fruition. This is why Isidorus and other medieval etymologists could actually derive *caballus* ("horse") from *cavare* ("to dig").[34] Today this seems not only fantastic, but also entirely unnecessary, if not gratuitous. But the horse was to them first of all the noble animal that represented the opening up of subterranean regions in order to bring forth into the light of day that which lay in heavy darkness. Hence "naturally" the horse came to be called *caballus*, because he was the digging animal *par excellence*!

In "The Magic Horse" the horse supplies not only a silvery brook, but also trees, villages, rich fields, and even a golden castle—a paradise, in short. This is the horse as creator, as demiurge: the cosmic horse. Any cosmic beast represents a dynamic (rather than moral) conception of the universe, as pointed out by H. G. Baynes in his discussion of the cosmic Chinese dragon: "In the West the dragon symbolizes the power of evil or the force of regression, for the Western mind is rooted in the idea that man's original nature is evil. In the East the dragon dwells on the highest mountains and is identified with clouds and flowing water, because the Eastern mind sees spiritual events as the interplay of natural elements. Hence the dragon, as symbol of the inexhaustible potential of natural energy, represents bene-

---

[33] Marie-Louise von Franz, "The Problem of Evil in Fairy Tales," in *Evil*, p. 105.
[34] Angelo de Gubernatis, *Zoological Mythology*, I, 353.

ficent spiritual power."[35] The cosmic beast expresses the idea of unity
—ecological unity—just as does the cosmic tree.[36] The biosphere is a
single, enormous organism, represented in the Upanishads as a cosmic
horse: "Verily, dawn is the head of the sacrificial horse, the sun his
eye, the wind his breath, universal fire his open mouth. The year is the
body of the sacrificial horse, the sky his back, the atmosphere his belly,
the earth the underpart of his belly. . . . The rising sun is his forepart,
the setting sun his hindpart."[37] This last cosmic comparison—"the
setting sun his hindpart"—appears in slightly altered form in Lorca,
when he says that at nine o'clock at night "the sky shines like the hindpart of a colt."[38]

The solar horse is the most commonly used form of the cosmic horse,
and the reasons for this are not far to seek. Ernest Jones sums these up
succinctly when he says that "the most important links connecting
the two ideas [of 'horse' and 'sun'] are probably those of irresistible
movement, luxuriant fertility and shining splendour."[39] Angelo de
Gubernatis's chapter on the horse in *Zoological Mythology* is devoted
almost entirely to the solar aspects of the horse symbol. His daily journey across the sky and nocturnal gallop back to the East are depicted as
a double horse, or horse of mutant coat: "The sun, in the beginning of
the night, rides a black horse, and afterwards a grey one . . . , but in the
morning . . . a white and luminous horse, which has a black tail."[40]
Gubernatis also notes the motifs of the golden horse[41] and of the red
horse[42] as variant symbols of the morning sun. This same animal is
described in Norse mythology in the following fashion: "Night rides
. . . on a horse called Hrímfaxi [Frosty-mane], and every morning he
bedews the earth with the foam from his bit. Day's horse is called
Skinfaxi [Shining-mane], and the whole earth and sky are illumined

[35] H. G. Baynes, *Mythology of the Soul*, p. 872.

[36] Rupert Allen, "Juan Ramón and the World Tree," *Revista Hispánica Moderna*
35 (1969): 306–322.

[37] Quoted by von Franz, "The Problem of Evil in Fairy Tales," p. 105.

[38] García Lorca, "Prendimiento de Antoñito el Camborio . . . ," in *RG*, pp. 445–
446.

[39] Ernest Jones, *Nightmare, Witches, and Devils*, p. 278.

[40] Gubernatis, *Zoological Mythology*, I, 290.

[41] Ibid., p. 295.

[42] Ibid., p. 296.

by his mane."[43] "Frosty-mane" bears a close resemblance to the beast of Lorca's cradlesong. This is the exhausted horse who suffers, as Lorca puts it, a "sorrow of snow" with hoofs wounded and mane frozen.

The double aspect of the solar horse also appears as a day rider and a night rider. In Greek mythology appear two brothers, a red horseman and a white horseman, who represent respectively the morning sun and the moon (white = silver).[44] In Oriental mythology these appear as charioteers who fight over possession of the fair Aurora, who is thought to be (and literally is) between them. Says Gubernatis, writing long before *Blood Wedding* was conceived (and some years before Lorca himself was conceived), these two rivals "may very naturally be [thought of] as contending for the possession of the bride when they have her between them."[45]

This observation bears no little relevance to the dramatic scheme of *Blood Wedding*, since the Bride is fought for by two rivals, one—the Groom—belonging to day while the other belongs to night. Leonardo, the night rider, sees his lover at night, and the climactic death scene in the forest takes place at night when the guilty lovers are sought out by the light of the moon.

Again, the Bride is saluted in the nuptial song as the fertile beginning of a new day; she will marry a golden Bridegroom, *la flor del oro*, a young man "of the finest gold."[46]

The sexual connotations of horseback riding are too well known to need much insisting upon. Lorca himself, in his celebrated poem, "The Unfaithful Wife," depicts copulation in such terms:

> That night I traveled
> the best of roads,
> mounted on a pearly white mare,
> without bridle and without spurs.[47]

[43] "Gylfaginning," in Snorri Sturluson, *The Prose Edda*, p. 38.
[44] Gubernatis, *Zoological Mythology*, I, 306–307.
[45] Ibid., p. 307.
[46] This is translated by Graham-Lujan and O'Connell as "a flower of gold"— either a mistranslation or arbitrary license. (See García Lorca, *Three Tragedies of Federico García Lorca*, pp. 98, 100.)
[47] García Lorca, "La casada infiel," in *RG*, pp. 434–436.

Ernest Jones mentions the frequency with which one meets this usage of the riding metaphor: ". . . in every language riding is one of the commonest euphemisms for coitus. . . . In German a man lacking in virility is called a 'Sonntagsreiter' ('Sunday rider') or a 'Bauerreiter' ('peasant rider'), and a name for the honeymoon is 'Stutenwoche' ('mare week')."[48]

The association of coition with horseback riding particularly relates to nighttime riding, not only because night is lovers' time, but also because there is a connection between sexual excitation and the dominance of the (moonlit) unconscious. The *lamia* is the mythical nocturnal fantasy produced out of sexual anxieties and appears in the form of a night rider: "The lamias are typical nightmares whose feminine nature is abundantly documented. Their universal peculiarity is that they *ride* their victim. Their counterparts are the spectral horses who carry their riders away at a mad gallop."[49]

Hence there is an important relationship between love and death, suggested by the notion of being "carried away"; and this is the principal ambivalence of the horse symbol. It relates to fertility and warmth (= sun), the sensuality thought of as characteristic of the tropics, and the joint motions of horse and rider readily yield an analogy to coition. This much identifies Leonardo as the night horse of the lullaby and as the sexual power of the drama. He is the "stud" who seeks out the affections of a woman socially recognized as belonging to another man. He is one of those described by Jeremiah: "They are become as amorous horses and stallions; every one neighed after his neighbour's wife" (5:8).

At the same time the horse symbol—above all the night horse—is an image of death. Being "carried away" by love merges into loss of self; and the love here dramatized by Lorca is a form of suicide. The last act of *Blood Wedding* depicts the love of Leonardo and the Bride in terms of a fatal commitment. It is a love-death attitude according to which love means death, not only because they believe that the furious villagers will hunt them down and slay them, but also because their final surrender to each other has meant a surrender to unconscious

[48] Jones, *Nightmare, Witches, and Devils*, p. 252.
[49] Jung, *Symbols of Transformation*, p. 249.

forces clamoring to be expressed. It is the "Way of the Blood" described by the three woodcutters; ". . . the union of the lovers is more than a simple act of physical sexuality whereby release from tension is achieved. . . . More profound instinctual depths are touched by it—realms beyond the scope of the conscious personality. . . . union with the beloved, intensified by the projection of the soul image, demands that the lover renounce himself and his limited personal ego and receive into himself another. This means a sort of spiritual death, in which he feels himself to be lost to himself, through union with something other than himself that is at once within him and beyond him."[50] This being "carried away" easily appears as an image of horseback riding, or as the funerary psychopomp who carries his victim away on horseback: ". . . the souls of the dead are fetched by horsewomen, the Valkyries. Modern Greek songs speak of Charon as riding on a horse. . . . sometimes the devil rides on a *three-legged* horse. The goddess of death, Hel, rides on a three-legged horse in time of pestilence."[51] The funerary aspects of the horse readily merge into the infernal aspects, and there is a good deal of material connecting horse and devil. The death-horse, the horse as a sexual symbol, these ideas naturally combine into a picture of the theriomorphic god of lust who carries man's soul to the perdition of the black world below. The devil-horse forms the natural counterpart of the god-horse, the solar force that carries up to heaven the spirit of man—as, for example, the rider of the White Horse in the Apocalypse (6:2).

There is no more appropriate symbol (unless it be the moon) for telescoping the two themes of love and death in *Blood Wedding*. The horse is Leonardo, the principal sexual force of the play, the night rider whose nocturnal activity will lead him to his death. The cradle-song depicts the horse in the double aspect of night and day; he has traveled all night long, is weary unto death, and weeps as he refuses to drink:

> Go to sleep, my carnation,
> for the horse refuses to drink.

---

[50] M. Esther Harding, *Psychic Energy*, p. 144.
[51] Jung, *Symbols of Transformation*, pp. 281–282.

Go to sleep, my rosebush,
for the horse is starting to weep.

The double theme of refusal to drink and weeping constitutes an allusion to mourning. It is the hero's own apprehension of the end to which he is fated. Gubernatis recalls this motif as typical of the stories concerning the heroic horse: ". . . as he exults by neighing over the good fortune of the hero who rides him, so he not only becomes sad, but sheds real tears when his rider is about to meet with misfortune."[52] The horses of the Roman legions are said to have wept and refused nourishment: "Suetonius . . . writes that the horses consecrated by Caesar to Mars and then set at liberty after the passage of the Rubicon, refused to eat and wept abundantly. . . . it is said that Caesar's horse itself shed tears for three days before the hero's death."[53] Gubernatis gives other examples of this affective relationship between the rider and the sorrowful steed that foresees his master's death.

In Lorca's cradlesong the horse, taken as a specialized form of a cosmic idea—the "horse of the dawn" (line 39)—must be seen, as noted, as two horses in one—the horse of day and the horse of night—as it undergoes the metamorphosis of the solar journey toward dawn. There is a circular transformation continually occurring as the one passes into the other, as the one fades away to be replaced by the other. The weary night horse must die to give way to his diurnal counterpart, just as Leonardo of the night is replaced by the Golden Bridegroom of the day. In fact there are really two Brides, the one who accepts the conventional courtship of the Groom (the conscious ego-personality) and the one who, in the middle of a wedding reception, flees with another man. By night the Bride belongs to the night rider, and the final scene depicts them in their appropriate setting, a nocturnal forest.

The night horse that expresses the sexuality of Leonardo weeps because his master must daily die to be replaced by the solar horse of another man; at the same time his mourning prophesies the actual death of Leonardo. His nocturnal death (and that of the Groom) is closely associated with the light of the Moon figure, who plays a considerable role in the final act. Why this is so must be considered in some detail,

[52] Gubernatis, *Zoological Mythology*, I, 349.
[53] Ibid., p. 350.

but for now it might be pointed out that the theme of the silvery death-dealing Moon is touched upon in the lullaby:

> . . . his mane frozen,
> within his eyes
> a silver dagger.

His "hot muzzle" is covered with "silver flies" (the flies of disintegration);[54] death looms, and the mantic horse sees it as the issue of a knife fight in a moonlit forest glade, for there is a "silver dagger" in the eyes of the prophetic beast.

Throughout the lullaby the symbolic motifs apply in a double sense. The song can be read simultaneously as a lullaby to the infant child, and as a description of Leonardo's activity and of the fate awaiting him. As cradlesong the causal relationship between horse and stream is expressed in terms of waking and sleeping: the child may sleep (because) the horse will not drink and (because) the horse is starting to weep. The steed of night has been vanquished and is dissociated from the dark river of sleep. He is the solar horse now and must go elsewhere ("Go off to the mountain"). The river does not pertain to him, is not a powerfully running impulse, but a sweetly flowing stream that sings when it reaches the pilings of the bridge—the bridge that itself suggests passage from this world into the other, the world of a gentle and untroubled sleep.

As descriptive of Leonardo, the song expresses the libidinal vigor of his nocturnal activity, when he rides to the "ends of the earth." At sunset the solar horse is metamorphosed into the horse of night, the horse of the moon, and is fated (like the horse of the dawn) to travel one path, and one path only. Shortly before his death Leonardo even tells his lover that he was nightly drawn to her side because that is where his horse had to carry him of its own accord, as it were. He did not guide the steed; it guided him:

> But I was riding horseback
> and the horse would go to your door.

[54] See my discussion of this fly symbolism in Lorca in Rupert Allen, *The Symbolic World of Federico García Lorca*, pp. 127–128.

This night horse, then, is Leonardo as the sexually driven male and is also the funerary beast or psychopomp that will carry him to the land of the dead. He "becomes," so to speak, the Moon of the last act; for the Moon too has always expressed both sexual activity and the descent into the land of the dead—for both mean a negation of the sunlit consciousness of day.

Lunar Symbolism

The figure of the Moon as a young woodcutter is introduced into the last act for the ostensible purpose of furnishing the light whereby the lovers can be hunted down. But he is given a special prominence, similar to that conceded to the two *duendes* in *Perlimplín*. He comes out alone after his arrival has been announced by the three woodcutters, and he has the following soliloquy:

> I am a round swan in the river,
> eye of cathedrals,
> false dawn on the leaves;
> they will not be able to escape!
> 5   Who is hiding? Who sobs
> through the underbrush of the valley?
> The moon leaves an abandoned
> knife in the air,
> which, being leaden ambush,
> 10   would be sorrow of blood.
> Let me enter! I come frozen
> along walls and window panes!
> Open roofs and breasts
> where I can warm myself!
> 15   I am cold! My ashes
> of somnolent metals
> seek the crest of fire
> along hills and streets.
> But the snow carries me
> 20   upon its shoulder of jasper,
> and I am drowned, hard and cold,
> by the water of the pools.
> But this night my cheeks
> will have red blood,

25   and the rushes bunched
at the feet of the wind.
Let there be no shadow nor thicket,
let them be unable to escape!
For I will enter into a breast

30   in order to warm myself!
A heart for me!
Warm! Let it spill forth
along the hills of my breast;
let me enter, ah, let me!

    (*To the branches*)

35   I want no shadows. My beams
must enter all places,
and let there be in the dark trunks
a sound of clarities,
so that this night my cheeks

40   may have sweet blood,
and the rushes bunched
at the feet of the wind.
Who is hiding? Out, I say!
No! They will not escape!

45   I will make the horse to shine
as a diamond fever.

    Cisne redondo en el río,
ojo de las catedrales,
alba fingida en las hojas
soy; ¡no podrán escaparse!

5   ¿Quién se oculta? ¿Quién solloza
por la maleza del valle?
La luna deja un cuchillo
abandonado en el aire,
que siendo acecho de plomo

10   quiere ser dolor de sangre.
¡Dejadme entrar! ¡Vengo helada
por paredes y cristales!
¡Abrid tejados y pechos
donde pueda calentarme!

15   ¡Tengo frío! Mis cenizas
de soñolientos metales

buscan la cresta del fuego
por los montes y las calles.
Pero me lleva la nieve
20   sobre su espalda de jaspe,
y me anega, dura y fría,
el agua de los estanques.
Pues esta noche tendrán
mis mejillas roja sangre,
25   y los juncos agrupados
en los anchos pies del aire.
¡No haya sombra ni emboscada,
que no puedan escaparse!
¡Que quiero entrar en un pecho
30   para poder calentarme!
¡Un corazón para mí!
¡Caliente!, que se derrame
por los montes de mi pecho;
dejadme entrar, ¡ay, dejadme!

(*A las ramas*)
35   No quiero sombras. Mis rayos
han de entrar en todas partes,
y haya en los troncos oscuros
un rumor de claridades,
para que esta noche tengan
40   mis mejillas dulce sangre,
y los juncos agrupados
en los anchos pies del aire.
¿Quién se oculta? ¡Afuera digo!
¡No! ¡No podrán escaparse!
45   Yo haré lucir al caballo
una fiebre de diamante.

The functional meaning of this soliloquy as a part of the "plot" has to be seen in terms of the earlier cradlesong: the two of them depict how the "wedding of blood" comes about and what it means as the brutal consequence of behavior dominated by instinct. They both express a series of motifs concerned with the death of night and life of day. The Moon among the foliage of the forest is a "false dawn," while the weeping horse is transformed into a horse of the dawn, just as the nighttime consciousness of the nocturnal rider will succumb to the daytime consciousness of the village. The Moon is like the blade of a knife poised in the air and waiting to destroy; the night horse of the lullaby carries in his eye the vision of a silver dagger, which is the silvery knife blade of the Moon. Both the horse and the Moon are "frozen"; blood runs high in both passages, and it is the Moon—the silver blade—that seeks it. The horse suffers a "sorrow of snow," and the cold moonlight is as cold as the snow.

The moon is a high-frequency symbol in Lorca, and there appears to be very little lunar tradition with which he is unfamiliar. His many uses of the moon are based variously on the principal characteristics popularly associated with it. The moon represents the realm of the unconscious, the disappearance of ego-consciousness, and so therefore the world of death, of insanity—and of creativity. While the moonlit night is regularly associated with lovers and romanticism, this superficial notion plays a relatively insignificant role in Lorca's poetry. In a prose piece he speaks, for example, of the moon's "feminine and romantic" light,[55] but this is a casual allusion to the popular, sentimental conception of "romantic" ("moon-June-spoon"). The connection between love and the moon is more deeply revealed by the tertium quid of the realm of the unconscious.

The world of the moon is as cold as death: "The Talmud refers the words, 'Though I walk through the valley of the shadow of death' . . . to him who sleeps in the shadow of the moon."[56] The world of the moon is naturally frigid in the absence of the sun and seems to reach down into the coldest deeps of instinct, the world of the serpent, the frog, and the tortoise; the world of aquatic plants and the vegetative nervous system; the world within, which is at the farthest remove from the daylight of ego-consciousness. John Layard makes note of Sanskrit compounds that are used to designate the cold moon: *Himkar*, "Creator of Snow," and *Shitānshu*, "Essence of Coldness."[57] The Moon of *Blood Wedding* is, before all else, the "Essence of Coldness,"

[55] García Lorca, "El convento," in *Monasterio de Silos*, in *OC*, pp. 1557–1558.
[56] Timothy Harley, *Moon Lore*, p. 197.
[57] John Layard, *The Lady of the Hare*, p. 124.

the quality that furnishes his principal reason for shedding his light in the forest:

> I come frozen. . . .
> I am cold!
> Let there be no shadow nor thicket,
> let them be unable to escape!
> For I will enter into a breast
> in order to warm myself!

The lovers, driven by instinct, thereby evoke the presence of the Moon; for the world of the moon is one of undifferentiated instinct, the lair of id, inhospitable to the warmth of human psychosexuality flowing into the stream of personal consciousness and enhancing its revelation of psyche. In his poem "The Moon Rises" Lorca relates that when the moon comes out "the impenetrable paths appear." "When the moon comes out ocean covers the land and the heart feels itself to be an island in the infinite." "Nobody eats oranges beneath the full moon," for "one must eat green, frozen fruit."[58] To surrender oneself to the moonlit night is to surrender to the deepest reaches of the unconscious, the forest world—or the aquatic world where the land creature awakens to find himself at the bottom of the ocean. Elsewhere has been quoted Lorca's statement to the effect that the creative act is like a hunting expedition: "The poet who is going to make a poem (I know from personal experience) has the vague feeling that he is going hunting at night in a very remote forest. . . . The moon, round like a hunting horn made of soft metal, sounds in the silence of the highest branches."[59] Nothing is sharply profiled; everything is dense and vague. Consciousness knows not what it really seeks; it only yields itself to the darkness. And such is the moonlit forest world of Leonardo and the Bride.

Ego-consciousness dwells in the hours of sidereal time, but the nocturnal vision lives in the timeless world of unconsciousness. Midnight is the hour when the unconscious is at its greatest strength, and it is

[58] García Lorca, "La luna asoma," in *Canciones*, in *OC*, p. 393.
[59] García Lorca, "La imagen poética de Góngora," in *OC*, p. 74. See Allen, *The Symbolic World of Federico García Lorca*, p. 90.

then that one slips away from the fraternal world of matching time-pieces. Writes Lorca:

> Over enormous moons
> Eternity
> is fixed at twelve o'clock midnight.
> And Time has gone to sleep
> forever in its tower.
> All the clocks
> deceive us.[60]

In that timeless realm one seeks the roots of all that is "really real," be-yond the maya of diurnal illusion, a kind of prison for Lorca:

> We live in glass
> cells,
> in a hive of air!
> We kiss through
> glass.
> Marvelous jail,
> whose door
> is the moon![61]

To walk through that door is to be released as from a prison into a new, "lunatic," uncompartmentalized universe, the universe of the child—which is why the child is characterized by Lorca as the one who "asks for the moon." To be an artist, says Lorca, "one must see with the eyes of a child and ask for the moon."[62] Similarly it is the saint—the man who escapes the prison of secularity built here and now—who awakens in the holy Becoming of lunar nonego:

> I imagine this afternoon
> that I am a saint.
> The moon was placed in my hands.
> I put it back
> into space

---

[60] García Lorca, "Meditación primera y última," in *La Selva de los relojes*, in *PS*, p. 613.
[61] García Lorca, "Colmena," in *Suite del agua*, in *PS*, pp. 594–595.
[62] García Lorca, "Imaginación, inspiración, evasión," in *OC*, p. 90.

and the Lord rewarded me
with rose and halo.[63]

This theme of lunar nonego as the portal to sacred reality appears in the soliloquy of the Moon figure where Lunus compares himself to the "eye of cathedrals," which means the rose window when seen at night (since "eye"—*ojo*—is used in this architectural sense in Spanish).

The diurnal and nocturnal worlds stand in an ambivalent, contradictory relationship; for from one end of the human scale sunlit day is life, whereas moonlit night is death. Daylight organizes and lets one live in the fullness of his steaming libido ("Nobody eats oranges beneath the full moon"); nighttime hurls each one alone into a deep jungle of "impenetrable paths."

But then again daylight leads one to overstep his organizing and he builds for himself a great airy hive and is trapped within a cell and impotently strains to kiss his neighbor through an impenetrable pane of glass. Here the high noon of human life means the hard glittering murder of all that is inwardly original and innocent. So does Lorca depict the Beheading of the Innocents: the cruel massacre of the children born within oneself can be opposed only by the Mother Earth that one carries within as a Presence of Instinct. When King Herod launched his attack against the Innocents, says Lorca, "maternal milk and the moon sustained the battle against the triumphant blood [letting]."[64] The high noon of glaring intellect massacres the newborn in a panic outburst of specious power—the specious Power of suppression wielded by the tyrant of the psyche. But true Power lies (as Wallace Stevens puts it) "in the waving of the wand of the moon, / Whose shining is the intelligence of our sleep."[65]

All to come lies waiting, concealed in the darkness of the creative unconscious, as in a fertilized egg. So can Lorca imagine the nighttime as a great broody hen, the cosmic fowl. The poet in *Don Cristóbal* says that "the moon is a chicken that lays eggs,"[66] meaning the same thing

[63] García Lorca, No. 4 of "Cuatro baladas amarillas," in *PC*, pp. 349–350.

[64] García Lorca, "Degollación de los Inocentes," in *OC*, p. 30.

[65] Wallace Stevens, "Someone Puts a Pineapple Together," No. 2 of "Three Academic Pieces," in *The Necessary Angel*, p. 84.

[66] García Lorca, *Retablillo de don Cristóbal*, in *OC*, p. 1036.

that Thoreau has in mind when he says: "The sun lights this world from without, shines in at a window, but the moon is like a lamp within an apartment. It shines for us. . . . Nature broods us, and has not left our germs of thought to be hatched by the sun. We feel her heat and see her body darkening over us. Our thoughts are not dissipated, but come back to us like an echo."[67] In like manner the Grimm story "The Singing, Soaring Lark" (a variant of the Cupid and Psyche legend) relates how the heroine finds and wins her true love with the help of a "moon egg": the sun cannot help her, but the moon says, ". . . here I give you an egg, break it when you are in great need."[68]

The moon then, as a symbol, possesses ambivalent meanings because the symbol alludes to psychic tendencies—and any psychic tendency easily and naturally turns into its apparent "opposite." Or, to put it another way, the label bestowed upon a psychic tendency (e.g., "love") represents an external, imperfect, and tentative diagnosis of endopsychic turmoil. What was called love turned out to contain a powerful substratum of hate; an act in the service of life turned out to be simultaneously the expression of a death wish.

But the *symbol* is not a label: it is the conscious representation of psychic ambivalence.

Lunar Transformations

General, ambivalent tendencies inhere in any symbol; but as they struggle endopsychically for primacy the symptomatic symbol changes its guises as an actor changes his makeup. The moon does not appear onstage simply as the moon, but as a peculiar *kind* of moon—as a male or as a female, to give a simple example.

One critic has expressed his disapproval of Lorca's use of the moon as a male figure in *Blood Wedding*, evidently believing it to be an arbitrary piece of fantasy on the part of Lorca: "By an inexplicable caprice, García Lorca gave to the voice of the [moon], which is expressed in the feminine gender [la Luna], the form of a woodcutter with a lantern in his hand. The moon, so feminine, of the poems of Lorca . . . loses in plasticity and in suggestiveness with this unexpected

---

[67] Thoreau, *Journal*, August 5, 1851, in *The Writings*, VIII, 372.
[68] "The Singing, Soaring Lark," *Grimm's Fairy Tales*, p. 404.

and infelicitous transformation."[69] Perhaps the transformation is less unexpected and infelicitous than the critic believes Lorca's symbolism to be. The symbolic guises of the moon are many, and gender is the least problem of lunar symbology. As a matter of fact, the study of lunar symbolism begins on the level of mere objects; for, as Alta Jablow points out, "all over Western Europe the moon in folklore is far more an object than a clearly personified character."[70] This holds equally in the work of Lorca. It is true that in some of his poems Lorca depicts the moon as being "so feminine," but it is not unusual for him to imagine the moon as a simple object or primitive animal. In his "Song for the Moon" Luna crawls slowly across the night sky like a white turtle.[71] In *Poet in New York* darkling consciousness appears so impervious to the fire of ego-consciousness that the lunar disk is like a sheet of asbestos hung in the sky.[72] The deathly moon is like a marble headstone.[73] It is the whitened skull of a horse,[74] by which one is no doubt to understand the skull of the solar horse that died at sundown. The wind that blows at night will cut itself against the knife of the half-moon,[75] and the consciousness that yields itself to the moon runs the risk of being dismembered by the sharp and stony fragments,[76] since each night presents a new chipped lunar blade. The moon is like a hunting horn made of soft metal,[77] and it is a chicken that lays eggs.[78]

These Lorcan fancies are not different in kind from those produced over the centuries by the popular imagination, which has seen the moon as buttocks,[79] egg,[80] mirror,[81] plate,[82] or any circular object of silver, notably coins; for the moon is symbolic silver, just as the sun is

[69] Alfredo de la Guardia, *García Lorca*, p. 293.
[70] Alta Jablow and Carl Withers, *The Man in the Moon*, p. 115.
[71] García Lorca, "Canción para la luna," in *Libro*, pp. 215–217.
[72] García Lorca, "Oda al rey de Harlem," in *NY*, p. 479.
[73] García Lorca, "Cementerio judío," in *NY*, p. 519.
[74] García Lorca, "Ruina," in *NY*, p. 511.
[75] García Lorca, "Canto nocturno de los marineros andaluces," in *PS*, pp. 641–642.
[76] García Lorca, "Fábula y rueda de los tres amigos," in *NY*, p. 474.
[77] García Lorca, "La imagen poética de Góngora," in *OC*, p. 74.
[78] García Lorca, *Retablillo de don Cristóbal*, in *OC*, p. 1036.
[79] Wilhelm Stekel, *The Interpretation of Dreams*, p. 115.
[80] "The Singing, Soaring Lark," in *Grimm's Fairy Tales*, p. 403.
[81] Benjamin Appel, *The Fantastic Mirror*, p. 11.
[82] Layard, *The Lady of the Hare*, p. 128, in ref. to the "white bowl."

symbolic gold, and a sympathetic attraction is considered to exist.[83] Just
as gold is solidified sunlight, so is silver a tangible piece of the moon.
There is an old superstition of "turning over the silver in our pocket
when seeing the new moon, in order to render the moon favourable to
us" (thus an English symbologist),[84] and that is why Lorca says that
when the moon comes out "the silver money sobs in our pocket";[85]
further, the poet of *Don Cristóbal* asks to be paid in silver coin because
he himself is a "poet of the night," and "silver coins seem to be illu-
minated by the moon."[86]

Popularly, not only is the moon thought of as similar in appearance
to various objects, but also the markings on its face are interpreted
variously: they are seen as a hare (this is no doubt the most widespread
belief),[87] toad,[88] boy or girl or both,[89] grandmother,[90] man or woman
or elderly couple;[91] they are seen as facial scars,[92] as dirt on its face,[93]
and as ashes—for, according to an Indian legend, the moon, "who is a
man, monthly falls in love with his wife's mother, who throws ashes in
his face,"[94] which recalls the Moon of *Blood Wedding* who, with his
"ashes of somnolent metals," seeks the warmth of Mother Earth.

For present purposes especial attention must be paid to the legends
according to which the man in the moon is a wood gatherer, or woodcutter. There may be some connection here with the natural tendency
to see the moon as an ax blade (a modern novelist observes how dark is
the night, "even with a hatchet moon in the sky")[95] or knife, since the
analogy of form creates a sympathy between the moon and cutting in-

[83] Ibid., p. 201.
[84] Ibid.
[85] García Lorca, "La luna asoma," in *Canciones*, in *OC*, p. 393.
[86] García Lorca, *Retablillo de don Cristóbal*, in *OC*, p. 1031.
[87] This is a major theme in Layard, *The Lady of the Hare*; see especially pp. 126–
128.
[88] Harley, *Moon Lore*, p. 69; Jablow and Withers, *The Man in the Moon*, p. 116.
[89] Sabine Baring-Gould, *Curious Myths of the Middle Ages*, p. 201; Jablow and
Withers, *The Man in the Moon*, pp. 19, 21; Rosetta Baskerville, *The Flame Tree
and Other Folklore Stories from Uganda*, p. 44; Harley, *Moon Lore*, pp. 36, 59.
[90] Layard, *The Lady of the Hare*, pp. 170–171.
[91] Harley, *Moon Lore*, p. 23.
[92] Jablow and Withers, *The Man in the Moon*, p. 120.
[93] Ibid., p. 22.
[94] Harley, *Moon Lore*, p. 33.
[95] Peter Beagle, *I See by My Outfit*, p. 246.

struments. In Ireland the practice has been reported of maidens pointing at the new moon with a knife and speaking an invocation. The knife is then placed under the pillow that night, and on the following day one is sure to meet one's true love.[96] Clearly this is a magic act meant to bestir unconscious forces through collaboration with the moon.

Whatever the connection, there are many old European stories about a woodcutter, or wood gatherer, who was punished for working on Sunday: ". . . he met a handsome man in Sunday suit, walking towards the church. The man stopped, and asked the faggot-bearer, 'Do you know that this is Sunday on earth, when all must rest from their labours?' 'Sunday on earth, or Monday in heaven, it's all one to me!' laughed the woodcutter."[97] Whereupon the Lord (for it was he) transported him to the moon ("yours shall be a perpetual moon-day in heaven") where one sees him yet with his faggot.

A further detail is added in a variant, relevant to the Moon figure of *Blood Wedding*: "In Tobler's account the man was given the choice of burning in the sun, or of freezing in the moon; and preferring a lunar frost to a solar furnace, he is to be seen at full moon seated with his bundle of sticks on his back."[98] Here is a clear depiction of the lunar figure of *Blood Wedding*: the moon in the form of a freezing woodcutter. And in *El público* Lorca gives further evidence of familiarity with this material: ". . . the winter moon can very well be a bundle of kindling covered with worms stiff from the cold."[99]

One should further consider the Sunday motif of the traditional legends, for the woodcutter in the moon is always there as punishment for violating the Sabbath. This has been given a Biblical source, for in Numbers 15:32 one reads: ". . . while the Israelites were in the desert, a man was discovered gathering wood on the Sabbath day." As punishment the unfortunate was stoned to death.

The connection here with the Moon of *Blood Wedding* appears to be the identification of the lunar death with Leonardo, the guilty lover.

---

[96] Harley, *Moon Lore*, p. 215.
[97] Ibid., pp. 21–22.
[98] Ibid., p. 22.
[99] García Lorca, *El público*, in *OC*, p. 1161.

Though the wedding arrangements are made on a Sunday, the ceremony takes place on Thursday. But the characteristic thing about the shocking behavior of Leonardo and the Bride is that they violate the solemn day. The sacraments have hardly been administered when Leonardo carries off the Bride—whereupon the scene is dominated by woodcutters: a trio of doom sayers, and then the Moon, in the form of a freezing woodcutter. Leonardo seems to have attracted to himself the entire weight of a legend.

But the symbolic intricacies do not end here. For one is still confronted by the fact that the Moon is a young man. Lorca is quite plain about this. The legendary stories about the man in the moon, however, make him out to be an old man; therefore, one must account for this Lorcan characteristic. Other things being equal, there was nothing to prevent Lorca from presenting the moon in the form of a woodcutter as ancient as the Beggar Woman. But an analysis of Lorca's representation of the moon will require one to consider the symbolism of the hermaphrodite.

The Hermaphrodite

". . . like the noises of the sea and of the
blood her precocious grandchild."[100]

There seems to be little doubt that the widespread connection between the moon and women has arisen because of the menstrual cycle[101] and because of the greater chthonic sympathy with Mother Earth traditionally attributed to women. Natural fertility and increase are always thought to be the province of women, and the earliest fertility rites are devoted to the Earth Mother. Pliny's description of the moon's alleged relationship to all this typifies the popular thinking of earlier times. Quoting Aristotle to the effect that "no animal dies except when the tide is ebbing," he says: "This is the source of the true conjecture that the moon is rightly believed to be the star of the breath, and that it is this star that saturates the earth and fills bodies by its approach and empties them by its departure; and that consequently shells increase

---

[100] James Agee, *A Death in the Family*, p. 6.
[101] Robert Graves, *The White Goddess*, p. 138.

in size as the moon waxes, and that its breath [*spiritus*] is specially felt by bloodless creatures, but also the blood even of human beings increases and diminishes with its light; and that also leaves and herbage . . . are sensitive to it, the same force penetrating into all things."[102] The association between instinct, blood, and the moon becomes evident here. As the tide ebbs and flows so does human blood and so, therefore, do instincts. When the blood "increases" it runs high and fast and threatens lunacy. In this sense the moon is a blood deity, meaning that to it the blood sacrifice is a necessity. Here one is dealing with the elementary dynamics of sacrifice; that which is at stake is sacrificed to its patron: "Among primitive people the sacrifice of any one species of food-animal is believed to lead to the increase of all food-animals of the same species."[103]

The moon, as the deity of night, is simultaneously the deity of the Earth realm, the telluric realm of blood and instinct; of ocean, swamp, and cave; indeed of all dark regions within or without the human psyche. Given the mysterious sympathy existing between the moon and women, in classical mythology the woman comes to be thought of as the moon in terrestrial form, just as the moon is woman in divine form—Luna, Selene, Diana, Hecate. Luna, as a matter of fact, is only one aspect of woman divinized as the *Triple Goddess*: "As Goddess of the Underworld she was concerned with Birth, Procreation and Death. As Goddess of the Earth she was concerned with the three seasons of Spring, Summer and Winter; she animated trees and plants and ruled all living creatures. As Goddess of the Sky she was the Moon, in her three phases of New Moon, Full Moon, and Waning Moon [i.e., girl, woman, hag]."[104]

This feminine trinity is indivisible and represents three different aspects of one thing: instinctual Becoming on earth, or change. Procreation, birth, death; the yearly round of seasons: these are reflected in the menstrual, or monthly, phases of Luna—Becoming made manifest in the night sky. And it is this chthonic realm that the Moon of *Blood Wedding* takes as his province, and also this same lunar realm in

[102] Pliny, *Natural History*, 2:221.
[103] Layard, *The Lady of the Hare*, p. 187.
[104] Graves, *The White Goddess*, p. 319.

which the destiny of Leonardo unfolds, since he is the secret night rider. The Moon will oversee the tragic climax when Leonardo rides off with his mate into the nocturnal forest; for Luna is the deity of both the vegetative realm and of death. Indeed, the last section of his soliloquy is an apostrophe to the forest itself.

The tragic ending of the play seems to be characterized by the woodcutters as a blood sacrifice to Earth: "One must follow the Way of the Blood." "But the blood which sees the light is drunk by the Earth." "Light" here is the light of the moon, and the blood spilled will rejuvenate and warm him:

> Open roofs and breasts
> where I can warm myself!
>
> . . . .
>
> But this night my cheeks
> will have red blood. . . .

His presence is a *fiat lux* to the forest—both the material forest in which he shines and the forest of the instinctual unconscious:

> (*To the branches*)
> I want no shadows. My beams
> must enter all places,
> and let there be in the dark trunks
> a sound of clarities,
> so that this night my cheeks
> may have sweet blood, . . .

The moonlight animates trees and plants since (as Pliny has explained) "leaves and herbage . . . are sensitive to it, the same force penetrating into all things."

The sacrifice to Luna takes the form of a libation of blood to the Earth by the light of the moon. It is a libation to the mechanism of fertility, the Becoming of woman: "The basic phenomenon behind woman's connection with blood and fertility is in all likelihood the cessation of the menstrual flow during pregnancy, by which means, in the archaic view, the embryo was built up. This intuitively sensed connection underlies the relationship between blood and fertility. . . . *The earth must drink blood if she is to be fertile.*"[105]

All this concerns the relationship between Luna and Woman, however. Yet in *Blood Wedding* Luna is in the form of Lunus as a young man. A criticism of this "inexplicable caprice" of Lorca's has already been cited, and perhaps it is not irrelevant to note at this juncture that in world mythology the gender of the moon, when personified, is not necessarily feminine or even usually so. In Scandinavian mythology the moon and the sun are brother and sister respectively, the son being named Mâni and the daughter Sol.[106] The Egyptians saw the moon as a male deity,[107] and in Teutonic mythology "down to recent times, our people were fond of calling the sun and moon *frau sonne* and *herr mond.*"[108] Even the Romans recognized a god Lunus.[109]

Nevertheless, it is a fact that many people think it strange to hear of the moon as a man. This seems to be so because any culture derived from Greco-Roman sources produces almost exclusively a feminine moon. Max Müller himself believed that the influence of classical models was the overwhelming cause of modern European belief in the Moon goddess,[110] and this would apply with especial force to the cosmopolitan (i.e., educated) concentrations of society.

If a European critic, then, quarrels with Lorca for introducing the audience to a masculine moon, it may very well be that this negative reaction itself is in some way a datum of the play. *Blood Wedding* is a stage drama, meant to have a direct impact upon a European audience, and evidently part of that impact includes the relative strangeness of a male moon. If this is the case, it would be pedantic to argue that Lorca uses a masculine moon because such a figure is "well known." On the contrary, it is probably closer to the truth to say that Lorca wanted to produce a bizarre effect. The audience for which he was writing commonly thinks of the moon as the Queen of Darkness; when they see

---

[105] Erich Neumann, *The Origins and History of Consciousness*, p. 55. My italics.
[106] Harley, *Moon Lore*, p. 24.
[107] Ibid., p. 83.
[108] Ibid., p. 82. Harley is quoting Jacob Grimm.
[109] Ibid., p. 83.
[110] Ibid., p. 82.

her as a youthful woodcutter, fainting and seeking sustenance, their reaction must be one of surprise: "Why, the Lady is a young man!"

That he is a youth with pale white face, rather than a virile figure in his prime or an old man (like our Man in the Moon), means that he produces an equivocal impression. The orb itself (as distinguished from the markings on its face) "ought" to be a woman, but instead Lorca, by an "inexplicable caprice," has created a moon that is (minimally) male. Thus the conclusion seems inescapable: the Moon figure is an ambiguous blend; "she" is an adolescent lad. "He" is a hermaphrodite, an androgyne.

The mythological notion of the hermaphrodite is not inspired by the carnival monster, of course, much less by the effeminate man or masculine woman. It is rather a symbolic ideal representing the perfect union of male and female elements.[111] Most of us are familiar with Plato's idea, in the *Symposium*, that the male and female represent the fragmented halves of an original unity. The notion of an original unity expresses the wholeness preexistent to the broken world of ego-consciousness in which all men now dwell: "This perfect state of being, in which the opposites are contained, is perfect because it is autarchic. Its self-sufficiency, self-contentment, and independence of any 'you' and any 'other' are signs of its self-contained eternality."[112] Male and female go about the earth seeking out the one true mate, and this is the world of love. It follows, then, that the deity ruling over the felicitous combination should represent that combination itself, the ideal fusion of male and female. This is the way Edmund Spenser depicts it in his *Faerie Queene*: when he describes "Great Venus Temple" it turns out that the "goddess" is actually androgynous. She is seen covered with a veil, which is to say that there is a "secret" here. Everyone thinks that Venus is the "goddess" of love, but such a belief shields the actual truth of the matter:

> The cause why she was couered with a vele,

---

[111] Mircea Eliade, in his essay "Mephistopheles and the Androgyne" (in *Mephistopheles and the Androgyne*, p. 100), observes a verbal distinction between "androgyne" (the symbol) and "hermaphrodite" (the anatomical reality); but it probably comes too late to strike root in symbology.

[112] Neumann, *The Origins and History of Consciousness*, p. 9.

Was hard to know, for that her Priests the same
From peoples knowledge labour'd to concele.
But sooth it was not sure for womanish shame,
Nor any blemish, which the worke mote blame;
But for, they say, she hath both kinds in one,
Both male and female, both vnder one name:
She syre and mother is her selfe alone,
Begets and eke conceiues, ne needeth other none.[113]

The veil conceals no "blemish," says Spenser: this is not a monster, but an ideal form of how things are. Love "syre and mother is her selfe alone," which, when one translates the symbol into the grosser form of the "beast with two backs," is simply a truism. Back in the archaic region of First Beginnings there is no Adam and Eve, but rather, as Delcourt puts it, "one Principle, . . . whose emanations descend in a series of steps to the multiple and the sensible. At the top of the ladder is a male and female power, dividing itself into a syzygy which in its turn procreates."[114]

Delcourt's use of the term "syzygy" ("yoked together") is entirely apposite here, since it is principally an astronomical term expressing a relationship (conjunction or opposition) between sun and moon. But Delcourt cites evidence to show that in post-Homeric times the moon itself "particularly" came to be revered as the divine syzygy, the "origin of mixed couples."[115] Layard recalls the belief that the moon is a eunuch,[116] meaning not "sexless," but of ambiguous sexuality. Lucian's second-century narration of a voyage to the moon describes it as productive of hybrid animals and reports that the Selenites "are not born of woman, but of man, because for their marriages they use men, since of women they know not even the name."[117]

The relative youth of Lorca's Moon figure is almost certainly connected with the ambiguous sexuality of the young, since adolescence marks the stage at which the "polymorphous perverse" tendencies of childhood begin to be resolved. Such is the ambiguous adolescent

---

[113] Edmund Spenser, *Faerie Queene*, Book IV, Cant. X, 41.
[114] Marie Delcourt, *Hermaphrodite*, p. 77.
[115] Ibid., p. 74.
[116] Layard, *The Lady of the Hare*, p. 190.
[117] Quoted in José Luis Martínez (ed.), *La luna*, p. 167. My translation.

character of Lorca's play *Five Years*, which has elsewhere been considered in some detail.

As the young man grows into the phallic stage, he more and more represses the feminine elements of personality culturally considered inappropriate to the behavior of the phallic male. But in no few cases there is a period during early adolescence when it is not at all clear which elements will be repressed and which encouraged.

The exemplary case of this adolescent ambiguity occurs in Hermann Hesse's *Steppenwolf*. Harry Haller, the protagonist, meets a childlike young woman—she could change her moods "with the facility of a gifted child"[118]—who strikes him as particularly androgynous. She asks him to guess her name, and "after a moment I saw something in her face that reminded me of my own boyhood and of my friend of those days. His name was Herman. For a moment it seemed that she had turned into this Herman."[119] When he asks her how it is that she can seem so like a boy, she tells him, in effect, that she is the carrier of his own psychological projection: "Oh, you did all that yourself. Doesn't your learning reveal to you that . . . I please you and mean so much to you . . . because I am a kind of looking glass for you, because there's something in me that answers you and understands you?"[120] The two of them form a spiritual syzygy, a masculine consciousness and a feminine unconscious. "It was the spell of a hermaphrodite. For she talked to me about Herman and about child hood, mine and her own, and about those years of child hood when the capacity for love, in its first youth, embraces not only both sexes, but all and everything, sensuous and spiritual, and endows all things with a spell of love and a fairylike case of transformation such as in later years comes again only to a chosen few and to poets, and to them rarely."[121] Such is Lorca's "poet of the moon" (*Don Cristóbal*), and such was Lorca himself: the *seer* who, by retaining the androgyny of his childhood, penetrates back beyond the fragmented and incomplete world of adult monosexuality. This sensitive condition is frequently and idly labeled "homosexual,"

[118] Hermann Hesse, *Steppenwolf*, p. 107.
[119] Ibid.
[120] Ibid., pp. 107–108.
[121] Ibid., p. 120.

which means little or nothing. Certainly the critics who have applied the label to Lorca have not thereby made a contribution of any kind. Spiritual androgyny is what Lorca most valued in himself, because it was the key to his creativity. To "grow up" in the conventional sense of the term would have been disastrous. It is the situation described by James Agee (at the age of 22), himself possessed of enormous poetic talent: "One thing I feel is this: that a great deal of poetry is the product of adolescence—or of an emotionally adolescent frame of mind: and that as this state of mind changes, poetry is likely to dry up. I think most people let it; and that the one chance is to keep fighting and trying as hard as possible."[122] What Agee calls "an emotionally adolescent frame of mind" is the spiritual hermaphrodism necessary to the endopsychic susceptibilities of the poet, strangely similar to the sensitivity of the visionary. Eileen Garrett, in her autobiography, confirms this: ". . . the people who possess these special sensitivities blend in their natures both the masculine and the feminine qualities. . . . I came to understand that the variations in sexual types were not to be despised."[123] This is the spiritual hermaphrodite of Lorca's *Five Years* who, according to the stage direction, must produce the impression of an effeminate young man: "If this role cannot be played by a very young actor, it should be played by a girl."[124] This is Lorca's way of solving the problem of how to represent onstage the hermaphroditic psyche: a lad who acts like a girl. In *Blood Wedding* it is the reverse— a "woman" (Luna) who appears to be a lad.

Psychologically the hermaphroditic principle is an outgrowth of the infantile spirit, for the child, like the beast with two backs, is "a recapitulation of the primordial human being *who is still at one with his instincts.*"[125] This same principle was recognized in alchemy as the *res bina*, or "double thing,"[126] which is the raw material with which the alchemist sets to work. This had to be so: fertile results, full realization of potential (spiritual gold), must always come from the manipulation of both male and female principles.

[122] James Agee, *Letters of James Agee to Father Flye*, p. 56.
[123] Eileen J. Garrett, *Adventures in the Supernormal*, pp. 113–114.
[124] García Lorca, *Así que pasen cinco años*, in *OC*, p. 1072.
[125] H. G. Baynes, *Mythology of the Soul*, p. 236. My italics.
[126] Herbert Silberer, *Problems of Mysticism and Its Symbolism*, p. 131.

The spiritual meaning of androgyny crops up again in the form of *ritual transvestism*, found in primitive puberty rites and marriage ceremonies. These are initiation rites, which means the crossing of a threshold into a new world. Ritual transvestism (exchange of garments) is a physical symbol alluding to the divine hermaphrodite. The wedding ceremony represents the union or yoking ($=$ syzygy), and each partner becomes half of a new whole: ". . . transvestism is not merely a prophylactic rite, a childish ruse to baffle demons, or simply a symbol of emancipation from a half-feminine past. It certainly [has] a positive value; it [has] power to promote health, youth, strength, longevity, perhaps even to confer a kind of immortality."[127] The fusion of man and woman into a new, double being, then, is presided over by the Honey Moon,[128] and the Moon figure of *Blood Wedding* alludes not only to the "wedding of blood" between Leonardo and the Bride, but also ironically to the exchange of vows between Bride and Groom. Properly the Moon "ought" to preside over the sacramental wedding of Bride and Groom since, after all, the divine hermaphrodite means sexual happiness and fertility: "The bisexual figure . . . is not a god of marriage considered as a contract, but . . . is protector of unions."[129] But Lorca's tragedy sets the two unions at odds, and there is no doubt as to which of these engenders anew the spectre of the sovereign dyad —no "protector" now, but the augury of death. He is both Eros and Thanatos.

The Symbolism of the Woodcutter

Here should be pointed out the analogy felt to exist between collective society and a forest. The forest commonly appears as a symbol of the unconscious in the sense that it is a vast region within which the differentiated ego finds itself lost. Such is the *selva oscura* in which Dante stumbles about; such are the "silent, dark, deep" woods of Robert Frost, who, as a responsible social entity with his "promises to keep," contents himself with only observing them from a distance.

---

[127] Delcourt, *Hermaphrodite*, p. 22.
[128] That "honeymoon" might have sprung originally from a negative expression ("waning love") does not nullify the underlying symbolism.
[129] Delcourt, *Hermaphrodite*, p. 60.

But to harp exclusively upon this kind of forest symbolism would suggest that one could not see the trees for the forest. The fact of the matter is that a forest is also a multitude of trees and so may be likened to a multitude of people. This is particularly true of the forest regularly exploited for use by the neighboring towns. The exploiter of the forest sees it as a domesticated thing; his view of it is an exploded view of myriad individuals and not a Gestalt for the unconscious mind. In the final analysis it all depends upon the degree of familiarity.

The tree itself has a complex and rich symbolism, both as a component of the forest and as an individual entity. As the latter it can be a symbol of the cosmos itself; it can be the habitation of a god or spirit; and it can be symbolic of the individual human being, since the tree is the largest being of the vegetative world just as man himself is symbolically the largest being of the animal kingdom. And the superiority of trees combined with their relative longevity makes them counterparts in the vegetative and animal worlds.

John Evelyn, a seventeenth-century English tree expert and a man of no little renown in his own day, had a good deal to say about the symbolism of trees in his classic *Discourse of Timber*; but being not only a cosmopolite but also a lover of the Trees (rather than generic forests), he favored the one-to-one correspondence. The tree, he says, "like man (whose inverted symbol he is) being sown in corruption, rises in glory, and by little and little ascends into an hard erect stem of comely dimensions, becometh a solid tower, as it were!"[130] He recalls the custom of the natalitial tree, practiced by the ancient Romans, according to which the parents would "plant a tree at the birth of an heir or son, presaging by the growth and thriving of the tree, the prosperity of the child."[131] And he describes the cultivation of the *seminary*, or tree nursery.[132] The word, much used as a metaphor for the education of young men, gradually lost its metaphorical value until now hardly anyone is aware that college students were commonly thought of as young saplings.

Thoreau was particularly fond of comparing trees to human beings,

---

[130] John Evelyn, *Silva: or, A Discourse of Forest-trees . . .*, II, 362.
[131] Ibid., p. 347.
[132] Ibid., p. 39 n.

whether individually or in stands: "A clump of white pines . . . impress me with a mild humanity. The trees indeed have hearts. . . . [They are] like a group of settlers with their children. The pines impress me as human."[133] On one occasion he uncharacteristically thinks it perhaps better to move among men than among trees: "It is narrow to be confined to woods and fields and grand aspects of Nature only. The greatest and wisest will still be related to men. Why not see men standing in the sun and casting a shade, even as trees?"[134] For Thoreau the man "with roots" is like a tree: "I love to see a man with a tap-root, though it make him difficult to transplant."[135]

According to Snorri Sturluson, men were created directly from trees: "When they were going along the sea-shore, the sons of Bor found two trees and they picked these up and created men from them. . . . The man was called Ask [Ash-tree] and the woman Embla [Elm?]; and from them have sprung the races of men who were given Mithgarth to live in."[136]

In recent years psychiatrists, says J. H. Plokker, have given attention to the tree as a useful way of symbolizing one's personality, and he describes the Tree Test (*der Baum-Test*) as it is used in experimental psychology. The way the subject draws a tree is considered to be a projection of his own self-image.[137]

To judge by evidence such as this, it is of importance to bear in mind the symbolic tree as representative of the individual human being. The forest of *Blood Wedding* no doubt symbolizes itself the instinctual realms into which the unhappy lovers have fled. But Lorca introduces woodcutters who discuss their case, and with this he adds a dimension to the conventional "dark forest" motif.

The woodcutter is not typically a man who is lost, like Dante, in a forest. In the fairy tale he is sometimes the subject of weird magic events, but not typically so. Rather one must see him as the agent through whom society exploits the trees. In this sense he represents the death of the tree, that is, the end of the tree that grows up into the

---

[133] Thoreau, *Journal*, December 20, 1851, in *The Writings*, IX, 145.
[134] Ibid., August 23, 1851, in *The Writings*, VIII, 421.
[135] Ibid., May 4, 1852, in *The Writings*, X, 16.
[136] "Gylfaginning," in Snorri Sturluson, *The Prose Edda*, p. 37.
[137] J. H. Plokker, *Art from the Mentally Disturbed*, pp. 194–195.

forest world as an autonomous entity. As such, seen from the tree's point of view, as it were, the woodcutter is akin to the symbolic figure of the Grim Reaper (and probably a variant of it). So does Thomas De Quincey describe him in order to depict the ravages of tuberculosis among the populace: "Are you aware, reader, what it is that constitutes the scourge . . . of Great Britain and Ireland? . . . it is pulmonary consumption. If you walk through a forest at certain seasons, you will see what is called a *blaze* of white paint upon a certain *élite* of the trees marked out by the forester as ripe for the axe. Such a blaze, if the shadowy world could reveal its futurities, would be seen everywhere distributing its secret badges of cognisance amongst our youthful men and women."[138]

This view of the woodcutter as the Grim Reaper is no doubt strengthened somewhat by the traditional association between the wooden coffin and the corpse that it holds. This is of special importance in the ancient Egyptian cult of Osiris, discussed at length by Erich Neumann, who considers as a "salient point" "the identity of the tree trunk and the wooden sarcophagus, the most important item in the Egyptian rites for the dead."[139]

If the moon represents the region of death and if the woodcutter is thought of as the Grim Reaper who stalks among the members of the forest, they find an element common to them both in the frequency with which the moon is likened to a hatchet or other cutting blade. Layard cites a Hottentot version of the story about the moon's argument with the hare (a story of great antiquity and universally known) in which the moon seized a hatchet and struck the hare with it ("Why the hare has a split lip").[140]

It is perhaps natural enough to associate the moon with cutting instruments—in Lorca a sickle[141] and a knife[142]—because to succumb to the dangerous impulses of the unconscious ("lunacy") is to "lose one's head." The moonlit atmosphere (note that Lorca's Moon soliloquy insists upon the light shed by the moon) drives one into lunacy

138 Thomas De Quincey, *Confessions of an English Opium-Eater*, pp. 421–422.
139 Neumann, *The Origins and History of Consciousness*, p. 230.
140 Layard, *The Lady of the Hare*, p. 166.
141 García Lorca, "Media luna," in *PC*, p. 347.
142 García Lorca, "Canto nocturno de los marineros andaluces," in *PS*, pp. 641–642.

ence, *Yerma* and *Blood Wedding* in direct fashion, and *Perlimplín* less so. *Yerma* presents a pure instance of grappling with the creative, "singing" attitude. *Blood Wedding*—otherwise a kind of *Cavalleria Rusticana*—abruptly, and at the climactic moment, finds itself prostrate before the apparition of the frail and grim hermaphrodite who threatens both to die and to kill. *Perlimplín* approaches (without addressing it directly) the "wedding problem" existent in the psyche of the poet, the confrontation between dry ego-consciousness and a merciless instinct heavy with desire.

Lorca once said in an interview that Perlimplín "cuckolds all the women in the world," which suggests, in the terms of this discussion, that brittle ego-consciousness will embrace death sooner than seek the goal of fidelity to the feminine unconscious, the source of creativity; for the task of creative union with the unconscious is beyond the powers, patience, and courage of all but a very few. Perlimplín is Everyman, and Belisa treats him as such. The challenge to establish a life-long union with the underworld of instinct is that "nightmare" of Prelimplín and of everyone, because somewhere people have learned to regard the unconscious as the foe of their coveted ego-tranquility. Somewhere they have learned that it is better for ego to grow old ungracefully ("withered—but safe!"). Better to earn the name of Yerma. Better to be a schlemiel.

But for the poet there is always the freezing Moon. For a Lorca the stasis of a sunshiny, timid, bachelor ego is no more a decently acceptable aim in life than it is for a Manolete or for a Flying Wallenda.

If we were to try to sum up (within the limits of the thinking in these pages) the largest meaning of Lorca as dramatist and poet, I believe we would have to see it in terms of how one becomes human in the face of instinct—*duende*. A very deep commitment to the animal within threatens to dehumanize us, while at the same time any alternative commitment holds the same threat. This is man's dilemma. One cannot be human without transcending instinct, nor can one be very human without bending to it. Only two ways allow resolution of the threatening impasse: love and art. Immersion in these commands the whole of the person, what is above and what is below.

BIBLIOGRAPHY

General

Adler, Gerhard. *Studies in Analytical Psychology.* New York: W. W. Norton, 1948.

Aelian. *On the Characteristics of Animals.* 3 vols. Cambridge: Harvard University Press, 1958–1959.

Agee, James. *A Death in the Family.* New York: McDowell, Obolensky, 1957.

———. *Letters of James Agee to Father Flye.* New York: G. Braziller, 1962.

Alarcón, Pedro Antonio de. *El sombrero de tres picos.* New York: Blaisdell Pub. Co., 1965.

Allen, Rupert. "Juan Ramón and the World Tree." *Revista Hispánica Moderna* 35 (1969): 306–322.

Alvarez, Alfred. *The Savage God: A Study of Suicide.* New York: Random House, 1970.

Andersen, Hans Christian. *Fairy Tales.* Edited by Svend Larsen. Odense, Denmark: Flensted, 1950.

Appel, Benjamin. *The Fantastic Mirror: Science Fiction across the Ages.* New York: Pantheon Books, 1969.

Arabian Nights. Edited by Andrew Lang. New York: David McKay Co., 1946.

Arizona Daily Star. August 8, 1971.

Asbjørnsen, Peter Christian, and Jørgen Moe. *Norwegian Folktales.* New York: Viking Press, 1960.

Baring-Gould, Sabine. *Curious Myths of the Middle Ages.* New York: University Books, 1967.

Baskerville, Rosetta. *The Flame Tree and Other Folklore Stories from Uganda.* New York: Negro Universities Press, 1969.

Bateson, Gregory, and Margaret Mead. *Balinese Character: A Photographic Analysis.* New York: New York Academy of Sciences, 1942.

Baynes, H. G. *Mythology of the Soul*. New York: Humanities Press, 1955.

Beagle, Peter. *I See by My Outfit*. New York: Viking Press, 1965.

Bettelheim, Bruno. *Symbolic Wounds: Puberty Rites and the Envious Male*. Glencoe, Ill.: Free Press, 1954.

Boswell, James. *London Journal (1762–1763)*. New York: McGraw-Hill, 1950.

Briffault, Robert. *The Mothers*. New York: Macmillan Co., 1931.

Cadalso, José. *Optica del cortejo*. Barcelona: Viuda Piferrer, 1790.

Camus, Albert. *The Fall*. New York: Knopf, 1956.

Clouston, W. A. *Popular Tales and Fictions*. 2 vols. Detroit: Singing Tree Press, 1968.

Consumers Union Report on Family Planning, The. Mount Vernon, N.Y.: Consumers Union of U.S., 1966.

Curtin, Jeremiah. *Tales of the Fairies and of the Ghost World*. Boston: Little, Brown and Co., 1895.

Dale-Green, Patricia. *Cult of the Cat*. London: Heinemann, 1963.

Darío, Rubén. *Obras completas*. Madrid: Aguado, 1950.

Dearden, Harold. *Devilish but True: The Doctor Looks at Spiritualism*. London: Hutchinson and Co., 1936.

Delcourt, Marie. *Hermaphrodite*. London: Studio Books, 1961.

De Quincey, Thomas. *Confessions of an English Opium-Eater*. Vol. 3 of *The Collected Writings of Thomas de Quincey*. 14 vols. Edinburgh: Adam and Charles Black, 1890.

Dowson, Ernest. *The Poetical Works of Ernest Christopher Dowson*. London: Cassell and Co., 1934.

Durkheim, Emile. *Suicide*. Glencoe, Ill.: Free Press, 1951.

Duyckaerts, François. *The Sexual Bond*. New York: Delacorte Press, 1970.

Eliade, Mircea. *The Forge and the Crucible*. New York: Harper, 1956.

————. *Mephistopheles and the Androgyne*. New York: Sheed and Ward, 1965.

Encyclopaedia Britannica, 1946 ed.

Evelyn, John. *Silva: or, A Discourse of Forest-trees* . . . 5th ed. 2 vols. London: H. Colburn, 1825.

Farberow, Norman L., and Edwin S. Shneidman, eds. *Clues to Suicide*. New York: Blakiston Division, McGraw-Hill, 1957.

————. *The Cry for Help*. New York: Blakiston Division, McGraw-Hill, 1961.

Finger, Charles J., ed. *Tales from Silver Lands*. Garden City, New York: Doubleday, 1924.

Franz, Marie-Louise von. "The Problem of Evil in Fairy Tales." In *Evil*. Edited by The Curatorium of the C. G. Jung Institute. Evanston, Ill.: Northwestern University Press, 1967.

Freud, Sigmund. *The Interpretation of Dreams*. Vols. 4 and 5 of *The Complete Psychological Works of Sigmund Freud*. London: Hogarth Press, 1953.

———. "Mourning and Melancholia." Vol. 14 of *The Complete Psychological Works of Sigmund Freud*. London: Hogarth Press, 1960.

———. *The Psychopathology of Everyday Life*. Vol. 6 of *The Complete Psychological Works of Sigmund Freud*. London: Hogarth Press, 1960.

García Márquez, Gabriel. *Cien años de soledad*. Buenos Aires: Editorial Sudamericana, 1970.

Garrett, Eileen J. *Adventures in the Supernormal*. New York: Creative Age Press, 1949.

Gibbs, Jack P., ed. *Suicide*. New York: Harper and Row, 1968.

Giraud, Albert. *Pierrot Lunaire*. Paris: Alphonse Lemerre, 1884.

Graves, Robert. *The White Goddess*. New York: Creative Age Press, 1948.

Grimm's Fairy Tales. Complete edition. New York: Pantheon Books, 1944.

Grimm's Fairy Tales. New York: Follett Publishing Co., 1968.

Gubernatis, Angelo de. *Zoological Mythology*. 2 vols. Detroit: Singing Tree Press, 1968.

Haag, Ernest van den. "The Case for Pornography Is the Case for Censorship and Vice Versa." *Esquire*, May 1967, pp. 134–135.

Harding, M. Esther. *Psychic Energy: Its Source and Goal*. New York: Pantheon Books, 1947.

Harley, Timothy. *Moon Lore*. Detroit: Singing Tree Press, 1969.

Harris, Frank. *My Life and Loves*. New York: Grove Press, 1963.

Herodotus. Translated by Canon Rawlinson. 2 vols. New York: C. Scribner's Sons, 1897.

Hesse, Hermann. *Steppenwolf*. Translated by Basil Creighton. New York: Holt, Rinehart, and Winston, 1929.

Huxley, Aldous. *The Doors of Perception*. New York: Harper and Bros., 1954.

Jablow, Alta, and Carl Withers. *The Man in the Moon*. New York: Holt, Rinehart and Winston, 1969.

Jacobs, Joseph, ed. *More English Fairy Tales*. New York: Schocken Books, 1968.

Jones, Ernest. *Free Associations*. London: Hogarth Press, 1959.

————. *Nightmare, Witches, and Devils*. New York: W. W. Norton, 1931.

Jung, Carl G. *Psychology of the Unconscious*. New York: Pantheon Books, 1957.

————. *Symbols of Transformation*. New York: Pantheon Books, 1956.

Kany, Charles E. *Life and Manners in Madrid: 1750–1800*. Berkeley: University of California Press, 1932.

Knowlson, T. Sharper. *The Origins of Popular Superstitions and Customs*. London: T. W. Laurie, 1910.

Lang, Andrew, ed. *Crimson Fairy Book*. New York: David McKay, 1947.

Layard, John. *The Lady of the Hare*. London: Faber and Faber, 1944.

Lifton, Robert Jay. *Death in Life: Survivors of Hiroshima*. New York: Random House, 1967.

MacManus, Diarmuid. *Irish Earth Folk*. New York: Devin-Adair Company, 1959.

Madsen, William and Claudia. *A Guide to Mexican Witchcraft*. Mexico City: Minutiae Mexicana, 1969.

Martínez, José Luis, ed. *La luna*. Mexico City: Ediciones Era, 1970.

Mead, Margaret. *Male and Female*. New York: W. Morrow, 1949.

Meerloo, Joost A. M. *Suicide and Mass Suicide*. New York: Dutton, 1962.

Megas, Georgios A., ed. *Folktales of Greece*. Chicago: University of Chicago Press, 1970.

Menninger, Karl, with Martin Mayman and Paul Pruyser. *The Vital Balance*. New York: Viking Press, 1963.

Milton, John. *Paradise Regained, the Minor Poems, and Samson Agonistes*. New York: Odyssey Press, 1937.

Moon, Sheila. *A Magic Dwells*. Middletown, Conn.: Wesleyan University Press, 1970.

Neumann, Erich. *Amor and Psyche*. New York: Pantheon Books, 1956.

————. *Depth Psychology and a New Ethic*. London: Hodder and Stoughton, 1969.

————. *The Origins and History of Consciousness*. New York: Pantheon Books, 1954.

Onians, Richard B. *The Origins of European Thought*. Cambridge: University Press, 1951.

Paredes, Américo, ed. *Folktales of Mexico*. Chicago: University of Chicago Press, 1970.

Plato. *The Dialogues of Plato*. Translated by B. Jowett. New York: Random House, 1937.

Pliny [Gaius Plinius Secundus]. *Natural History*. 10 vols. Cambridge: Harvard University Press, 1938.

Plokker, J. H. *Art from the Mentally Disturbed*. Boston: Little, Brown, 1965.

Radin, Paul. *The Trickster: A Study in American Indian Mythology*. With commentaries by Karl Kerényi and Carl Jung. New York: Philosophical Library, 1956.

Resnik, H. L. P., ed. *Suicidal Behaviors*. Boston: Little, Brown, 1968.

Rosten, Leo. *The Joys of Yiddish*. New York: McGraw-Hill, 1968.

Silberer, Herbert. *Problems of Mysticism and Its Symbolism*. New York: Moffat, Yard and Company, 1917.

Snorri Sturluson. *The Prose Edda*. Translated by Jean Young. Berkeley: University of California Press, 1964.

Spenser, Edmund. *Faerie Queene*. Oxford: The Clarendon Press, 1909.

Stekel, Wilhelm. *The Interpretation of Dreams*. New York: Liveright, 1943.

Stevens, Wallace. *The Necessary Angel*. New York: Knopf, 1951.

Strauss, Walter A. *Descent and Return: The Orphic Theme in Modern Literature*. Cambridge: Harvard University Press, 1971.

Tasso, Torquato. *La Gerusalemme liberata*. Florence: La Nuova Italia, 1946.

————. *Jerusalem Delivered*. Translated by Edward Fairfax (1600). New York: Capricorn Books, 1963.

Thass-Thienemann, Theodore. *Symbolic Behavior*. New York: Washington Square Press, 1968.

Thoreau, Henry David. *Journal*. Vols. 7–20 of *The Writings of Henry David Thoreau*. New York: Houghton, Mifflin and Co., 1906.

Verlaine, Paul. *Choix de poésies*. Paris: Bibliothèque-Charpentier, 1907.

Voragine, Jacobo de. *La leyenda dorada*. 2 vols. Madrid: Biblioteca Hispania, 1913.

Waterman, Philip F. *The Story of Superstition*. New York: Grosset and Dunlap, 1929.

Wentworth, Harold, and Stuart Berg Flexner. *Dictionary of American Slang*. New York: Thomas Y. Crowell Co., 1960.

Zimmer, Heinrich. *The Art of Indian Asia: Its Myths and Transformations*. 2 vols. New York: Pantheon Books, 1955.

Bibliography Related to Federico García Lorca

Alberich, José. "El erotismo femenino en el teatro de García Lorca." *Papeles de Son Armadans* 39 (1965): 9–36.

Allen, Rupert C. *The Symbolic World of Federico García Lorca*. Albuquerque: University of New Mexico Press, 1972.

Aratari, Anthony. "The Tragedies of García Lorca." *Commonweal*, August 12, 1955, pp. 472–475.

Auclair, Marcelle. *Enfances et mort de García Lorca*. Paris: Editions du Seuil, 1968.

Babín, María Teresa. "Narciso y la esterilidad en la obra de García Lorca." *Revista Hispánica Moderna* 11 (1945): 48–51.

Barea, Arturo. *Lorca, el poeta y su pueblo*. Buenos Aires: Losada, 1956.

Borel, Jean-Paul. *El teatro de lo imposible*. Madrid: Ediciones Guadarrama, 1966.

Cannon, Calvin. "The Imagery of Lorca's *Yerma*." *Modern Language Quarterly* 21 (1960): 122–130.

Carbonell Basset, Delfín. "Tres dramas existenciales de Federico García Lorca." *Cuadernos Hispanoamericanos* 64 (1965): 118–130.

Chabás, Juan. *Historia de la literatura española contemporánea*. Havana: Cultural, 1952.

Chandler, Richard, and Kessel Schwartz. *A New History of Spanish Literature*. Baton Rouge: Louisiana State University Press, 1961.

Cobb, Carl W. *Federico García Lorca*. New York: Twayne Publishers, 1967.

Correa, Gustavo. *La poesía mítica de Federico García Lorca*. Eugene: University of Oregon Press, 1957.

Da Cal, Ernesto G. and Margarita, eds. *Literatura del siglo XX: Antología selecta*. New York: Holt, Rinehart and Winston, 1955.

Descola, Jean. *Historia literaria de España*. Madrid: Editorial Gredos, 1969.

Díaz-Plaja, Guillermo. *Federico García Lorca: Su obra e influencia en la poesía española*. Madrid: Espasa-Calpe, 1961.

Díez-Canedo, Enrique. *Artículos de crítica teatral: El teatro español de 1914 a 1936*. Mexico City: J. Moritz, 1968.

Elizalde, Ignacio, and Rosendo Roig. *Literatura española contemporánea*. Zaragoza: Editorial Hechos y Dichos, 1965.

Fergusson, Francis. *The Human Image in Dramatic Literature*. Gloucester: Peter Smith, 1969.

Fusero, Clemente. *García Lorca*. Milan: Dall'Oglio, 1969.

García Lorca, Federico. *Five Plays: Comedies and Tragicomedies by Federico García Lorca.* Translated by James Graham-Lujan and Richard O'Connell. New York: New Directions, 1963.

————. *Obras completas.* Madrid: Aguilar, 1967.

————. *Three Tragedies of Federico García Lorca: Blood Wedding, Yerma, Bernarda Alba.* Translated by James Graham-Lujan and Richard O'Connell. New York: New Directions, 1947.

Gassner, John. *Masters of Drama.* New York: Dover Publications, 1954.

Guardia, Alfredo de la. *García Lorca: Persona y creación.* Buenos Aires: Sur, 1941.

Honig, Edwin. *García Lorca.* Norfolk, Conn.: New Directions, 1944.

Lewis, Allan. *The Contemporary Theatre.* New York: Crown Publishers, 1971.

Lima, Robert. *The Theatre of García Lorca.* New York: Las Americas Publishing Co., 1963.

Lott, Robert. "*Yerma*: The Tragedy of Unjust Barrenness." *Modern Drama* 8 (1965): 20–27.

Machado Bonet, Ofelia. *Federico García Lorca: Su producción dramática.* Montevideo: Impr. Rosgal, 1951.

Martínez Nadal, Rafael. *El público: Amor, teatro y caballos en la obra de Federico García Lorca.* Oxford: Dolphin, 1970.

Mora Guarnido, José. *Federico García Lorca y su mundo.* Buenos Aires: Losada, 1958.

Nourissier, François. *F. García Lorca: Dramaturge.* Paris: L'Arche, 1955.

Oliver, William. "The Trouble with Lorca." *Modern Drama* 7 (1964): 2–15.

Río, Angel del. "Federico García Lorca." *Revista Hispánica Moderna* 6 (1940): 193–260.

Sánchez, Roberto G. *García Lorca: Estudio sobre su teatro.* Madrid: Ediciones Jura, 1950.

Schonberg, Jean-Louis. *Federico García Lorca: L'homme, l'oeuvre.* Paris: Plon, 1956.

Skloot, Robert. "Theme and Image in Lorca's *Yerma.*" *Drama Survey* 5 (1966): 151–161.

Stamm, James R. *A Short History of Spanish Literature.* Garden City, N.Y.: Doubleday, 1967.

Time, December 16, 1966, p. 87.

Umbral, Francisco. *Lorca, poeta maldito.* Madrid: Biblioteca Nueva, 1968.

Valbuena Prat, Angel. *Historia de la literatura española*. 8th ed. 4 vols. Barcelona: Editorial Gustavo Gili, 1968.

Vázquez Ocaña, Fernando. *García Lorca: Vida, cántico y muerte*. Mexico City: Editorial Grijalbo, 1962.

Williams, Raymond. *Drama from Ibsen to Brecht*. New York: Oxford University Press, 1969.

Zdenek, Joseph W. "La mujer y la frustración en las comedias de García Lorca." *Hispania* 38 (1955): 67–69.

INDEX